Narratives of Becoming Leaders in Disciplinary and Institutional Contexts

Also Available from Bloomsbury

Academics' International Teaching Journeys, *edited by Anesa Hosein, Namrata Rao, Chloe Shu-Hua Yeh and Ian M. Kinchin*
Early Career Teachers in Higher Education, *edited by Jody Crutchley, Zaki Nahaboo and Namrata Rao*
Cosmopolitan Perspectives on Academic Leadership in Higher Education, *edited by Feng Su and Margaret Wood*
Social Theory and the Politics of Higher Education, *edited by Mark Murphy, Ciaran Burke, Cristina Costa and Rille Raaper*
Leadership in Higher Education from a Transrelational Perspective, *Christopher M. Branson, Maureen Marra, Margaret Franken and Dawn Penney*
Professors as Academic Leaders, *Linda Evans*
Academic Identities in Higher Education, *edited by Linda Evans and Jon Nixon*
Academic Working Lives, *edited by Lynne Gornall, Caryn Cook, Lyn Daunton, Jane Salisbury and Brychan Thomas*

Narratives of Becoming Leaders in Disciplinary and Institutional Contexts

Leadership Identity in Learning and Teaching in Higher Education

Edited by
Anesa Hosein, Namrata Rao and Ian M. Kinchin

BLOOMSBURY ACADEMIC
LONDON • NEW YORK • OXFORD • NEW DELHI • SYDNEY

BLOOMSBURY ACADEMIC
Bloomsbury Publishing Plc
50 Bedford Square, London, WC1B 3DP, UK
1385 Broadway, New York, NY 10018, USA
29 Earlsfort Terrace, Dublin 2, Ireland

BLOOMSBURY, BLOOMSBURY ACADEMIC and the Diana logo are trademarks of
Bloomsbury Publishing Plc

First published in Great Britain 2023
Paperback edition published 2024

Copyright © Anesa Hosein, Namrata Rao and Ian M. Kinchin and contributors, 2023

Anesa Hosein, Namrata Rao and Ian M. Kinchin and contributors have asserted their right under the Copyright, Designs and Patents Act, 1988, to be identified as Author of this work.

For legal purposes the Acknowledgements on p. xvi constitute an extension of this copyright page.

Cover designer: Grace Ridge
Cover image: © John M Lund Photography Inc/ Getty Images

All rights reserved. No part of this publication may be reproduced or transmitted in any form or by any means, electronic or mechanical, including photocopying, recording, or any information storage or retrieval system, without prior permission in writing from the publishers.

Bloomsbury Publishing Plc does not have any control over, or responsibility for, any third-party websites referred to or in this book. All internet addresses given in this book were correct at the time of going to press. The author and publisher regret any inconvenience caused if addresses have changed or sites have ceased to exist, but can accept no responsibility for any such changes.

A catalogue record for this book is available from the British Library.

A catalog record for this book is available from the Library of Congress.

ISBN: HB: 978-1-3501-8261-5
PB: 978-1-3501-9930-9
ePDF: 978-1-3501-8262-2
eBook: 978-1-3501-8263-9

Typeset by Newgen KnowledgeWorks Pvt. Ltd., Chennai, India

To find out more about our authors and books visit www.bloomsbury.com and sign up for our newsletters.

Contents

List of Figures	vii
List of Tables	viii
List of Contributors	ix
Foreword	xii
Jill Jameson	
Acknowledgements	xvi

Introduction: Learning and Teaching Leadership Journeys in
Institutional and Disciplinary Contexts   1
   Anesa Hosein and Namrata Rao

Part 1 Becoming Institutional Leaders

1 Social Capital and Social Networks as Leadership Transition from a Disciplinary to Institutional Context   15
   Courtney DeMayo Pugno

2 A Journey from Scholarship to Leadership: The Education of an Educator   31
   Patrick B. O'Sullivan

3 The Changing Perspectives of an Academic Leader: Looking from Outside to the Inside and from Inside to the Outside   49
   Celia Popovic

4 Examining a Leadership Journey through a Lens of 'Integrated Scholarship'   65
   Mike McLinden

Part 2 Becoming Leaders in the Discipline

5 Finding the Space for Disciplinary Leadership in Biological Sciences   85
   Amalia Hosein

6 Developing a Learning and Teaching Leadership Profile in a Specialist Arts Institution   101
   Louise H. Jackson

7 Finding a Path to Leadership in Science by Choosing to Be Different: The Road Not Taken 119
   Susan Rowland
8 Building a Bridge from Chemistry to Educational Leadership: Overcoming the Valley between the Two Cultures 139
   Paulo Rogério Miranda Correia
9 Education and Leadership in Physics: Making Every Step of My Journey Count 153
   Alison Voice

Part 3 The Future of Learning and Teaching Leadership

10 Reflections on Disciplinary and Institutional Leadership: Crossing the Abyss 171
   Ian M. Kinchin

Index 183

Figures

4.1 A summary of the four types of 'integrated scholarship' outlined in the report of the Boyer Commission (Boyer, 1990; Boyer Commission, 1998). Figure adapted from McLinden et al. (2015)   69
7.1 Levels of culture (adapted from Schein, 1984)   127
7.2 The Gartner Hype Cycle (adapted from Fenn and Blosch, 2018)   131
8.1 Concept map to highlight the main aspects of my journey   148
9.1 Schematic showing the life cycle of students in higher education, developed by my research group to represent our diverse yet intertwined research activities   163
10.1 A concept map of the potential contributions of centralized and distributed leadership models to the development of adaptive expertise (modified from Kinchin, 2017)   177

Tables

0.1 Contributors and Their Contexts 5
3.1 Stages of Development Using the Lens of Perry's Theory of
    Intellectual and Ethical Development (Perry, 1970, 1998) 51

Contributors

Patrick B. O'Sullivan is Director of the Center for Teaching, Learning and Technology at California Polytechnic State University, San Luis Obispo, USA. Prior to that, he served seven years as founding director of the Illinois State University's integrated teaching centre and technology support unit, also called the Center for Teaching, Learning and Technology. He earned a PhD in communication from UC Santa Barbara in 1996 and began his academic career as an assistant professor in the Department of Communication at Illinois State University. His teaching and research focused on social uses of communication technologies, and he earned tenure in 2002.

Courtney DeMayo Pugno completed her PhD in medieval history at the University of Houston, USA in 2010, researching educational culture in the High Middle Ages. She joined the faculty of Heidelberg University in Tiffin, Ohio, in 2010 as Assistant Professor of History and, in 2018, created the college's first Center for Teaching Excellence. In 2019, she expanded the centre into the Owen Center for Teaching and Learning, a holistic institution that serves students and faculty through faculty development programmes, instructional technology, accessibility services, academic support, academic advising and library services.

Amalia Hosein is Assistant Professor at the University of Trinidad and Tobago (UTT), Trinidad and Tobago. She started her career in biological sciences as a tutor and demonstrator in biochemistry and genetics at the University of the West Indies, St Augustine. She became one of the first staff members of the newly developed biomedical engineering programme in 2008, after which she moved to the Marine Sciences Unit in 2020. She started as a research assistant on the UTT telemedicine project and the UTT cardiovascular wellness project. As the Vice Chair for the Institute of Electrical and Electronics Engineers, Trinidad and past Tobago chapter, and the Chair for Women in Engineering (WIE), she advocates for the underprivileged and against injustice among the poor and voiceless. As the Chair for WIE, she is working on breaking the glass ceiling of women in leadership among tertiary institutions through research and networking.

Anesa Hosein is Senior Lecturer and the Head of Educational Development and Research at the University of Surrey's Institute of Education, UK. Anesa is interested in how marginalized identities affect higher education participation for both students and academics. Her current research revolves around investigating migrant academics as well as students' mental health.

Louise H. Jackson is Associate Dean (Academic Development) at the Institute of Contemporary Music Performance, UK. She was previously Head of Learning Enhancement at Trinity Laban Conservatoire of Music and Dance in London. In 2013, she was awarded a National Teaching Fellowship, the highest award for teaching in the UK. Her areas of interest in research include critical pedagogy and its use in arts education, inclusive practice and access to and participation in higher education, and higher educational development.

Ian M. Kinchin is Professor of Higher Education in Surrey Institute of Education at the University of Surrey, UK, where he is engaged in the professional development of university teachers. Ian has published research in the fields of zoology, science education and academic development. He has a PhD in science education and a DLitt in higher education.

Mike McLinden is Emeritus Professor in Education at the University of Birmingham, UK. With over thirty years of experience as an academic, he has extensive experience as a teacher, university lecturer, researcher and senior manager. He is a co-founder of the Vision Impairment Centre for Teaching and Research at the University of Birmingham. Mike's research interests in the field of inclusive education have been primarily concerned with facilitating equitable inclusion for children with disabilities. His pedagogical research interests have focused on equitable participation for students with disabilities and the development of 'research-informed' pedagogical practice through integrated critical enquiry.

Celia Popovic is Associate Professor in the Faculty of Education at York University, UK. She was the founding Director of the Teaching Commons at York and is now engaged in teaching undergraduate and graduate courses in post-secondary education and researching in the field. The author, editor or co-editor of five books, numerous chapters and articles in peer-reviewed journals, she is both a scholar and a teacher. In 2018 she was inducted into the Staff and Educational Development Association Roll of Honour; in 2019 she was awarded the Educational Developers' Caucus Distinguished Educational Developer Award; and in 2021 she was recognized as a York University Research Leader.

Namrata Rao is Principal Lecturer in Education at Liverpool Hope University, UK, where she coordinates the School of Education's postgraduate taught programmes. Her key areas of research and publication include (but not restricted to) various aspects of learning and teaching in higher education that influence academic identity and academic practice. She is a senior fellow of the Higher Education Academy, an executive member of the British Association of International and Comparative Education and a member of the research and development group of the Association for Learning Development in Higher Education. Her recent publications include a co-edited book, *Early Career Teachers in Higher Education: International Teaching Journeys* (2021), published by Bloomsbury.

Paulo Rogério Miranda Correia is Associate Professor in Didactics at the University of São Paulo (USP), Brazil, and teaches and researches within the School of Arts, Science and Humanities. He has been involved in researching the application of concept maps to teaching and learning since 2005. His current research considers ways to optimize the use of concept maps in understanding human cognitive architecture and changes in knowledge structures. Paulo was the chairman of the *Sixth International Conference on Concept Mapping* (*CMC2014*), organized by USP and the Institute for Human & Machine Cognition. In 2019, he led the USP and Coursera partnership to launch the first MOOC dedicated to developing novices' skills of learning and collaborating using concept maps.

Susan Rowland is Associate Dean Academic and Deputy Executive Dean in the Faculty of Science at the University of Queensland, Australia. She is responsible for strategic oversight of all matters relating to Teaching & Learning, academic administration, and academic management of student administration across the Faculty, which serves over 8,000 students each year. Originally a biochemist, Susan is now a social scientist using qualitative research methodologies. Her research group examines the student experiences of science-authentic learning pedagogies, the development of employability in science students and the impact of teaching-focused academics in the sciences. She works with her colleagues to change the culture and practice of science teaching and is a principal fellow of the Higher Education Academy (HEA, now Advance HE).

Alison Voice is a Professor of Physics Education in the School of Physics and Astronomy at the University of Leeds, UK. She is a Chartered Physicist, National Teaching Fellow and Senior Fellow of the Higher Education Academy. Having held the role of Director of Student Education in her school for many years, she has now founded a research group in physics education to further pursue her passion for evidence-based pedagogy and to lead and inspire staff and students to develop their own research in this area.

Foreword

Leadership in higher education is sometimes identified as residing only in the top management positions of universities and colleges. Yet, if we consider Peter Northouse's much-cited definition of leadership as a 'process whereby an individual influences a group of individuals to achieve a common goal' (2019, p. 43), we can see immediately that in Northouse's terms the process of leadership is not necessarily enacted only by those individuals who are assigned to occupy senior levels of management. It may, and does, exist in many other places within higher education institutions. Leadership is also not necessarily always linked to a level of management or administrative institutional position, group or individual per se, but may also readily be a process activated by or emerging through the work of both faculty and institution-wide academic staff who carry out a teaching and learning leadership process that influences one or more groups of students to achieve the shared goals of learning.

Leadership is also, in more recent theories, not necessarily linked to particular traits of personality, character, physique or demographic background, but may emerge and be impressively in evidence in both the most predictable and the most unexpected situational contexts. The spontaneity and enigmatic nature of leadership, its elusive qualities and paradoxically powerful blend of transparency and complexity have fascinated scholars for centuries. This has, seemingly inexorably, led to a massive global accumulation of literature on almost every aspect of leadership functioning. One would have thought there was almost nothing new left to say, considering how many books and articles on the subject of leadership have already been written.

And yet there is more to say. There is indeed much more to say on areas that have been relatively glossed over so far in leadership studies. One important area hitherto disappointingly under-recognized is the academic leadership of teaching and learning in higher education. There remains a stubborn tendency in the literature on leadership in higher education to focus more on leadership research linked to assigned management roles rather than focusing on emergent and assigned leadership of teaching and learning. This neglect of attention to academic pedagogical leadership needs to be addressed.

Hence I welcome this highly original book, *Narratives of Becoming Leaders in Disciplinary and Institutional Contexts: Leadership Identity in Learning and Teaching in Higher Education*, which begins to map out some unique narratives that address this deficit of attention to the critically important work of academic leaders of teaching and learning. Bringing together the personal stories of nine emerging and established teaching and learning leaders in higher education, the book recounts an analysis of the theoretically informed experiences of academic leaders from Australia, Brazil, Canada, Trinidad and Tobago, the UK and the United States. Edited by Anesa Hosein, Namrata Rao and Ian M. Kinchin, the book takes us imaginatively through the subjective individual evolutionary pathways of leadership discovery that these nine academics experienced within their national, disciplinary and institutional situations.

The metaphor of the leadership journey comes to life through these narratives recounting personal and professional transitions, dilemmas and complexities of navigating the terrain of disciplinary and institutional leadership. In 'Part 1: Becoming Institutional Leaders', four chapters explore original perspectives in making the transition from an academic faculty disciplinary role to university-wide interdisciplinary leadership.

In Chapter 1, Courtney DeMayo Pugno of Heidelberg University provides an exploration and framework for others to understand her leadership journey – using social capital and social networks – in making the transition from an institutional faculty member to two different institutional teaching and learning leadership positions. This theme of the leadership journey is taken up again in Chapter 2 by Patrick O'Sullivan of California Polytechnic State University, who draws on his own experience to describe his rewarding transition from disciplinary scholarship to a wider whole-university transdisciplinary academic leadership position as an educator passionate about promoting higher education's moral and social responsibilities through scholarly teaching in his role as director of a university teaching centre.

The leadership journey is explored yet again in a different way through an analysis of the multiple and dichotomous identities of leaders in learning and teaching in Chapter 3 by Celia Popovic of York University. Celia applies Perry's theory of intellectual and ethical development as a framework to analyse the challenges, conflicts and synergies of differing identities in the development of leadership. Conscious engagement with challenges in personal development on the leadership journey as an active scholar emerges again in further exploration in Chapter 4 by Mike McLinden, University of Birmingham, who applies Boyer's four types of scholarship to analyse the 'practice and praxis of scholarship', providing insights for others wishing to overcome the challenges of navigating an academic leadership journey.

Providing a fascinating contrast to Part 1, five chapters in 'Part 2: Becoming Leaders in the Discipline' explore original perspectives on the leadership journey in becoming an academic faculty disciplinary leader.

In Chapter 5, Amalia Hosein of the University of Trinidad and Tobago writes from the unique perspective of making an academic leadership journey in the biological sciences within a small island developing state. Amalia draws together reflections on how governance, social and professional networks affected her agency to overcome challenges in the leadership journey from a graduate teaching assistant to an assistant professor. The journey of developing a specialist disciplinary leadership profile in learning and teaching is the subject of the next reflection by Louise Jackson, Institute of Contemporary Music Performance, in Chapter 6. Louise reflects on the particular challenges of developing ethical leadership in learning and teaching in the context of working with performer-teachers distinguished by their artistic reputational expertise in the specialist arts sector.

Susan Rowland of the University of Queensland joins the leadership journey debate in Chapter 7 in a different way, writing about overcoming colleagues' suspicious reactions and developing collegiality through a cultural change regarding their responses to her unusual decision to take an alternative teaching-focused academic pathway. Ten years later, her decision to develop teaching rather than research in the sciences is still resulting in a rewarding cultural environmental change. Chapter 8 by Paulo Rogério Miranda Correia of São Paulo University also explores an alternative academic leadership journey in moving between the two cultures of the sciences and humanities, drawing on C. P. Snow's 1959 discussion of stark differences between the scientific and humanities pathways. Paulo's leadership journey to bridge the uncertain dark valley between chemistry and education developed his resilience and empathy in coping with a career change. Career development as an academic leader in a specialist discipline is also the focus of Alison Voice of the University of Leeds in Chapter 9. Alison reflects making every step count on her journey to become a senior academic pedagogical leader in physics, overcoming challenges and disciplinary battles regarding gender stereotypes to build up her own portfolio of skills and experiences as an educational leader.

Rounding off the book in 'Part 3: The Future of Learning and Teaching Leadership', Chapter 10, by Ian Kinchin of the University of Surrey, provides an interesting and wise reflection drawing together disciplinary and interdisciplinary institutional leadership perspectives. Ian outlines helpful academic guidance on the development of an inclusive, philosophically and epistemologically plural academic stance regarding Santos's 'ecology of knowledges' to promote both the 'being' of disciplinary excellence and the 'becoming' of developing responsive institutional leadership in empathetic understanding of and care for others.

The unique strengths of this excellent book are to bring together institutional and disciplinary perspectives in a series of profoundly thoughtful reflections on different academic leadership journeys. These *Narratives of Becoming Leaders in Disciplinary and Institutional Contexts* are greatly to be valued in developing the emergent field of academic and pedagogical leadership, enriching our understanding of the field of leadership in higher education in new ways.

Prof. Jill Jameson
London, December 2021

Reference

Northouse, P. G. (2019), *Leadership Theory and Practice*, 5th edn, London: Sage.

Acknowledgements

The origins of this book idea are rooted in the reflections of our own academic journeys as each of us have strived for learning and teaching leadership positions within our disciplinary and institutional context – the joys we experienced, the challenges we overcame and the success we achieved as we positioned ourselves as learning and teaching leaders within our unique contexts. These initial personal experiences and the curiosity to obtain a wider view of the challenges and successes experienced by others in their learning and teaching journeys within their unique disciplinary and institutional contexts led to the conception of this book idea. However, it has been the support, encouragement and faith demonstrated in our idea by Alison Baker, senior publisher for education and linguistics, which made it possible to bring this project to fruition, for which we are most grateful. We would also like to record our thanks to Anna Elliss, editorial assistant for education at Bloomsbury.

Without the honest and inspiring stories of the challenges and achievements in the learning and teaching journeys within their institutional and disciplinary contexts shared by the contributors, this book would have not taken its current form; therefore, we extend our special thanks to all contributors from across the world. Your stories have been special and inspirational and would offer much value to others seeking to pursue the path of learning and teaching leadership within their unique institutional contexts. We would like to express particular gratitude to J'annine Jobling for her helpful comments on the final draft of the manuscript. In addition, we are very grateful for the funding offered by Liverpool Hope University, which supported the proof-reading of the volume at a pressured time. Finally, we would like to thank our families and friends for giving us the space to undertake this academic pursuit and for their unwavering support to see us through the book's completion.

Introduction: Learning and Teaching Leadership Journeys in Institutional and Disciplinary Contexts

Anesa Hosein and Namrata Rao

Background

How do academics become leaders in learning and teaching? And how do they navigate their way to learning and teaching leadership positions within their disciplinary and institutional contexts? This is the central question that this book seeks to explore. Often leadership in learning and teaching in academia is associated with formal leadership positions such as the vice-chancellors, heads of department and deans of faculty. Whilst these leadership positions are typical and well defined across academia, the journeys to these formal leadership positions are less defined and known. Sometimes one might garner what a leader may have done in their journeys to leadership positions by looking at their profile pages, their publication lists or projects they have been on and previous positions they have occupied and trying to piece together their leadership pathways (Macfarlane and Chan, 2014). However, such an analysis of an individual's profile in making sense of their leadership journeys does not make explicit the challenges they navigated, the dead-ends they may have come to, the u-turns they have had to make and when they were able to set their sat-nav in the desired direction and navigate seamlessly (if we may be so bold to utilize a road metaphor). Neither does it provide an insight into what drove them to become leaders: their values, their philosophies or critical incidents in their lives – indeed what made them leaders before they acquired the formal leadership positions. It is this leadership journey itself, the various twists and turns that we would like to discover, including the beginnings, the in-betweens and the ongoing challenges. However, understanding such learning and teaching leadership journeys tends to reflect on individuals who have 'already made it' to positions of power, and these offer only a fraction of insights into the journeys of leaders. It does not make explicit the journeys of those who chose not to take up positions of power, but who rather were leaders in learning and teaching without occupying specific high-profile positions. These include the so-called middle leaders based on their job duties (Branson, Franken and Penney, 2015, 2016) and those early career leaders who demonstrate leadership through their learning and teaching.

In this book, we want to elucidate the diversity in learning and teaching leadership journeys, which include individuals occupying the highest positions of power within their institution, those who lead their discipline and those who may be at the in-betweens of their leadership journeys – who often do not occupy formal leadership positions but demonstrate learning and teaching leadership in their day-to-day lives. We are not concerned with their leadership approaches or their qualities (Bryman, 2007; Dopson et al., 2016), although that in itself is insightful, but rather with the journey of being and becoming a leader within their institutions and disciplines (Juntrasook, 2014). We take the stance that everyone's journey is unique, but it is bounded by the social and cultural rules and norms of their institutions and their respective disciplines. Each leadership journey, we contend, shares some commonalities and can be underpinned by some theory or philosophy that explains their leadership disposition and approaches and has shaped their unique pathways as leaders. Thus, to understand the journey, each contributor in this book was invited to consider their journey from a theoretical or conceptual perspective alongside detailing the practical aspects of their leadership journeys. This was not meant to generalize the journey, as warned by Tan (2020), but rather to make sense of how social norms and practices have shaped them as learning and teaching leaders. Being reflective is a key tenet (Schön, 1987) of any teacher and, therefore, is central to any learning and teaching leadership journey. We do not become leaders in isolated bubbles; these are inherently influenced by a range of social, psychological, philosophical, historical and economic factors that are part of the educational ecosystem (Bandyopadhyay et al., 2021). For a more critical and holistic understanding of an individual's leadership journey, an appreciation of the various factors which exercise influence in shaping these journeys is needed.

At both institutional and disciplinary levels, people are influenced by the social milieu that they are a part of. Universities, like any other organization, have particular social environments and networks that academics must negotiate, survive and possibly thrive in (McMurray and Scott, 2013). The university environment is informed by its philosophies, strategies and/or missions, which shape its structures, strategic direction and day-to-day functioning. Using a more hegemonic approach, the most visible difference which is often identified in contemporary universities is between that of teaching-focused versus research-focused universities. The philosophies of these universities would be uniquely different, and how an academic negotiates and creates their learning and teaching leadership profile within these distinct academic environments may be dependent on how teaching is viewed and celebrated within their institution. There are countless anecdotal studies on how teaching is and can be devalued in an institutional system where research is highly valued, and both activities are part of a zero-sum game (Bak and Kim, 2015; Hosein, 2017). But the whole academic landscape pits teaching-focused and research-focused universities against each other, with the latter always having higher prestige due to the position they occupy on the league tables, which themselves offer greater recognition to the research rather than teaching activity of the institutions. Therefore, academics may not celebrate their leadership achievements or recognize how much they have contributed to changing learning and teaching both institutionally and more widely across the higher education landscape. In fact, much of the literature on leadership within higher education does not focus on learning and teaching exclusively, but instead places a greater focus on administrative leadership that combines wider administrative, research and teaching leadership activities (Bryman, 2007; Dopson et al., 2016; Macfarlane and Chan, 2014). This book seeks to shift this narrative with a view to recognizing, celebrating and surfacing all the achievements (the good, the bad and the ugly) of academics who identify themselves as learning and teaching leaders. Once more using the road metaphor, it is important to recognize that these journeys are not smooth, but often bumpy and rough; individuals may negotiate potholes, punctures and engine trouble in establishing legitimacy as learning and teaching leaders within their institutional contexts. It requires considerable resilience, willingness to change and often to travel and lay out new roads, being innovative and listening to the oncoming traffic in order for these individuals to be successful in their leadership journeys, rather than packing it up and returning to the safety of their metaphorical learning and teaching home.

Autoethnographic and Personal Narrative

Throughout this book, the contributors explore their leadership journeys and how these have been shaped by their institutional and disciplinary contexts, and in doing so, we have encouraged them to use personal narratives. We have gone further as editors to ensure that these personal narratives adopt an autoethnographic approach.

Ellis, Adams and Bochner (2011) define autoethnography as 'an approach to research and writing that seeks to describe and systematically analyze (*graphy*) personal experience (*auto*) in order to understand cultural experience (*ethno*)' (p. 1, original emphasis). As Chang (2008) explains, autoethnography combines 'cultural analysis and interpretation with narrative details' (p. 46). It was not sufficient that these journeys reflected an itinerary approach, that is, a step-by-step retelling of their different points in journeys. It was important that each contributor contextualized their leadership journey and explained the university, discipline and/or their country culture to help make better sense of their leadership. In this way, these leadership journeys became a collection of cultural analyses of the higher education landscape.

Through the autoethnographic approach, the contributors can surface the unknown or hidden cultural elements of leadership journeys. Hence, whilst the contributors have traversed different pathways in their journeys, their knowledge about these pathways is tacit. However, through a reflection on and analysis of the contexts of their pathways, they can make this tacit knowledge explicit, in a way that is almost a discovery to them about themselves and the contexts they work within. Through an analysis of their journeys, the contributors can delve deeper into understanding the reasons and processes behind why they took certain pathways and are able to illuminate these for us, as they take us along on their journeys. It allows the reader then to reflect on their own context and situation and how they may shape their own leadership journey and what might be the points of convergence and divergence in their own journey with those journeys shared in this book.

About the Contributions

We, therefore, see these contributions as an important collection of work on leadership in learning and teaching from across the world, including North America, South America, the Caribbean, Europe and Australia, which elucidates

Table 0.1 Contributors and Their Contexts

Author	Country	Context
Courtney DeMayo Pugno	United States	University-wide
Patrick O'Sullivan	United States	University-wide
Celia Popovic	Canada	University-wide
Mike McLinden	UK	University-wide
Amalia Hosein	Trinidad and Tobago	Biological sciences
Louise Jackson	UK	Music
Susan Rowland	Australia	Biochemistry
Paulo Rogério Miranda Correia	Brazil	Chemistry
Alison Voice	UK	Physics

the experience of working within unique institutional and disciplinary contexts. Each contributor has also provided some recommendations or lessons learnt from their leadership journey. In this book, we have divided the contributions into two parts (Table 0.1).

Institutional Contributions

In the first part, we have four leadership journeys that show contributions to the university at an institutional level, such as working in a central learning and teaching centre. The contributors to this section are as follows:

Courtney DeMayo Pugno explores how her leadership was influenced by her social capital and knowledge of social networks. She demonstrates how she utilized her social capital in the form of a practical, working knowledge of the institution's culture in her transition from faculty to institutional leadership in teaching and learning.

Patrick O'Sullivan tracks how his traditional faculty career unexpectedly veered towards an academic leadership position as director of a university teaching centre. He highlights how his journey required evolving his professional identity from a disciplinary researcher who taught students in a narrow specialty to a transdisciplinary faculty development leader who mentors peers towards more effective instruction.

Celia Popovic shares how her multiple identities affected her leadership journey. She looks at the concept of leadership journey through dichotomous identities and the conflicts and synergies inherent by holding these dichotomous identities: faculty vs institution-wide role, immigrant vs native, teaching-intensive vs research-intensive.

Mike McLinden engages with the concepts of practice and praxis of scholarship and conscious engagement. Through conscious engagement, he explores his leadership journey using Boyer's four types of scholarship. He provides insights into the individual challenges and issues he encountered when undertaking leadership roles and the distinctive nature of his 'scholarship' at key milestones.

Disciplinary Contributions

In the second part of the book, we have five leadership journeys of individuals working within their disciplines who may also have some university-wide contributions. A summary of their journeys is as follows:

Amalia Hosein elucidates her leadership journey in biological sciences within the small island developing state (SIDS) of Trinidad and Tobago. Using the concepts of structure and agency, she explores how governance and societal structures, at both the university and disciplinary levels, affected her agency in being innovative in learning and teaching. She delves into how the value of social and professional networks in SIDS can create change and acceptance in her leadership journey.

Louise Jackson explores her leadership of learning and teaching within a specialist arts institutional context where performer-teachers are employed because of their artistic reputation. She focuses on the challenges of working in the specialist arts sector where learning and teaching is subordinate to the perception of prestige of this artistic reputation. Leadership is explored in relation to seemingly progressive and performative educational contexts that perpetuate an uncritical approach to learning and teaching.

Susan Rowland elaborates on her leadership journey which began with her desire and decision to be different. She shares her journey from a difficult biochemistry research pathway to a fortuitous new academic track at her university. She explores her journey as a new teaching-focused academic in the sciences and the way she built a leadership role in an environment where her colleagues' attitudes to a teaching-focused academic in the sciences have evolved from suspicion to acceptance and collegiality.

Paulo Rogério Miranda Correia frames his leadership journey as a bridge between the cultural differences in sciences and humanities. He explains how changing from one to the other implies walking through a dark valley, treating the uncertainty and the unknown as companions. He focuses on how he dealt with the methodological shock in developing a new hybrid identity as he moved from chemistry to education.

Alison Voice demonstrates how her leadership journey in physics was shaped by her identity as a female academic, which required her to counter stereotypes and often having to act as a role model. She explains how having a profile in pedagogical research as opposed to scientific research meant she had to battle with long-held disciplinary traditions for promotion.

Importance of Institutional Perspectives

Academics moving between countries and universities with different institutional and national cultures may be stunted or accelerated in their leadership journeys by adverse and favourable cultures they negotiate. In our previous edited book, *Academics' International Teaching and Learning Journeys* (Hosein et al., 2018), international academics shared via their narratives the challenges in understanding the teaching and learning cultures of their home and host countries as they moved from one institutional and national context to another. No doubt such a shift in cultures occurs even at a smaller geographical scale when academics move from, for example, a teaching-focused to a research-focused university and are faced with a culture shock due to the differing expectations and conceptualizations of learning and teaching leadership. Celia Popovic explores her transition and culture shock in moving countries and institutions in greater depth within her chapter. Academics' learning and teaching journeys may be also influenced by their country's geographical position, culture and higher education philosophies. For example, Courtney DeMayo Pugno explores her journey in a small liberal arts college in the rural American Midwest and shows how in such small teaching-focused institutions developing social capital via the use of social networks can create change in learning and teaching institutionally.

Indeed, within the institution itself, there may be policies that influence how academics manage their learning and teaching leadership journeys. For example, institutions may actively encourage academics to engage in formal and informal learning and teaching development programmes or offer mentorship schemes for early career academics which focus on teaching mentorship alongside research mentorship (Rao, Hosein and Raaper, 2021). This, therefore, demonstrates the value the institution places on learning and teaching and how the institutional culture may offer opportunities for academics to explore learning and teaching more fully, rather than engaging with it at a more instrumental level. Increasingly now teaching track positions are offered in institutions, which allow progression opportunities for individuals with a particular interest in leadership in learning and teaching (Hosein, 2017). This demonstrates a further shift in the philosophies of some universities and the increasing recognition and importance being offered and placed on learning and teaching leadership. For example, Patrick O'Sullivan details his journey from being on a research track position to a teaching track position within his university and how the latter resonated with what he considered his purpose as an academic. New institutional policies or gaps in institutional policies which are not always directly related to teaching can influence teaching; for example, an institutional policy to increase recruitment from different geographical or social territories and opening up new programmes can create opportunities for academics to step in and lead. Or, for example, the recognition of a shortcoming in an institution's approach to understanding learning and teaching can also create the opportunity to lead. This is what Mike McLinden explores in his chapter, where he discusses how he, together with like-minded colleagues, set up a teaching and research centre focused on the creation of a more integrated approach to critical inquiry, rather than having teaching and research as separate and discrete activities.

Importance of Disciplinary Perspectives

The learning and teaching leadership journey is often influenced by the disciplinary context. Shulman (2005) speaks about signature pedagogies, that is, the key approaches that individuals use in their disciplines to teach. These are often related to the troublesome knowledge or threshold concepts in the discipline and implementing teaching approaches and methods for developing these. These approaches can lead to the development of academic tribes and territories (Becher and Trowler, 2001) and promote beliefs on how things should be done and how it has always been done. For example, Louise Jackson explores how the prestige of her institution, a specialist dance college, challenged her leadership journey in learning and teaching in various ways.

A learning and teaching leader needs to navigate the disciplinary territories to introduce or bring about change and often faces diverse challenges, such as the inability to permeate into and influence pedagogical cultural networks (Kinchin et al., 2018). Therefore, for a leader to create change, they will need to make the most of their social networks, using both their strong and weak connections to influence people (Rienties and Hosein, 2020). Both Courtney DeMayo Pugno and Patrick O'Sullivan touch upon the importance of these within the institutional context. For example, Amalia Hosein elucidates how the power structure networks in biological sciences within a SIDS can inhibit growth and how she was able to use her strong connections at the lower level of the institutional hierarchy networks to influence learning and teaching at the higher level of the institutional hierarchy, where she had weaker connections.

There is also the issue of crossing disciplines. Learning and teaching by its very nature is within the realm of social sciences, as it deals with working with people, that is, staff and students. However, for those in the 'hard disciplines' such as the physical sciences (Biglan, 1973), to bridge the gap into the social sciences and to appreciate the craft of teaching is in itself a threshold concept (Meyer and Land, 2003). Most universities now have teacher training programmes for higher education staff, which require academics from traditional 'hard disciplines' to engage in different ways of thinking and different ways of evaluation and observation. Indeed, it requires the academics to use more reflective practices (Schön, 1987). The different ways of thinking can sometimes be challenging, and when trying to bridge the gap, some may struggle with this new conceptualization of learning and teaching, which involves a unique approach closer to those in the social sciences. This in turn poses some newer challenges for academics in these 'hard' disciplines who try to establish themselves as learning and teaching leaders. Paulo Rogério Miranda Correia explores this in his chapter about creating a new hybrid identity through his journey as a learning and teaching leader in chemistry. Susan Rowland highlights in her chapter how the crossing over to social sciences enabled her to have a language and vocabulary to explain teaching practices within her discipline of biochemistry and, in so doing, helped give a voice and sensemaking of teaching practices to those who are not social scientists.

Academics based within the various disciplines can become leaders in learning and teaching at the departmental level. However, the discipline is wider than the institution, and hence disciplinary leadership in learning and teaching could go beyond institutional boundaries, even though in their own departments they may be still bounded to some extent by the institutional culture. The promotion of particular approaches to learning and teaching in a discipline may involve multiple stakeholders such as professional accreditation boards, government bodies and employers (Hosein and Harle, 2017). These professional and government bodies and employers, as well as researchers and academics in various institutions, form a network that disciplinary learning and teaching leaders must engage with. Disciplinary leaders may then have a stronger loyalty to the discipline rather than acting as a leader within their institution. Alison Voice, for example, writes about how her growing reputation as a learning and teaching leader in physics meant that she was invited into the national quality assurance panel to help determine the pedagogy and content of all physics degree programmes in the UK.

Conclusion

Paulo Coelho, the Brazilian novelist, once said in an interview in 2008, 'Everybody has a creative potential and from the moment you can express this creative potential, you can start changing the world.' We would like to think about learning and teaching leaders in the same way; everyone has a leadership potential, and from the moment they express this leadership potential, they can start changing the world of learning and teaching. In this book, we follow the meandering ways that each individual academic followed, harnessed or enhanced to realize their leadership potential and to change their professional world. We hope that you enjoy reading their leadership journeys and will discover the different paths to being and becoming leaders in learning and teaching.

References

Bak, H.-J. and Kim, D. H. (2015), 'Too Much Emphasis on Research? An Empirical Examination of the Relationship between Research and Teaching in Multitasking Environments', *Research in Higher Education*, 56 (8): 843–60. https://doi.org/10.1007/s11162-015-9372-0.

Bandyopadhyay, S., Bardhan, A., Dey, P. and Bhattacharyya, S. (2021), 'Education Ecosystem', in *Bridging the Education Divide Using Social Technologies*, 43–75, Singapore: Springer.

Becher, T. and Trowler, P. R. (2001), *Academic Tribes and Territories*, 2nd edn, Buckingham: The Society for Research into Higher Education and The Open University Press.

Biglan, A. (1973), 'The Characteristics of Subject Matter in Different Academic Areas', *Journal of Applied Psychology*, 57 (3): 195–203.

Branson, C. M., Franken, M. and Penney, D. (2015), 'Middle Leadership in Higher Education: A Relational Analysis', *Educational Management Administration and Leadership*, 44 (1): 128–45. https://doi.org/10.1177/1741143214558575.

Branson, C. M., Franken, M. and Penney, D. (2016), 'Reconceptualising Middle Leadership in Higher Education: A Transrelational Approach', in J. McNiff (ed.), *Values and Virtues in Higher Education Research: Critical Perspectives*, 155–70, Abingdon: Routledge.

Bryman, A. (2007), 'Effective Leadership in Higher Education: A Literature Review', *Studies in Higher Education*, 32 (6): 693–710. https://doi.org/10.1080/0307507070 1685114.

Chang, H. (2008), *Autoethnography as Method*, Abingdon: Routledge.

Dopson, S., Ferlie, E., McGivern, G., Fischer, M., Ledger, J., Behrens, S. and Wilson, S. (2016), *The Impact of Leadership and Leadership Development in Higher Education: A Review of the Literature and Evidence*, London: Leadership Foundation for Higher Education. www.advance-he.ac.uk/knowledge-hub/impact-leadership-and-leaders hip-development-higher-education-review-literature-and.

Ellis, C., Adams, T. E. and Bochner, A. P. (2011), 'Autoethnography: An Overview', *Forum Qualitative Sozialforschung/Forum: Qualitative Social Research*, 12 (1): article 10. www.qualitative-research.net/index.php/fqs/article/view/1589/3095.

Hosein, A. (2017), 'Pedagogic Frailty and the Research-Teaching Nexus', in I. M. Kinchin and N. E. Winstone (eds), *Pedagogic Frailty and Resilience in the University*, 135–49, Rotterdam: Sense Publishers.

Hosein, A. and Harle, J. (2017), 'The Vulnerability of a Small Discipline and Its Search for Appropriate Pedagogy: The Case of Medical Physics', in E. Medland, R. Watermeyer, A. Hosein, I. M. Kinchin and S. Lygo-Baker (eds), *Pedagogical Peculiarities: Conversation at the Edge of University Teaching and Learning*, 69–85, Leiden: Brill.

Hosein, A., Rao, N., Yeh, C. S.-H. and Kinchin, I. M. (2018), *Academics' International Teaching Journeys: Personal Narratives of Transitions in Higher Education*, London: Bloomsbury.

Juntrasook, A. (2014), ' "You Do Not Have to Be the Boss to Be a Leader": Contested Meanings of Leadership in Higher Education', *Higher Education Research and Development*, 33 (1): 19–31. https://doi.org/10.1080/07294360.2013.864610.

Kinchin, I. M., Rao, N., Hosein, A. and Mace, W. (2018), *Migrant Academics and Professional Learning Gains: Perspectives of the Native Academic – Research Report*, London: Society for Research into Higher Education. https://srhe.ac.uk/wp-content/uploads/2020/03/Kinchin-Rao-Hosein-Research-Report.pdf.

Macfarlane, B. and Chan, R. Y. (2014), 'The Last Judgement: Exploring Intellectual Leadership in Higher Education through Academic Obituaries', *Studies in Higher Education*, 39 (2): 294–306. https://doi.org/10.1080/03075079.2012.684679.

McMurray, A. and Scott, D. (2013), 'Determinants of Organisational Climate for Academia', *Higher Education Research and Development*, 32 (6): 960–74. https://doi.org/10.1080/07294360.2013.806446.

Meyer, J. and Land, R. (2003), *Threshold Concepts and Troublesome Knowledge: Linkages to Ways of Thinking and Practising within the Disciplines*, Enhancing Teaching-Learning Environments in Undergraduate Courses Project, Occasional Report 4, Edinburgh: University of Edinburgh School of Education. www.etl.tla.ed.ac.uk/docs/ETLreport4.pdf.

Rao, N., Hosein, A. and Raaper, R. (2021), 'Doctoral Students Navigating the Borderlands of Academic Teaching in an Era of Precarity', *Teaching in Higher Education*, 26 (3): 454–70. https://doi.org/10.1080/13562517.2021.1892058.

Rienties, B. and Hosein, A. (2020), 'Complex Transitions of Early Career Academics (ECA): A Mixed Method Study of with Whom ECA Develop and Maintain New Networks', *Frontiers in Education*, 5 (137). https://doi.org/10.3389/feduc.2020.00137.

Schön, D. (1987), *Educating the Reflective Practitioner*, San Francisco, CA: Jossey-Bass.

Shulman, L. S. (2005), 'Signature Pedagogies in the Professions', *Daedalus*, 134 (3): 52–9. https://doi.org/10.1162/0011526054622015.

Tan, Y. (2020), 'Academics' International Teaching Journeys: Personal Narratives of Transitions in Higher Education', *Compare: A Journal of Comparative and International Education*, 50 (4): 617–18. https://doi.org/10.1080/03057925.2019.1642025.

Part 1
Becoming Institutional Leaders

1

Social Capital and Social Networks as Leadership Transition from a Disciplinary to Institutional Context

Courtney DeMayo Pugno

Educational developers often start as faculty members and transition to leadership in teaching and learning (Muir and Craig, 2017). For many, the shift can be overwhelming. The transition alters power dynamics among faculty colleagues and friends, restructures personal and professional relationships and transforms interactions between individuals at multiple levels of the institutional organization.

For me, the transition from being a faculty member to the director of the Centre for Teaching Excellence (CTE) and then to executive director of a coupled Teaching and Learning Centre occurred at a non-elite SLAC (small liberal arts college) in the rural American Midwest. My shift in roles was facilitated, and leadership enhanced, by social capital (information, resources, cultural norms and behaviours, emotional connections and reciprocity with colleagues) and social networks (social relationships between different people, all of whom interact with one another). My social networks and social capital helped me move from being a full-time faculty member to a part-time faculty developer, and then from a part-time faculty developer to a full-time campus leader in teaching and learning. The centre I created focused on building social capital and social networks among interdisciplinary groups of faculty members. In my experience, social capital supported and eased my transition from faculty member to campus leader in teaching and learning, helped make my leadership of the new Owen Center for Teaching and Learning successful and shaped my personal approach to leadership.

This chapter sits at the intersection of literature on social capital and social networks in higher education and my experiences. I hope my insights will be of value to other educational developers so that they too can use social capital and social networks to advance teaching and learning on their campuses. Knowledge of the institution's teaching and learning culture and the existing faculty networks was of vital importance to building strategic and relevant programming, and using cohort-based and peer-to-peer faculty development activities to establish and enhance social capital and social networks encouraged faculty engagement with the new centre.

Institutional Context

Founded by the members of the German Reformed Church (now United Church of Christ) in Tiffin, Ohio, in 1850, Heidelberg University attracts mostly lower-income, first-generation students. With a total enrolment of around thousand mostly residential undergraduate students and 200 graduate students in counselling and business, Heidelberg's faculty consists of about sixty full-time and sixty part-time faculty members, distributed across seventeen academic departments and thirty-four majors. Like many other small colleges in the United States, Heidelberg's faculty evaluation process emphasizes teaching effectiveness and institutional service over research. Academic departments range in size from one to six full-time professors, requiring nearly all faculty members to teach broadly. Heidelberg's faculty manual includes SoTL (Scholarship of Teaching and Learning) as professional development and/or professional activity, reflecting the importance of teaching effectiveness and excellence in faculty evaluation (Heidelberg University, 2020). This focus on teaching, however, did not translate to consistent and widespread support for pedagogy improvement.

Until 2018, teaching support was overseen exclusively by the faculty development committee (FDC), a rotating group of four elected faculty members. Because the members of FDC taught a full course load (four courses per semester) and the committee had rotating membership, the programming initiatives and activity level varied from year to year and generally consisted of a daylong workshop at the start of each semester. In the absence of campus-wide, extended faculty development opportunities, instructors developed their own pockets of peer teaching support (ASIIP Co-Chairs, 2017).

In the 2015–16 academic year, the vice president for academic affairs/provost launched a campus-wide self-study, the Academic Strategic Initiatives for Improvement (ASIIP). Every faculty member participated in groups reviewing teaching practices, academic support resources and academic programmes.

ASIIP's goal was to re-evaluate Heidelberg's practices and offerings to be more competitive and relevant, reflecting the pressures facing many small schools in the United States (Grupp, 2014, p. 45). The subcommittee tasked with evaluating the institutional resources and support for teaching compiled a Teaching Resources/Support Wish List, which included the creation of a Centre for Teaching and Learning (CTL) with staff devoted specifically to supporting faculty pedagogy (Subcommittee on Teaching Resources, 2016).

ASIIP initiated my transition from being a faculty member to first director of a CTE and then executive director of the Owen Center for Teaching and Learning. I sought out the first opportunity and was recruited for the second. Pursing the directorship of the CTE was a natural outgrowth of my career trajectory and one likely to resonate with readers who teach at small colleges. Although I was trained as a specialist – a Medieval historian – my teaching responsibilities at Heidelberg were broad. Between 2010 and 2018, I taught fifteen different history courses, covering different topics, periods and geographic regions. Teaching so widely changed the way I thought about my discipline and the purpose of my teaching; I wasn't teaching future historians who would go to graduate school and earn PhDs, but rather future citizens who needed the transferrable skills (critical thinking and reading, analytical writing) my discipline helped them develop. By shifting my pedagogy to a focus on skills rather than content, I realized that I loved teaching more than I loved history, which made research on the Middle Ages less interesting than research on pedagogy.

Social Capital and Social Networks Defined

French sociologist Pierre Bourdieu defined social capital as 'the sum of the resources, actual or virtual, that accrue to an individual or a group by virtue of possessing a durable network of more or less institutionalized relationships of mutual acquaintance and recognition' (Bourdieu and Wacquant, 1992, p. 19). Nan Lin defines social capital as the 'investment in social relationships with expected returns in the marketplace' (2001, p. 19). Benbow and Lee draw on this definition, defining social capital as 'valued, actionable resources accessed and mobilized through personal relationships' (2019, p. 72). Social capital encourages the flow of information and reflects an individual's access to resources, functioning simultaneously as an individual asset that benefits one person (through increased prestige or promotion, for example) and as a shared resource that benefits a particular group or an entire community (Lin, 1999).

Putnam explains that social capital also helps promote community cohesion through shared norms, cultural institutions and activities, highlighting the connection between social structures or organizations and social cohesion. In Putnam's analysis, it is the 'social organization such as networks, norms, and social trust that facilitate coordination and cooperation for mutual benefit' (2000, p. 21). Cooperation and trust is the positive result of social capital; the ability to accumulate, transfer or otherwise utilize that social capital comes from an individual's membership within a social network, that individual's location within any organization (including a community) and that individual's ability to move between and among different social networks, both within and outside the community or organization.

The accumulation, transfer or deployment of social capital occurs through the creation of connections that either bond or bridge communities together. Bonding networks consist of close-knit relationships between members and are characterized by reciprocal relationships based on mutual trust, cooperation and support; bonding networks are particularly useful for accessing resources and providing emotional support (Barthauer, Spurk and Kauffield, 2016). Bridging networks connect one group to another, allow members to move across and between social networks and are especially useful in the transfer of information (Barthauer, Spurk and Kauffield, 2016). In bridging networks, individuals serve as the connectors between different communities or constituencies within an institution. Both bridging networks and bonding networks are valuable to educational developers. Network membership shapes the way an individual understands their role in a community, their knowledge of institutional fit and norms of behaviour; provides (or limits) their access to resources; and provides important transactional or process knowledge about rules, strategies and approaches. For educational developers, these networks are extremely important, 'increasing the skillset and resource base that educational developers can provide to the instructors with whom they work' (Ingram, 2019, p. 66).

Social Capital and Social Networks in Educational Development

As leaders in teaching and learning, educational developers should understand the function of social capital in higher education and the specific institutional context. Such knowledge can provide helpful insights when developing a strategic plan for a new centre, taking on a new leadership role and for planning programmes. Several recent studies reflect both the theoretical and practical significance of social capital to educational development.

In their conceptual model, Wright et al. (2018) acknowledge the importance of social capital to the effective functioning of centres for teaching and learning. In their paper 'The Four Rs', the authors write about the significance of responsiveness, relationships, resources and research, and although the authors do not specifically discuss social capital, their key concepts are deeply tied to either social networks or social capital. In the authors' model, being responsive to the needs of the community is likely the most important of the Four Rs, as responsiveness helps build the centre's credibility and cultivates the sense of mutual trust (a type of social capital) necessary for a CTL to work closely with faculty clients. Relationships, with constituents at all levels of the institution's organizational structure, are necessary for every educational developer, but especially those new to their positions (Wright et al., 2018). For example, at Berea College, relationships between the CTL and different campus offices at all levels of the institution helped guide the CTL's work in a new direction (Wright et al., 2018). Relationships, or social networks and the social capital they produce, are what enable centres for teaching and learning to do their work. Resources, another form of social capital, are essential for a CTL, as a centre's effectiveness is shaped by its ability to both manage and navigate various types of resources (Wright et al., 2018). Research, the fourth R in this conceptual model, emphasizes knowledge of evidence-based teaching practices, yet another type of social capital important to the work of educational developers (Wright et al., 2018). For Wright et al., social networks and social capital are necessary components of their 'Four Rs' model for guiding centres for teaching and learning.

Other studies that investigate the role of faculty developers on small college campuses focus on the positioning of a CTL as an institutional hub. Grupp argues that faculty developers at small institutions can 'lead from the middle' because they work at the intersection of faculty, instructional and organizational development, placing the CTL at the convergence of multiple campus networks (2014, p. 54). Effective CTL leadership requires 'understanding the roles and responsibilities of the faculty developer within the organisational context' (Grupp, 2014, p. 54). In Grupp's analysis, the strategic location of a CTL and its placement at the intersection of different networks will enable the CTL to bridge networks within the organization and use social capital in the form of institutional knowledge to advocate for change. Though Grupp (2014) doesn't use the terms social capital or social networks, her recommendations are all types of social capital important to the work of educational developers: knowledge of current research, the design and execution of quality programming, allies and positive relationships within campus, an understanding of the organizational structure and context, and the active participation in and/or support of activities that enhance teaching and learning.

There is also some literature in educational development that connects the development of social capital to specific programmes. Susanne Morgan's analysis of a new faculty mentoring programme at Ithaca College is one such example. Morgan (2014) argues that mentoring groups commonly transfer social capital through increased clarity about institutional norms and practices. The new faculty mentoring programme Morgan created at Ithaca drew on the social capital of mentors – people 'whose relationships are characterized by reciprocity and trust have higher social capital than those with more functional or hierarchical relationships' – and transferred that social capital to new faculty members through a deliberately designed mentoring programme (Morgan, 2014, p. 82). Within Ithaca's mentoring programme, the process of connecting new faculty members to senior colleagues, and working intentionally to construct bonding networks between them, facilitated the transfer of social capital from the senior member to the junior member and successfully integrated new colleagues into the institution.

Understanding social capital and social networks can, therefore, afford faculty developers important advantages in understanding and executing their role. My personal experiences in the transition from being a faculty member to creator and director of the CTL, when viewed through the lens of social capital and social networks, may serve as an exemplar for others as they embark on their own journeys into educational development.

From Faculty to Leadership in Teaching and Learning

Like many educational developers, my shift in campus roles occurred through serendipity, but my transition was aided, and my leadership shaped and enhanced, by social capital. The process by which this transition occurred reflects the three stages of developing beneficial social capital articulated by Lan Nin and summarized by Benbow and Lee (Benbow and Lee, 2019; Lin, 2001):

> *Stage 1: Precursors and preconditions* – an individual develops beneficial social ties. In my experience, this stage occurred during my time as

a faculty member, during which I learned about the institution and developed my own social networks and social capital.

Stage 2: Access and mobilize – the individual utilizes the social capital developed in stage 1. For me, this stage occurred during the design, planning and launch of the CTE at Heidelberg University, during which I drew upon those social networks and utilized my social capital to help ensure the success of the CTE.

Stage 3: Benefits and rewards – the individual reaps the returns on the social capital developed in stage 1 and deployed in stage 2. In this stage, I merged the CTE with our student support centre, creating a new CTL that paired pedagogy and technology support for faculty with advising, accessibility and learning support for students (Benbow and Lee, 2019).

Because these three stages of social capital development mirror my own personal experience with the transition from being a faculty to an educational developer/campus leader on teaching and learning, I will discuss my experiences in the context of these three phases.

Stage 1: Building Social Capital as a Faculty Member

Stage 1, during which I developed my social networks and social capital, lasted from 2010 to 2017. I laid the groundwork for my transition to leadership in teaching and learning by acclimating myself to the campus community and developing personal knowledge of the institutional culture, systems and practices like all new faculty members must. I was also introduced to the social capital of the institution, identifying the existing networks of faculty, staff and administration. Part of learning to navigate those existing networks was identifying who the central actors (people with the most connections to others in the institution) were at the institution (Kezar, 2014). Similarly, identifying who the faculty opinion leaders were (people whose opinions were influential over the ideas or attitudes of others) was also of great importance (Kezar, 2014). It was important for me to identify the central actors and opinion leaders because those were the colleagues best equipped to help me succeed as a new faculty member.

At the time I was hired, our college did not have a formal new faculty mentoring programme; instead, new faculty members were assigned faculty mentors who had no training, no shared curriculum, nor any official institutional guidance. The mentoring programme was disjointed and inconsistent, which made identifying and working with mentors more important to me and necessary to my success as a faculty member. At the time, I was not aware that the work I was doing to identify and connect with campus mentors would support my transition to leadership. I only thought in terms of creating social networks that could help me establish myself as a faculty member. Because there was no structured mentoring programme to support new faculty members, it was both necessary and expedient for me to seek out guidance from established colleagues, who could help me learn institutional norms, campus rules and practices, and social relations that would help create my own beneficial social capital.

To establish relationships, I created my own social networks. Some of this was accomplished organically, developing from informal interactions with colleagues. Some of it was intentional; one of the opinion leaders I sought out as a mentor, for example, was a woman who introduced me to a group of female junior faculty members who worked together to promote one another's scholarly pursuits, to help crowdsource solutions to shared problems and to provide advice to one another as we navigated a campus that was dominated by elderly white men. This network helped me navigate unfamiliar gendered dynamics on campus and provided much needed peer-to-peer support. Other networks developed out of service to the institution; in my fourth year, for example, I served on a task force to design a co-curricular programme. Service on this task force allowed me to develop a close relationship with two other faculty members on the task force who were emerging as campus opinion leaders and were beginning to take on more leadership roles. These examples are representative of the types of social networks and social capital I developed; my networks were based on affinity groups, shared interests and shared experiences. By tapping into these networks, I created beneficial social capital through new social relations and increased knowledge of campus politics, norms and culture.

The final component of stage 1 was the Academic Strategic Initiatives for Improvement (ASIIP) self-study, described above. ASIIP was a pivotal moment in my transition from faculty to leadership in teaching and learning; I participated in the ASIIP task force focused on teaching first-year students and ended up serving as the de facto leader of that group. As part of that work, I conducted extensive research on evidence-based pedagogical practices, surveyed faculty to learn about current institutional practices and wrote recommendations on how to bridge the divide between what Heidelberg faculty were doing and what they should have been doing. Improving faculty pedagogy in courses for first-year students was particularly important because of institutional goals to improve student retention and graduation rates.

The report on first-year teaching included recommendations on pedagogy revisions, which also connected with the report from the faculty charged with reviewing campus support for teaching and learning. Ultimately, the ASIIP self-studies provided four recommendations that shaped the creation of the CTE:

1. Creating a central repository for resources and materials relating to supporting teaching and learning;
2. Assigning or hiring personnel dedicated to the support of teaching and learning, including an instructional technologist;
3. Creation of a campus Teaching and Learning Centre;
4. Revising institutional practices regarding teaching of first-year students (ASIIP Co-Chairs, 2017).

These recommendations were crafted by faculty drawn from across the college and signalled widespread recognition of a general need for better support for teaching and learning.

Some of the recommendations implied that the institution as a whole suffered from a lack of social capital and inadequate social networks. One of the subcommittees, titled 'Teaching Conversations', was charged with reviewing the institutional culture relating to teaching and determined that 'isolated, single and small collaborative efforts towards teaching excellence are already in place at HU [Heidelberg University]' (ASIIP Co-Chairs, 2017, pp. 3–4). The efforts already underway did not translate into wider institutional change or institutional initiatives. This failure to scale up teaching improvement programmes implies that the participants and leaders lacked the social capital necessary to tap into broader campus networks and mobilize a wider cross-section of faculty members. My participation in ASIIP, and my leadership on the group investigating teaching practices for first-year students, helped establish my credibility as an expert in pedagogy and a campus leader in teaching and learning, both of which enhanced the social capital I drew upon to create the CTE.

Stage 2: Creating the CTE

In stage 2, in which I accessed and mobilized the social capital I developed in stage 1, I designed and implemented the college's first CTE. In the design and execution of the campus CTE, I tapped into my understanding of the faculty's needs, my institutional experience and knowledge and my understanding of the college culture to prioritize programmes and activities. Drawing on my social capital allowed me to meet the needs of my colleagues and provide support to new faculty members and those seeking to improve their pedagogy. The programmes I used to launch the CTE focused on encouraging greater interaction and cooperation between faculty members as a way of building wider social networks, helping colleagues learn from and help one another, thereby facilitating more effective collaborative and mutual action among colleagues.

In 2018, the CTE debuted with two cohort programmes: a faculty learning community (FLC) and a new faculty mentoring programme. I chose these programmes for several reasons: they reflected priorities identified in the campus-wide self-study; they helped create interdisciplinary faculty networks; they had a high likelihood of short- and long-term success, which could help grow my social capital as a leader and which resonated with my experiences as a faculty member. Both programmes brought together interdisciplinary groups of faculty members around shared areas of focus and helped bridge existing networks to build positive social capital and create teaching and learning links to promote relationships outside each participant's home department (Rientes and Kinchin, 2014). I placed less emphasis on individualized consultations because group programmes provide a safer environment for implementing change and because I wanted to build social capital and networks among programme participants (Kezar, 2014, p. 97).

New faculty mentoring was of particular importance to me and to the faculty committees I consulted when I designed the CTE. As someone who had to create her own mentoring relationships, I wanted to ensure new colleagues were better supported than I was as a new faculty member. Well-planned mentoring programmes provide new colleagues with the information, resources and support they need to be successful, which positively impacts retention and job satisfaction among faculty. Therefore, the CTE in 2018 launched a new faculty mentoring programme, loosely modelled on the University of Findlay's Teaching Partners Programme (Denecker, 2014).

The new faculty mentoring programme focused on learning institutional norms and culture, which Morgan (2014) rightly points to as one of the benefits of a mentoring programme. The mentoring programme also provided better mechanisms for information sharing across academic departments because new faculty members were grouped into interdisciplinary small groups that worked with a faculty mentor from outside their home departments. Interdisciplinary mentoring allowed new faculty members to build connections and share information across academic departments, which, as Claudia Gonzalez-Brambila (2014) points out, is one of the most important benefits of social capital. The relationship between mentoring programmes and social capital is easily apparent, as mentoring is one way that an individual can build social ties necessary to navigate a particular context (Benbow and Lee, 2019). Like the mentoring programme designed at Ithaca College, mentors were selected because they possessed high social capital in the form of knowledge and relationships (Morgan, 2014); at Heidelberg, mentors were recruited from the faculty opinion leaders rather than central actors to ensure a separation between the mentoring programme and faculty evaluation. The interdisciplinary and formative nature of the programme provided new colleagues with a place to ask questions, gain insights into departmental dynamics, develop strategies for navigating conflict and receive developmental feedback on their teaching, which built bonding networks between mentors and new faculty members. The creation of these networks, combined with the transfer of knowledge and information from mentor to new faculty member, helped new colleagues create their own social capital.

Like the design of the new faculty mentoring programme, the FLC I implemented was informed by my social capital, specifically my knowledge of institutional priorities, needs and culture. Based on a report of the ASIIP first-year teaching task force (discussed above), I designed an interdisciplinary FLC in which participants would revise courses for first-year students. FLC participants built social capital as they formed bonds with each other, established shared norms and engaged collectively in common scholarly activity (Carpenter et al., 2011).

The FLC successfully created bonding networks between participants, as revealed by final reports used to assess the programme. One participant used language indicative of a bonding network, stating 'having a group of diverse, but like-minded colleagues to provide support, feedback, and some accountability really helped reduce the anxiety and risk associated with making significant course changes' (Pruneski, 2018, p. 5). Another noted the positive social capital the FLC created, stating 'I think the most beneficial component was that it created a sense of community across campus' (Pistorova, 2018, p. 3). Another stated, 'I also found the camaraderie of working within the FLC group as both motivating me to complete my task and rewarding in making me feel more of a member of the faculty community at large' (Svoboda, 2018, p. 5). Finally, another participant discussed the culture of mutual trust fostered in the FLC's bonding network:

> I appreciated the members' honesty in sharing both their successes and failures in the classroom. I think our willingness to be open about our own frustrations

> brought about some great discussions, collaborations, and ideas to make improvements in our courses. Sharing our experiences made me realize that I am not the only one facing certain challenges and obstacles in the classroom. I also really enjoyed getting to know my colleagues from different disciplines and departments. (Roerdink, 2018, p. 4)

By carefully aligning the CTE's initiatives with the needs of my institution, I used my social capital to inform and develop programmes. In this, my social capital helped establish my reputation as a leader who could identify campus needs, plan and implement high-impact programming and effect change. Both the new faculty mentoring programme and the FLC established my role as an effective leader and garnered greater support from colleagues and cultivated buy-in from institutional leadership, who were pleased to see that the programmes I initiated had a positive impact on faculty teaching, faculty morale and student learning. The evaluation of both programmes demonstrated their success, not only in achieving their individual programme goals but also in building social capital among participants. Dissemination of that data, through a public presentation on the outcomes of the FLC and through the CTE's annual report, which was shared with faculty and administration, further demonstrated accountability and transparency, which in turn helped solidify my position as a capable leader of the CTE and build my social capital.

Stage 3: Expanding the CTE into a CTL

In the winter of 2019–20 (in the midst of the Covid-19 pandemic), I merged the CTE with the college's academic support centre, creating a coupled CTL that supported all students and faculty. The merger was the result of personnel changes and my growing social capital as the leader of the CTE. At this stage, I reaped the rewards of my social capital by expanding the scope of the teaching centre to create a CTL that reframed the CTE's mission, vision and functional areas. The merger between the CTE and campus academic support was rooted in my awareness that 'the solutions to issues involving persistence, academic momentum, and equity are as much related to curriculum, course design, pedagogy, and assessment as they are to student support services' (Mintz, 2020). The creation of a coupled CTL also allowed me to build networks between faculty and academic support staff by bringing faculty development, instructional technology, academic support, student accessibility services, academic advising and the library together into a single CTL that supported all aspects of faculty teaching and student learning.

For the Owen Center for Teaching and Learning to be successful, I once again used my knowledge of Heidelberg's recent practices, institutional culture and campus demographics to build strong strategic relationships across campus, particularly with athletics. Approximately 60 per cent of Heidelberg's students participate in intercollegiate sports, so the coaching staff play a huge role in the lives of our students. By recruiting the coaches as partners in supporting student success, I signalled a collaborative approach to working with different functional areas. My first strategic partnership was with the athletic director, who invited me to present the centre's new direction and organization at a coaches' meeting, my first meeting outside academic affairs to discuss the reorganization of the CTL. In this meeting, I shared the plan for the Owen Center for Teaching and Learning, asked the coaches for feedback on the organizational structure and asked them how my staff could better support student athletes. I recruited a director of academic support from among the coaching staff; this individual now acts as a bridge between academic affairs and athletics, facilitating the flow of information between these two areas of the organization and promoting collaboration between the CTL and athletics to support student success.

In addition to building better relationships with athletics, I used my social capital to further improve faculty investment and involvement in academic support. Academic support was fully separated from classroom teaching, making collaboration between academic support and faculty more difficult. To bridge the divide between faculty and academic support, I revised the programmes to promote more faculty involvement and improved information sharing by reporting attendance at academic support programmes such as Supplemental Instruction and Academic Coaching. I recruited a faculty member to oversee the Writing Center, thereby building a bridge between the English Department and the CTL; I hired a faculty member to establish a support centre for mathematics, building a similar bridge between the Maths Department, the Education Department and the CTL. By integrating faculty into the structure of academic support programmes, I used my social capital to implement programmatic revisions that benefitted both students and faculty.

Much like the division between academic support and faculty, academic advising for incoming students was also entirely separate from departmental faculty advising. Faculty found this disconnect troubling, as it separated students from potential faculty mentors and highlighted inconsistency in academic advising practices. Poor information sharing between academic departments and professional academic advisors led to contradictory or inconsistent advice. Keenly aware of the shortcomings of Heidelberg's previous advising system,

I integrated faculty members into the centralized advising system for first-year students, further bridging the centralized system of advising with faculty advising in business, social sciences, education, humanities and the arts.

The integration between faculty, athletics and student support provides better support for all constituencies at Heidelberg University. Designing and implementing the merger of two separate centres provided opportunity for me to build stronger relationships with faculty, staff and administration by using my social capital to improve existing systems and better support students and faculty. The expansion of the CTE into the CTL allowed me to assert a larger leadership role on campus and – though this transition is still currently underway – to establish the Owen Center for Teaching Learning as the central node in a campus-wide network of support for all aspects of teaching and learning. By drawing on my own social capital to inform the restructuring of the CTL, I was able to reap the rewards of my social capital to advance my position as a leader in teaching and learning.

Conclusions

Faculty members who are considering shifting from faculty to a position of leadership in teaching and learning, especially at small colleges, would do well to consider how existing networks, relationships and institutional knowledge can facilitate that transition. Drawing on your own social capital to assess institutional needs and align your actions with institutional priorities can allow faculty members to successfully navigate a transformation in their campus roles. Additionally, faculty members who have already transitioned from a teaching role to an administrative role in teaching and learning can leverage their social capital to ensure the success of their centres. By using social capital to create intentional programmes grounded in your institution's unique culture and needs, and by using those programmes to encourage the development of social capital and social networks among community members, faculty members can navigate the transition to effective leadership in teaching and learning, one which fosters connections, relations and cross-institutional working across the various aspects involved in staff and student learning and teaching support.

References

ASIIP Co-Chairs (2017), 'ASIIP Update: Academic Strategic Initiatives for Improvement', Heidelberg University.

Barthauer, L., Spurk, D. and Kauffield, S. (2016), 'Women's Social Capital in Academia: A Personal Network Analysis', *International Review of Social Research*, 6 (4): 195–205.

Benbow, R. and Lee, C. (2019), 'Teaching-Focused Social Networks among College Faculty: Exploring Conditions for the Development of Social Capital', *Higher Education*, 78: 67–89.

Bourdieu, P. and Wacquant, L. J. D. (1992), *An Invitation to Reflective Sociology*, Chicago: University of Chicago Press.

Carpenter, A., Coughlin, L., Morgan, S. and Price, C. (2011), 'Social Capital and the Campus Community', *To Improve the Academy*, 29: 201–15.

Denecker, C. (2014), 'The Teaching Partners Programme: A Place for Conversation, Collaboration, and Change', *Journal of Faculty Development*, 28 (1): 25–31.

Gonzalez-Brambila, C. (2014), 'Social Capital in Academia', *Scientometrics*, 101: 1609–25.

Grupp, L. (2014), 'Faculty Developer as Change Agent: A Conceptual Model for Small Institutions and Beyond', *Journal on Centres for Teaching and Learning*, 6: 45–58.

Heidelberg University Board of Trustees (2020), *Heidelberg University Faculty Manual*, Tiffin, OH: Heidelberg University.

Ingram, E. (2019), 'The Impact of Social Capital on Educational Developers', *New Directions for Teaching and Learning*, 159: 65–74.

Kezar, A. (2014), 'Higher Education and Social Networks: A Review of Research', *Journal of Higher Education*, 85 (1): 91–124.

Lin, N. (1999), 'Building a Network Theory of Social Capital', *Connections*, 22 (1): 28–51.

Lin, N. (2001), *Social Capital: A Theory of Social Structure and Action*, New York: Cambridge University Press.

Mintz, S. (2020), 'Why We Need Centers for Educational Innovation, Evaluation, and Research', *Inside Higher Ed*, 30 November, https://www.insidehighered.com/blogs/higher-ed-gamma/why-we-need-centers-educational-innovation-evaluation-and-research.

Morgan, S. (2014), 'Mentoring and Support for New Faculty: Enhancing Social Capital Using Communities of Practice', *Learning Communities Journal*, 6: 75–92.

Muir, G. and Craig, J. (2017), *Getting Started in an Educational Development Career: From Faculty to Small College CTL Director*, Nederland, CO: POD Network.

Pistorova, S. (2018), *FLC Final Report*, Tiffin, OH: Heidelberg University.

Pruneski, J. (2018), *FLC Final Report*, Tiffin, OH: Heidelberg University.

Putnam, R. D. (2000), *Bowling Alone: The Collapse and Revival of American Community*, New York: Simon & Schuster.

Rientes, B. and Kichin, I. (2014), 'Understanding (In)formal Learning in an Academic Development Programme: A Social Network Perspective', *Teaching and Teacher Education*, 39: 123–35.

Roerdink, A. (2018), *2018 FLC Final Assessment*, Tiffin, OH: Heidelberg University.

Subcommittee on Teaching Resources (2016), *Teaching Resources/Support Wish List: Academic Strategic Initiatives for Improvement*, Tiffin, OH: Heidelberg University.

Svoboda, S. (2018), *FLC Final Report – Svoboda THR 150*, Tiffin, OH: Heidelberg University.

Wright, M., Rudder Lohe, D., Pinder-Grover, T. and Ortquist-Ahrens, L. (2018), 'The Four Rs: Guiding CTLs with Responsiveness, Relationships, Resources, and Research', *To Improve the Academy*, 37 (2). https://quod.lib.umich.edu/t/tia/17063888.0037.206/--four-rs-guiding-ctls-with-responsiveness-relationships?rgn=main;view=fulltext.

A Journey from Scholarship to Leadership: The Education of an Educator

Patrick B. O'Sullivan

Introduction

This chapter examines my journey that began as a traditional academic (teaching, scholarship, service) and then veered towards an academic leadership position in faculty development (directing a university teaching centre). It is a pathway that may offer a tremendously rewarding alternative for academics who are passionate about scholarly teaching and motivated to make a difference for an entire university community. My journey is distinct but not unique, and the details may prompt colleagues to envision a similar path.

The challenges along the way contribute to the rewards that the trek provides: transitioning from largely autonomous faculty priorities to interdependent, collaborative leadership responsibilities; bridging the professor/scholar culture and the 'dark side' of administrative culture; embracing the responsibility to self-educate in a different discipline to create a professional development curriculum; evolving my professional identity from being a disciplinary researcher who teaches students in a narrow specialty to a transdisciplinary educator who mentors peers across the broad landscape of professional fulfilment. What had originally seemed to be a temporary detour became my enduring new direction as I transformed myself from a researcher largely unprepared to teach effectively into an educator able to integrate both the teaching and scholarship dimensions of my responsibilities as an academic.

At a time when universities around the world are reassessing outdated rationales for traditional organizational structures and re-envisioning what today's students need for the world they will be shaping (Bok, 2006; Davidson, 2017), informed leadership for our evolving teaching mission is critical.

A leadership role in a university teaching centre is at the heart of institutional change towards greater fulfilment of higher education's moral mandate and social responsibilities.

Becoming a Scholar

Becoming what is known as an 'academic' requires as much a cultural indoctrination as does a scholarly education. The metamessages of graduate school – the implicit lessons that shadow the official curriculum – are possibly the most important to understanding the distinctive (and sometimes counterproductive) threads running through the culture of academia. My years spent in an American doctoral programme included brief yet powerful episodes of stumbling over unstated rules, violating unarticulated values and watching while my seemingly benign and reasonable assumptions and expectations were shattered with prejudice. Collectively, they function to resocialize graduate students to better fit into the norms and values of their programme's faculty – both for better and for worse. In my programme, and perhaps in many others, one of those values was to elevate research above teaching.

One of my core motivations for pursuing a doctorate was to teach at the university level. For a decade after earning a bachelor's degree, I worked as a journalist on a regional daily newspaper. A caring journalism professor at the state university in town had noticed my published stories in the local daily newspaper and invited me to teach several journalism classes. The experience was a revelation for me: not only was I not horrible at it, sharing my professional knowledge and experience with undergraduates stirred something deep and rewarding. This experience opened a new possible vista for my life, and with my mentor's guidance, I left my job at the newspaper and entered graduate school. I first earned a master's degree at one university and then entered a doctoral programme at another. All along, my intention was to return to my mentor's university and teach journalism alongside him.

In my doctoral programme, however, subtle messages kept reminding me to keep my interest in teaching to myself. In this programme's culture, I encountered cues that speaking openly about an interest in teaching was interpreted by faculty as a sign that you were not on the trajectory of the favoured graduate students. In the hierarchy of the graduate students, those at the top of the pecking order were seen as having the most promise to follow closely in their doctoral advisor's footsteps as a noted researcher. For professors in my programme at a research-intensive university, what mattered most was the potential for graduate students to publish a significant volume of scholarly articles in selective high-prestige journals. Working as a teaching assistant to these professors gave me intimate insights into how marginally they considered their teaching assignments. They devoted minimal energy to prepping class sessions and even less to updating their courses or refining their teaching methods. If these professors were productive in their scholarly work, their undergraduate teaching only had to be passable for them to be considered successful in their academic assignments. This is less of a criticism and more of a candid observation, as my professors were being responsive to the values of the dominant academic culture.

These experiences told me that I was a stranger in a strange land: a graduate student aspiring to a teaching career seeking a degree in a doctoral programme populated with professors (and classmates) who saw research as the most valued enterprise. In many ways, my experiences tracked those of a sojourner from one culture entering a different culture (Kim, 2001). So, I suppressed my overt expressions of interest in teaching and focused on research. It was not a complete capitulation, however, as I came to appreciate the challenge of exploring ideas and the rewards of working to answer questions that could add to capital 'k' Knowledge. As it turned out, I was reasonably successful at scholarly research. By the time I finished my doctoral degree, I had two sole- or first-authored academic publications and two dissertation awards. I was well prepared for a scholarship-centric position at a research university, just as the dominant academic culture had directed.

Although I successfully navigated the mismatch between my goals for graduate school (becoming a skilled educator) and my actual preparation (becoming a skilled researcher), that same disconnect emerged again when I ventured into the academic job market in the mid-1990s. The plum openings for assistant professor posts at prestigious research universities were scant and highly competitive. Most recruitments were for mid-sized public universities where teaching was a significant portion of the responsibilities, and that's where many of us landed. The result is that many in my generation of new PhDs (including me) began our academic careers largely unprepared for the teaching responsibilities of a university appointment. Worse, we were all largely unaware of our limited knowledge and skills for teaching. As a result, we launched our teaching careers confident that modelling our own professors' attitudes and approaches towards teaching was sufficient to meet our professional obligations and our students' needs (see chapter 9 in Derek Bok's 2013 book on higher education). It soon became apparent to me in my early years as an assistant professor that modelling our professors' attitudes and approaches would not suffice to meet my responsibilities as an educator.

Being an Academic

The disconnect between my graduate school preparation and my university teaching responsibilities played out in memorable ways. The stresses and challenges of those first days, the first weeks, the first semester and the first year are vivid even now, twenty-five years after starting my first tenure track position. I recall leaving from my last class of each day completely drained. Walking from the classroom through the faculty office corridors past my colleagues, I maintained a veneer of confidence and competence. Once inside my office, I closed the door behind me to keep my real feelings private. With lights off, I would lay on the floor with my eyes closed, breathing deeply to try to dissipate the tension and anxiety swarming my mind and taxing my body. Usually after fifteen to twenty minutes, I would be able to wearily pull myself up off the floor and get back on the computer to prep the next day's classes. This was my routine for much of my first year, although the intensity of the exhaustion gradually lessened over time.

At the time, I figured that I was the only one feeling such exhaustion. No one else had ever described anything similar. As a new assistant professor, I certainly did not share this with my senior colleagues. I did not want to let anyone think that perhaps they made a mistake in hiring me, and I certainly did not want to feed a perception that I was not on a pathway towards tenure and success. I felt like an imposter, fearing that I would one day be revealed as an incompetent fraud. I later learned that what I felt was common enough to have a name (the 'imposter syndrome') and an extensive literature (e.g. Bravada et al., 2020). The only reason it did not overcome me is because I was so determined to fake it until I could make it.

What was not immediately apparent to me then, but is so clear to me now, is why I was so exhausted. I was expending prodigious amounts of energy coping with my uncertainty and anxiety about teaching. So many questions and precious few insights to apply: what should I do with the next class session? Why use one method and not another? How would I know whether or not I'm on the right track? In hindsight, if I had fully bought into my graduate programme's model of university teaching, I would have been far less stressed because I would have been more confident despite my ignorance. As it was, the stresses came from being vaguely aware of my limitations but unsure about what they were and with few ideas about what to do about them. The intensity of stress would gradually dissipate to a degree over the next several years. My teaching methods evolved gradually but also fitfully and only with a great deal of energy. I relied on mostly trial-and-error changes guided by good intentions, decent instincts about human motivation and occasional insights gleaned from a colleague or an article.

What I did not have, but could have used, was mentoring – formal or informal – from knowledgeable colleagues. Teaching was not a topic of conversation among my fellow faculty. I detected, and then accepted, the prevailing cultural norm that everyone outwardly assumed everyone else was teaching well enough so there was no need to discuss it with each other. Our classroom spaces were considered our private domain. In my nine years of teaching three courses each semester, no colleague ever visited my class for any reason. Classroom observations of junior faculty by senior colleagues are commonly a part of annual evaluations at many universities, but not in my programme. Even asking someone to observe and give feedback on your teaching was too close to an admission that you were not already excellent – like everyone else was supposed to be. Showing a sign of weakness to senior faculty could be hazardous in a department where they could be a crucial voice and consequential vote regarding tenure and promotion decisions. In this culture, you were assumed to be an effective teacher because the research publications on your curriculum vitae constituted sufficient evidence that you were a qualified educator.

The dominant accepted indicators of teaching effectiveness were the formal, end-of-term student evaluations. These were strictly confidential among fellow faculty members. I do not recall ever seeing any of my colleagues' average scores, and I never shared mine with my colleagues. Don't ask, don't tell. A discussion about the validity and value of student ratings of teaching is for another time and place. Suffice it to say that as the (deeply flawed, severely biased, sadly incomplete but pragmatically dominant) source of official feedback on teaching, they nevertheless carry significant weight for each educator's self-perception of their abilities (Blum, 2020; Feldman, 2019). Add to that the massive consequences that those strange little numbers have for retention, promotion and tenure ('RPT') and the distortion is amplified.

According to my own teaching evaluations over the years, I was an adequately adequate teacher: not stellar, not horrible – but consistently solid. Of course, like most faculty, I had no real data-driven insights into why my ratings were what they were or what I might do to improve them. I cared deeply about my students, and I was dedicated to their success. However, all I had to draw on were my own experiences as a student, my largely unguided experiences in graduate school as a teaching assistant, a few lecturer assignments and my graduate school mentors' models – all wrapped up in my best intentions. I did sometimes conclude that I did not have the 'teacher gene', that mysterious capability that some professors seemed to possess that enabled them to be a brilliant teacher with no apparent 'training' and little apparent effort. I was good enough in the classroom, and my scholarly productivity was sufficient to earn tenure and promotion. Next, I set my sights on working towards becoming a full professor.

A Split in the Road

You would have heard the adage 'Luck is where preparation meets opportunity'. In hindsight, I was lucky to have recognized the opportunity when it arose and was fortunate that my preparation had qualified me for a position that I had not even known would exist. The opportunity came in a small item appearing in the campus newsletter inviting faculty applications for the director of a newly reconstituted teaching centre for my campus. I had only a vague idea of what the position would entail, but I met the minimum qualifications: I was tenured and my interest in teaching had influenced the focus of my scholarly work (e.g. O'Sullivan, Hunt and Lippert, 2004). At the time, the idea of taking on this position seemed like a detour from the path towards full professorship. A colleague and close friend pestered me to apply despite my ambivalence, and I will forever be grateful for his persistence and confidence in me.

It became apparent to me that this career move was an opportunity to apply much of what I had studied, researched and taught for the prior fifteen years. This would be a chance to leverage my scholarly work and draw on my fifteen-plus years of experience in college classrooms to try make a real and lasting difference for faculty peers across the university. Intrigued by the challenge, I applied.

I was actually a bit stunned when the e-mail offering me the job arrived in my inbox. Apparently, the search committee members thought that I was worth a try. What they surely did not appreciate (or even have the background to assess) was the breadth and depth of my ignorance of education models, theories, methods and trends. In short, I was experienced and well-intentioned but mostly clueless – and mostly unaware of how much I needed to learn. With a sincere intent to make the most of this unexpected opportunity, I accepted the offer to become director of the Center for Teaching, Learning and Technology. With that, I took an unexpected offramp from the highway of a traditional faculty career and veered into an unfamiliar academic territory.

Facing False Dichotomies

Responses from colleagues to the announcement of my new position were revealing. Two patterns emerged. The first was captured in versions of the same question from colleagues: 'But won't you miss teaching?' My response was invariably along the lines of: 'Yes, but I won't miss the grading!' After a few instances of fielding this question, I started to add: 'Actually, I will continue to teach – just not undergraduates in departmental curriculum courses.' That elaboration did little to mollify some of my peers that I was not making a big mistake. The other type of reaction from colleagues was that I was abandoning my membership in the faculty culture. Invocations of the phrase 'going to the dark side' indicated that some saw this career choice as a betrayal of my faculty tribe. Becoming an administrator was akin to defecting from the *Rebel Alliance* to join *Darth Vader and the Empire*.

This reaction was disconcerting because I had never bought into the us-versus-them narrative that pitted noble and oppressed faculty against disconnected and arrogant campus leadership. In my mind, this was yet another false dichotomy much like those I had recognized in other areas of academia: art versus science, theory versus practice, mind versus body, emotion versus cognition, qualitative versus quantitative methods and, in my discipline, the false dichotomy between mass communication and interpersonal communication (O'Sullivan, 1999). I had found that the most intriguing questions, and the most productive answers, are at the intersections of what have been accepted as disparate components of reality. If this career choice meant I would be distancing myself from some of my colleagues, I would accept that. I also recognized that the faculty/administration dichotomy was a manufactured cultural divide that I would have to bridge when reaching out to faculty about their teaching.

This new position also focused me on another false dichotomy that has long hindered higher education's contributions to society: research versus teaching. In my experience, research and teaching were considered zero-sum enterprises: time and effort spent on one is a direct trade-off for the other. In my doctoral programme in the 1990s, our research skills were vastly more important than our teaching skills. Our faculty mentors knew that our potential for research productivity would be the key to us landing a position, bolstered by the assumption that we would be striving for a prestigious research-intensive university post. The other less prominent reason was because their slim and outdated knowledge of effective undergraduate teaching practices meant that they had little capacity or motivation to provide mentoring in teaching. In my time as a tenure-line faculty member, time and energy devoted to developing teaching effectiveness had to compete with that allocated to scholarly productivity – and research always seemed to take priority over teaching in evaluation criteria.

In my teaching centre position, I quickly came to appreciate more fully just how false the divide was between teaching and research. In my own experience, my teaching (at least the way I had conducted it) was a clear complement to my scholarship. I had the advantage of regularly teaching courses that I had developed based on my area of specialty (communication technologies and social interaction). Designing and updating these courses constantly provided interesting and timely questions to consider in my research. Keeping the course current required me to constantly update examples and to swap dated references with emerging developments. That helped me stay tuned into the social and cultural consequences of new technologies relevant to my scholarship.

Perhaps the most common way that faculty expect to bridge teaching and research is by bringing their own research into their classes. I was able to do that, given my advantage of having teaching assignments that closely aligned with my scholarly interests. Research findings, theories and models (my own and those of others found in my manuscript's reference lists) informed my courses' contents. Conversely, I can point to several of my publications and numerous conference presentations that sprung from the spontaneous 'aha!' moments sparked by students' insightful questions or observations. For example, a graduate student's offhand questions to me about online flaming sparked a thought process that eventually became a publication (O'Sullivan and Flanagan, 2003). I can also note timely examples and new concepts that I brought into my classes from my sustained mucking around in areas that piqued my research interests.

An even more vivid, and promising, way of bridging the teaching/research dichotomy emerged early in my new position at the teaching centre. Over the years, my path to improvement was based primarily on trial and error, applying ideas that occurred to me in response to a problem, or borrowing a method from a colleague. I recognized that some of my colleagues had reputations as excellent teachers and somehow routinely received stellar student evaluations. However, what made them so effective remained a mystery. Perhaps to help me rationalize my comparative mediocrity, I may have rationalized that some people were just born to be good teachers. That I did not happen to be one of them I could more easily attribute to the happenstance of poor luck with the genetic lottery.

It was not long after stepping into the position at the teaching centre that what I learned began to dismantle the 'some are just born to teach' fallacy. Coming from my disciplinary expertise, I recognized that I had limited knowledge of teaching models, principles and practices. So, I did what academics do: I began online searches for relevant literature. By mining bibliographies and reference lists, the constellation of useful materials expanded – the more I found, the more I recognized was there to explore. I gradually realized that I had just begun to wade into a significant reservoir of research literature on instructional principles and practices. Unaware at the time, I was exploring what Boyer (1997) had established was a legitimate and valued form of academic scholarship: the scholarship of teaching and learning.

Thus began a gradual but powerful transformation of my thinking: I began to realize that the capacity to be an effective educator was not some mysterious talent bestowed on a select few. Effective teaching was a learnable accumulation of knowledge and skills available to anyone willing to do the work needed over the years. It seems so obvious to me now, but it was a powerful awakening that recast my view of myself as an educator – I realized that I, too, had the capacity to become a more effective teacher. My well-intentioned, relatively uninformed and only marginally effective trial-and-error method of improvement resulted in slow and fragmented progress. It also left me with a nagging self-doubt about my capacity to ever become an excellent teacher despite how important that was to me. I felt like an underachiever as an educator, which only accentuated the stresses and corroded the sense of accomplishment in my academic career. The existence of a path to improve my teaching by building on insights from so many talented, dedicated educators was exciting and energizing. Now I understood that the imposter syndrome that had shadowed me throughout my academic career was based on a fundamental misunderstanding of what it takes to become an excellent educator. Scholarly teaching was something that I could learn, not something that I had to have been born with. I wasn't an imposter; I was an educator in the making. For me this was a game changer.

Becoming an Educator

Transitioning to the teaching centre position, I pivoted to the questions essential for my new responsibilities: does any of my personal and professional journeys apply to my colleagues in academia? Have they been facing similar cultural challenges and pragmatic barriers? Are my experiences unique to me, or might others also be as delighted as I was about the possibilities for improving their teaching? Can I draw on my own two decades of experiences in the trenches as a college educator to design and implement programmes and services that could be responsive to the needs and goals of my fellow faculty members? And, ultimately, have I found myself in a position to make a real and critical difference for enhancing my university's ability to fulfil its promise to the 20,000 undergraduates who come to campus each year in search of rich, transformational and rewarding learning experiences?

My answer to each of those questions was 'I sure think so!' I was in an academic leadership job that I hadn't known even existed, learning things I didn't know were there to learn about effective teaching and university-level leadership, and was committed to solving challenges that I hadn't known were broadly shared among faculty. Adjusting to this new career direction was persistently difficult and constantly exhilarating. A side benefit was that it also provided me with a modest but important degree of distance from my prior career path to gain valuable new perspectives on the faculty life and academic culture that had been my identity and my purpose for the prior twenty-five years.

As intriguing as all of that was, I also needed to consider another important question: what do I need to learn to be successful? The opportunity to explore the rich, inspiring wealth of models and methods for effective teaching was a challenging and appealing chance to again flex my intellectual curiosity in a literature outside my disciplinary terrain. It was also an unexpected second chance to return to my original purpose for applying to a graduate school. Although I had been a teaching assistant in a graduate school, an instructor at several universities and a tenure track/tenured faculty member at a quality state university, I now began to recognize the chasm more clearly between my initial intentions and my current reality. The distance between my ambition to be an inspiring teacher and my actual capabilities was real. Being a published scholar with years of experience in college classrooms was insufficient for me to be the teacher that I wanted to be, contrary to what I had been socialized to believe. It took an unexpected detour from the traditional academic career path, accompanied by a significant realignment of my identity and values as an academic, to finally begin closing the gap between my lived experiences as a faculty member and my original vision for my purpose in higher education. Taking on this new role was the beginning of my education to become an educator.

From the start, I envisioned using my personal experiences as a guide. My goal was to establish a teaching centre that could provide for my colleagues the informed support and motivation that I had needed but never found. I had a LOT to learn. To be able to provide direction for the teaching centre's staff and to shape the programmes and services, I needed to engage with the scholarly teaching literature as I had done in my disciplinary research literature. I also had the benefit of discovering a professional organization called the Professional and Organizational Development Network (commonly referred to as 'POD').[1] My experiences with the members of POD online and in person at conferences confirmed for me that I had finally found my tribe: fellow academics devoted to better instruction and committed to practising a culture of generosity for each other and our faculty colleagues.

What I have learned in my new career direction – now sixteen years and counting – has provided me a 30,000-foot view of higher education of multiple universities where I have studied and worked, and of university teaching that I never would have achieved in a traditional faculty career. I have come to better understand why higher education evolved into the way it is now and some of the resulting shortcomings (Blum, 2017; Bok, 2006; Davidson, 2017). I learned how faculty development (the general term used to encompass the work of improving university teaching) and teaching centres can play a critical role in bringing university teaching into the twenty-first century (Gillespie and Robertson, 2010; Schroeder, 2011). In contrast to an insular department life, where my professional and social world was limited to a handful of colleagues, I found myself becoming an engaged member of an expansive community of peers from all disciplines and from across the university. Working first hand with the many talented, dedicated and stellar colleagues has filled me with deep optimism about my current university and for higher education in general.

My responsibilities in the teaching centre also led to working relationships with other campus leaders: chairs, associate deans, deans, associate provosts and even (occasionally) provosts and campus presidents. It also clarified for me that most of those in campus leadership positions are senior faculty who were the product of the same culture that had shaped my mentors and me – a culture that remains relatively uninformed about the rich resources for models and methods of effective teaching.

Those insights and relationships helped me to better understand the vagaries in my own faculty career. They were also critical for forming my goal of promoting a cultural change at my university towards one where faculty had clear pathways to become effective educators. My faculty experiences are essential to my ability to design programmes and engage colleagues in ways that could evolve faculty knowledge, skills and attitudes towards improving instruction. This work is essential if higher education is going to meet the needs and goals of current and future generations of students.

Leadership responsibilities in a teaching centre also prompted me to focus on expanding and deepening my knowledge of scholarship-based instructional methods that are effective and appropriate for current cohorts of college students. I uncovered nuggets of wisdom and precious artefacts of insights just about everywhere I turned. I discovered clever and practical models to 'backward' design students' learning experiences (Fink, 2013; Wiggins and McTighe, 2005) instead of teaching by telling learners what they should know. Ken Bain (2004) introduced me to the concept of creating a natural learning environment in the ways that the best college teachers do. I learned how to adopt active learner-centred teaching to replace traditional subject/topic-centred or teacher-centred teaching (Blumberg, 2009; Nilson, 2016). I came to appreciate and implement simple but powerful methods for formative assessment of learning (Angelo and Cross, 1993; Barkley and Major, 2016) that were also excellent methods to prompt self-directed learners towards active learning steeped in reflection (Bean, 2011; Nilson, 2006). What I learned about emerging insights from neuroscience prompted a greater focus on redesigning instruction for more effective, transformational learning (Brown, Roediger and McDaniel, 2014), including for the neurodiversity among students (Armstrong, 2010; Cain, 2013). More recently, I've deepened my knowledge about new perspectives on Maslow's Hierarchy with which educators can help provide a more equitable foundation of support so that all learners can be successful (Kaufman, 2020). All of these, completely applicable to the university classroom, are also tremendously valuable not only in identifying relevant topics for the centre's programming and services but also in the nuanced work of designing and facilitating workshops and providing effective guidance to faculty.

Mixed with that excitement was also a touch of regret. As much as I was delighted with each finding, each discovery prompted an ache of recognition of how much difference each would have made for me earlier in my academic career. Teaching college students would undoubtedly have been less stressful, less exhausting, more successful and more fulfilling if I had been prepped with at least some of these concepts and guided by experienced and thoughtful educators. I could not help but think of the hundreds of students in my courses who would have had learning experiences far closer to my aspirations. In short, I could have been a much better educator much sooner. That this could also be true for my colleagues became the core motivator for my work as the teaching centre director: to provide for them what I had needed to become the teacher that I aspired to be, so that they could become the teacher that they sought to become.

Just a couple of years into my new position, an exchange with a faculty member on the final day of a 'Reinvent Your Course' summer workshop helped confirm that my regrets were not unique. On last-day reflections, participants one by one talked expansively and warmly about what they had gained from the experience. A veteran colleague, who had signed up for the workshop despite being only a year or two away from retirement, looked glum. I approached him, saying that he looked rather unhappy and invited him to share. He said he did in fact learn a lot and was so very glad to be in it. 'So why do you look unhappy?' I asked. He shot back, 'Where was this (workshop) thirty years ago?' He explained that everything that he had learned made so much sense and generated for him a genuine excitement about his fall classes. But even as he envisioned how strong his future classes would be, he said he could not stop thinking of how apparent all that he had not known about effective teaching during his lengthy faculty career was. He explained that he felt he had let his students down now that he understood so many ways he could have been a much better teacher. All I could do was to empathize with him by recounting my own feelings of remorse at what I had not done for my own students, but could have done with this kind of guidance and encouragement. When he mused about putting off his retirement so he could put what he had learned into practice, I took it as a good sign.

What I hadn't anticipated from my education as an educator was the degree to which what I learned was essential – sometimes transformational – for my professional and personal self as a life-long learner. For example, I recognized that my willingness to take on this new career direction was evidence of a growth mindset (Dweck, 2006), even as I recognized that early in my career I had unwittingly embraced a fixed mindset about my teaching. What I learned about effective 'backward design' for curricular planning prompted me to 'start with the end in mind' in my administrative and life tasks by first clarifying objectives and assessments before identifying how to proceed (Wiggins and McTighe, 2005). Exploring the not-yet-known is at the core of the scholarly enterprise, yet it was nevertheless reassuring to learn about the rewards of embracing struggles, errors and failures (Schulz, 2010) as resources for accomplishments (rather than a source of shame) in all aspects of my life. What I learned about metacognition (Nilson, 2016) and emotion in learning (Cavanaugh, 2016) prompted me to embrace mindfulness (Siegel, 2010) as an administrator, educator, colleague, spouse and parent. What I learned about neuroscience provided me with a greater appreciation for the neurodiversity in myself and among others (Armstrong, 2010; Cain, 2013). What I learned about perceptual and analytical biases inherent in the human mind helped me to be aware of my many privileges and how to become a better ally for social justice (DiAngelo, 2018; Steele, 2010). The result is that at this late stage of my career I am more authentically 'me' and more fulfilled as a father, husband, son, sibling, friend and colleague as well as a teacher and educational leader (Brown, 2018; Palmer, 1998).

Conclusion

My experiences earning a doctorate and navigating a faculty career path through tenure continue to provide me with vivid insights essential to my effectiveness as an educational leader. I have lived the shortcoming of how graduate students are prepared for university-level teaching. Now my current role has allowed me opportunities to bring scholarship-informed principles and practices of effective instruction (what I call 'the science of the art' of teaching) to my faculty colleagues. I value deeply the entire range of experiences I had as a faculty member, including the struggles. But I know now that a conventional academic career could never have been as rewarding as my role in educational development leadership. I have never looked back at my career choices with regret, especially because I am always eagerly looking ahead to what I can learn next to become a better mentor for my fellow educators. My professional and personal purpose now is to motivate and support higher education scholars to become effective educators in the ways that our students need and deserve. My professional growth and personal rewards that come with this commitment are vast, deep and accumulating every day.

Perhaps one day, if graduate school preparation for teaching improves and universities' support and expectations for faculty's instructional expertise become the norm, this job will diminish in importance. Until that happens, the need for other academics to choose paths similar to mine remains acute. Higher education must be moved from its inertia of tradition if it is to meet the changing needs of today's learners for an education that prepares them for careers and lives in the twenty-first century. I believe that university teaching centres and the faculty who become educators that lead them are well positioned to help make that change happen. For such education development leaders to be successful in their careers, they would need to move from a fixed mindset of being a disciplinary researcher to becoming a transdisciplinary educator with a flexible mindset willing to cross the disciplinary boundaries. Such leaders need to be willing to engage with the scholarship of learning and teaching and to build structures that encourage a cultural change to motivate academics to embrace teaching as a meaningful and rewarding aspect of their professional career.

Note

1 The POD Network (https://podnetwork.org) is North America's largest educational development community devoted to improving teaching and learning in higher education. The network has more than 1,400 members representing every US state and more than thirty countries.

References

Angelo, T. and Cross, P. (1993), *Classroom Assessment Techniques: A Handbook for College Teachers*, 2nd edn, San Francisco, CA: Jossey-Bass.
Armstrong, T. (2010), *The Power of Neurodiversity: Unleashing the Advantages of Your Differently Wired Brain*, Cambridge, MA: Da Capo Press.
Bain, K. (2004), *What the Best College Teachers Do*, Cambridge, MA: Harvard University Press.
Barkley, E. F. and Major, C. H. (2016), *Learning Assessment Techniques: A Handbook for College Faculty*, San Francisco, CA: Jossey-Bass.
Bean, J. (2011), *Engaging Ideas: The Professor's Guide to Integrating Writing, Critical Thinking and Active Learning in the Classroom*, 2nd edn, San Francisco, CA: Jossey-Bass.
Blum, S., ed. (2020), *Ungrading: Why Rating Students Undermines Learning (and What To Do Instead)*, Morgantown: West Virginia University Press.
Blum, S. (2017), *'I Love Learning; I Hate School': An Anthropology of College*, Cornell, NY: Cornell University Press.
Blumberg, P. (2009), *Developing Learner-Centered Teaching: A Practical Guide for Faculty*, San Francisco, CA: Jossey-Bass.
Bok, D. (2006), *Our Underachieving Colleges: A Candid Look at How Much Students Learn and Why They Should Be Learning More*, Princeton, NJ: Princeton University Press.
Bok, D. (2013), *Higher Education in America*, Princeton, NJ: Princeton University Press.
Boyer, E. (1997), *Scholarship Reconsidered: Priorities of the Professoriate*, Princeton, NJ: Princeton University Press.

Bravata, D. M., Watts, S. A., Keefer, A. L., Madhusudhan, D. K., Taylor, K. T., Clark, D. M., Nelson, R. S., Cokley, K. O. and Hagg, H. K. (2020), 'Prevalence, Predictors, and Treatment of Impostor Syndrome: A Systematic Review', *Journal of General Internal Medicine*, 35 (4): 1252–75.

Brown, B. (2018), *Dare to Lead*, New York: Random House.

Brown, P. C., Roediger, H. L. and McDaniel, M. A. (2014), *Make It Stick: The Science of Successful Learning*, Cambridge, MA: Belknap Press.

Cain, S. (2013), *Quiet: The Power of Introverts in a World That Can't Stop Talking*, New York: Random House.

Cavanaugh, S. R. (2016), *The Spark of Learning: Energizing the College Classroom with the Science of Emotion*, Morgantown: West Virginia University Press.

Davidson, C. N. (2017), *The New Education: How to Revolutionize the University to Prepare Students for a World in Flux*, New York: Basic Books.

DiAngelo, R. (2018), *White Fragility: Why It's So Hard for White People to Talk about Racism*, Boston: Beacon Press.

Dweck, C. S. (2006), *Mindset: The New Psychology of Success*, New York: Random House.

Feldman, J. (2019), *Grading for Equity: Why It Matters and How It Can Transform Schools and Classrooms*, Thousand Oaks, CA: Corwin Press.

Fink, D. (2013), *Creating Significant Learning Experiences: An Integrated Approach to Designing College Courses*, San Francisco, CA: Jossey-Bass.

Gillespie, K. J. and Robertson, D. L., eds (2010), *A Guide to Faculty Development*, 2nd edn, San Francisco, CA: Jossey-Bass.

Kaufman, S. B. (2020), *Transcend: The New Science of Self-Actualization*, New York: TarcherPerigee.

Kim, Y. Y. (2001), *Becoming Intercultural: An Integrative Theory of Communication and Cross-Cultural Adaptation*, Thousand Oaks, CA: Sage.

Nilson, L. B. (2006), *Creating Self-Regulated Learners: Strategies to Strengthen Students' Self-Awareness and Learning Skills*, Sterling, VA: Stylus.

Nilson, L. B. (2016), *Teaching at Its Best: A Research-Based Resource for College Instructors*, 4th edn, San Francisco, CA: Jossey-Bass.

O'Sullivan, P. B. (1999), 'Bridging the Mass-Interpersonal Divide: Synthesis Scholarship in HCR', *Human Communication Research*, 25 (4): 569–88.

O'Sullivan, P. B. and Flanagan, A. (2003), 'Reconceptualizing "Flaming" and Other Problematic Messages', *New Media and Society*, 5 (1): 69–94.

O'Sullivan, P. B., Hunt, S. and Lippert, L. (2004), 'Mediated Immediacy: A Language of Affiliation in a Technological Age', *Journal of Language and Social Psychology*, 23 (4): 464–90.

Palmer, P. (1998), *The Courage to Teach: Exploring the Inner Landscape of a Teacher's Life*, San Francisco, CA: Jossey-Bass.

Schulz, K. (2010), *Being Wrong: Adventures on the Margin of Error*, New York: HarperCollins.

Schroeder, C., ed. (2011), *Coming in from the Margins: Faculty Development's Emerging Organizational Development Role in Institutional Change*, Sterling, VA: Stylus.

Siegel, D. J. (2010), *Mindsight: The New Science of Personal Transformation*, New York: Bantam Books.

Steele, C. M. (2010), *Whistling Vivaldi: How Stereotypes Affect Us and What We Can Do*, New York: Norton.

Wiggins, G. and McTighe, J. (2005), *Understanding by Design*, 2nd edn, Alexandria, VA: Association for Supervision & Curriculum Development.

3

The Changing Perspectives of an Academic Leader: Looking from Outside to the Inside and from Inside to the Outside

Celia Popovic

Introduction

I am currently an associate professor at York University, Toronto. This is not where I expected to be when I started my career in the mid-1980s. In this chapter I shall describe the journey of my career, as it relates to my development as a leader. In so doing, I reflect on this journey through the lens of being an outsider in many contexts. I use Perry's Theory of Intellectual and Ethical Development ([1970] 1998) as a guiding framework in reflecting on my journey.

My career has seen me move in a circle in that I was first a lecturer, then became an educational developer and am now a lecturer again. Educational development is a specialized field in further and higher education (HE, or post-secondary education [PSE] in North America), which can be summarized as supporting those who teach to provide the best learning experience for students (Baume and Popovic, 2016).

After graduating in the mid-1980s with a BA in English and American studies, I worked for six years as a corporate trainer. I became a lecturer in further education (FE) for a couple of years before moving into HE as an educational developer, having completed an MEd and later an EdD. In the mid-2000s I became a manager as head of a teaching support centre. In 2011, I moved from the UK to a similar role in Canada. Finally, in the waning years of my career, I find myself an associate professor at a Faculty of Education in a Canadian university.

In this chapter I look at the five stages of my FE/HE career through the lens of Perry's Theory of Intellectual and Ethical Development ([1970] 1998), telling my tale and highlighting the challenges and issues faced at each stage and identifying the strategies and strengths that I developed to overcome those challenges. I also use metaphors of journey and maps, but of course, the end point of that journey is ever shifting.

Perry suggests there are nine positions that learners move through in their intellectual development. Some learners stop at a position before reaching the final level; some do so in one area while achieving different levels in others. To summarize these nine positions, Perry describes the movement from dualism or received knowledge (positions 1 and 2), to multiplicity or subjective knowledge (positions 3 and 4), to relativism or procedural knowledge (positions 5 and 6), to commitment or constructed knowledge (positions 7, 8 and 9). I apply this framework in reflecting on my experiences as a professional in three aspects: as a teacher, as an educational developer and as a manager.

The nine positions can be summarized as follows:

- *Position 1:* The student sees the world in polar terms of we-right-good vs other-wrong-bad. There is a right answer, the teacher knows that right answer and the learner can, too, if they work hard enough. As a leader, I interpret this as a belief that there is a right way to lead others, and that it is relatively simple to determine what is right and what is wrong.
- *Position 2:* The student perceives diversity of opinion and uncertainty and accounts for them as unwarranted confusion in poorly qualified authorities, or as mere exercises set by authority 'so we can learn to find The Answer for ourselves'. As a leader, I interpret this as maintaining the idea there is a right answer to every situation and any diversity is a test for the leader to find the 'correct' approach.
- *Position 3:* The student accepts diversity and uncertainty as legitimate but still temporary in areas where authority 'hasn't found The Answer yet'. S/he supposes authority grades him/her in these areas on 'good expression' but remains puzzled as to standards. As a leader in this position, I would try to find the correct path from a range on offer.
- *Position 4:* (a) The student perceives legitimate uncertainty (and therefore diversity of opinion) to be extensive and raises it to the status of an unstructured epistemological realm of its own in which 'anyone has a right to his own opinion', a realm which he sets over against authority's realm where right–wrong still prevails, or (b) the student discovers qualitative contextual relativistic reasoning as a special case of 'what They want' within authority's realm. A leader in this position may interpret the diversity of

Table 3.1 Stages of Development Using the Lens of Perry's Theory of Intellectual and Ethical Development (Perry, 1970, 1998)

Stage	Metaphor	Identity/identities	Perry stage	Leadership style
1. Instructor in FE (teaching)	Lost	Bewildered, imposter syndrome	Dualism moving towards multiplicity	Self-informed, seeking out examples
2. Educational developer in HE (educational development)	Found a map	Increasing confidence, belonging	Teaching multiplicity to relativism Educational development – dualism towards multiplicity	Community-contributing service Sharing Exploring
3. Manager in UK (management)	Improved the map	Bigger view/changed perspective	Educational development – multiplicity Management – duality towards multiplicity	Team Inclusive Lead by example
4. Manager in Canada (management)	Created a new map based on the old one allowing for new contours and landmarks	New location, some things familiar, some very different	Relativism to commitment	Team national/international Influencing policy Empathic leadership
5. Professor in Faculty of Education (teaching)	Maps become globe, new maps developed by others	New identity, based on the old, moved from one side of the desk to the other I know who I am	Commitment	Elder At peace Collegial Community Collaboration

leadership approaches as evidence that any leadership approach is valid, including their own.

- *Position 5:* The student perceives all knowledge and values (including authority's) as contextual and relativistic and subordinates dualistic right–wrong functions to the status of a special case, in context. A leader in this position may argue that the end justifies the means, or that an action is determined by the specifics of a situation, rather than an underlying system of values.
- *Position 6:* The student apprehends the necessity of orienting himself in a relativistic world through some form of personal commitment (as distinct from unquestioned or unconsidered commitment to simple belief in certainty). A leader in this position acknowledges the need for values or a moral compass on which to base their decisions.
- *Position 7:* The student makes an initial commitment in some area. The leader identifies the values or morals that inform their practice.
- *Position 8:* The student experiences the implications of commitment and explores the subjective and stylistic issues of responsibility. The leader takes this awareness further by embodying, not just espousing, their beliefs.
- *Position 9:* The student experiences the affirmation of identity among multiple responsibilities and realizes commitment as an ongoing, unfolding activity through which he expresses his lifestyle. The leader does the same (Perry, 1970, pp. 9–10, with the addition of viewing the positions through the lens of a leader).

1. Feeling Lost: Dualism Moving towards Multiplicity – Lecturer in FE in the UK

My move into FE was sudden and fragmented. Graduating into a recession in the UK in the mid-1980s, I first worked as a trainer for a software company. While I enjoyed the teaching element of the role, I nurtured a desire to work in PSE. A friend suggested that I could get work as a lecturer despite having just a BA, no teaching qualifications and six years of experience as a trainer in IT systems. One week later, it was the start of the autumn term, and I was a casual lecturer, working part time in four different FE colleges in the UK. As a new lecturer, I was keen to find ways to improve my teaching. There was no requirement for me to seek out this support and no help in finding it.

As a casual lecturer I belonged to no one. I had four managers, yet I had none. The 'managers' in this context were programme leads or heads of department tasked with finding tutors for GCSE and A-level programmes, the UK national exams usually taken at the end of grade 10 and grade 12 high school education. I was hired on the basis of my curriculum vitae and later, because I had met the expectations, could be trusted with another group. I had no feedback on my performance, other than the exam grades for the students. I had no sense of the objectives of the institution or the department. In one case, I never met anyone face to face apart from the students. The hiring was done by phone; the class was in the evening. I went to the allotted room, met the students and went home again. The only college employee I met was the caretaker, who was the literal gatekeeper as he held the key to the room but not the key to teaching.

In another college, where I taught several classes in the daytime, I did meet with permanent lecturers. I quickly learned not to ask for help from my 'colleagues' as one of them told me firmly on the first day that I wasn't to ask for lesson plans: 'Why should we do your work for you?' was the off-putting remark.

In this context it was not easy to find a path for myself, let alone exercise leadership. I was keen to ensure that I was doing the job properly, sitting firmly in position one of Perry's list. I decided to take a City and Guild Certificate in Adult Learning, a decision that was well made. I attended classes in person and met with other interested teachers as well as the course directors. It was this experience that led to my subsequent career, although I didn't anticipate it at the time. I found that I was fascinated by the content of the course – how students learn, what teachers can do to improve the chances of success, how to structure classes – but also by the notion that teaching is a skill that can be learnt. While the lack of support and oversight was isolating, it did bring an advantage as well. The only responsibility I had was to myself and my students. I ensured I turned up early to class, had a plan for the session and the term as a whole and prepared myself as best I could. But I was not burdened by the responsibilities that came later.

In this time, I learnt to be organized, self-reliant and resourceful. Some of the skills I brought with me; others I learnt from trial and error. I was learning my craft as a teacher, not just in terms of teaching skills but also in terms of understanding the culture of FE. I found solace in the work of Veblen ([1899] 2009), from which I learnt to think critically about norms and mores of a culture which served to keep newcomers in a position of outsiders. When, later, I came across Perry's Theory of Intellectual and Ethical Development (1970), I was able to identify my own nascent development as a lecturer as being at the stage of dualism, but I was moving towards one of multiplicity. According to Perry, the first stage of intellectual development finds the learner seeking answers. The world is viewed as a series of problems with right and wrong answers. Gradually, as the learner develops an awareness that there may be more than one answer, they move to a position of multiplicity. For me, this was manifested in my desire to find an answer to my question – what is the best way to teach? I thought the more experienced colleagues knew the answer. As I progressed my way through the City and Guilds course, I became aware that there were multiple ways to teach. I absorbed the message that student-centred learning (SCL) was ideal, and I was distraught by the realization that I had not taken this approach in my early classes. In my dualistic view, SCL = right, everything else = wrong. As I gained experience as a lecturer, I realized that there are multiple ways to teach, and I began to appreciate the complexity inherent in the question 'how should one teach?'

2. Educational Developer in HE in the UK: Finding a Map

In my first HE appointment, I joined a friendly team that provided support to instructors wanting to incorporate technology into their teaching. I felt at home. I saw the same people in the same room each day and had engaging work with people sincerely interested in teaching. This was my first educational development role, although I did not know to call it that then. Routes into educational development are diverse, and often unplanned, as was mine. The haphazard career paths of developers have been widely documented and discussed (Baume and Popovic, 2016; Little, Green and Felton, 2019; Zhou and Felton, 2019).

I was a junior member of the team, but I was respected for the skills and knowledge that I brought with me. While much of my work was with individual lecturers, or working on my own, I was also part of a team. I drew on the experience I had in industry in navigating my way through team meetings. I attended meetings that were well run and meetings that were not. I tried to identify the factors that helped and those that hindered, such as keeping to time, staying on point and ensuring quieter members had as much opportunity to speak as the more dominant 'usual suspects'. At this stage, much of my learning was informal and experiential. When I moved to my next post, I found a very different culture. This university seemed to me to be an odd combination of newness and cutting edge, structured around notions of academic freedom and tradition found in Oxbridge.

In my first three posts, I was hired on an 'academic-related' contract. This meant that I was recognized as doing scholarly work of some kind, but I was not regarded as a fully-paid-up member of the elite (an academic). As a junior employee, I thought I had little kudos or power. Yet, if that were the case, why was I sometimes regarded as a threat? I remember one occasion when I had been asked to run a session on learning outcomes and curriculum alignment. I was in a room with forty to fifty participants, all of whom were subject experts and experienced teachers. A learning outcomes–based curriculum rather than content-led was a new idea for them. One of the lecturers interrupted the workshop to ask me to explain my academic qualifications, to justify why they should listen to me. While I could understand the desire to ensure that I was credible, it was an uncomfortable experience. I had a Master's in Education at that point and was midway through a doctorate. I knew I was a legitimate person to run the workshop, and so I calmly explained my credentials. Afterwards I wondered how that lecturer would have felt had a student publicly challenged them in the same way. It is highly unlikely that a student would do that. The power imbalance would not only prevent a student from challenging, but in the context of a medical school, the perceived danger to that student's future career would reduce any chance of dissent.

On another occasion, when working with clinical doctors (medicine in the UK is taught in part by faculty in the medical school and in part by practising medics in the field), I was challenged in an equally disturbing but different way. I was in a reception with around fifty doctors, a dozen administrators and some visitors. From one side of the packed room, a booming voice rang out: 'Hey Popovic! I hear you think I should be using the internet in my teaching. So how am I supposed to do that?' Aside from sheer rudeness, the aggression of this took me by surprise. I was aware that everyone had stopped talking and were looking at either me or the questioner. I took a breath, walked slowly and calmly over to where he was standing and, in a normal volume, invited him to meet with me to discuss his needs. I didn't allow my emotions to show; I maintained a professional demeanour; and I felt I took control. But I was shaking inside.

The doctor was at least twenty years older than me, accustomed to other people following his instructions without question, a figure of authority and power. At the time, I felt attacked and that his intention was to humiliate me. In retrospect, I think he felt threatened or at least irritated by an outsider entering his domain and disrupting a teaching process that, as far as he was concerned, had no need for disruption. On the other hand, he may have been sincerely interested in how the internet might impact his teaching and had no regard for social norms. Whether he was or not, he never took up my invitation to meet with me.

Teaching in HE often triggers emotional reactions. There is a fine line between sharing ideas and appearing to preach. The power relationships are not always explicit and can change according to context. Perry's stages help me to understand my own journey, but also that of others. It is possible that medic was seeing teaching and learning through the lens of dualism, where a new method, 'the internet', challenged his practice: rather than seeing it as an opportunity, it was perceived as a threat.

I sought out peers in similar positions both within and beyond the institution. One of my colleagues, a senior professor, took a nurturing approach, treating me like his doctoral or postdoctoral student. He encouraged me to be scholarly, to see myself as a scholar and to push the boundaries of the job description. I think without his encouragement I may not have seen myself as a scholar, rather as a technician and provider of support. As I reflect on this, I realize this has been a pattern throughout my career. This is a question of identity as much as behaviour or outcome. The choice of employment category exemplifies this tension – are educational developers scholars or staff; are we there as a support to academics; or are we academics in our own right? (Baume and Popovic, 2016).

I also sought out support from the professional organization – Staff and Educational Development Association (SEDA). As my career has developed, so too has the prevalence of educational development. The earliest teaching support centres seem to date from the 1970s, with the first in the UK founded by Lewis Elton in 1967 at the University of Surrey. In the 1980s, when I began my career, there were still very few teaching centres. Over the decades since then, educational development has expanded such that now there are very few universities in the UK or Canada that offer no support at all. Along with this expansion came the critical mass to warrant the formation of a professional organization. SEDA took on that role, and for me was a godsend when I discovered it in the early 2000s. In SEDA I did not need to explain the challenges; other members faced the same. Better still, there were people ready and eager to share their wisdom, to explore, to challenge, to take risks. Through the biannual conferences, the resources and the networks, I found 'my tribe' (Becher and Trowler, 2001). I launched myself into a frenzy of activity, joining committees, volunteering to review conference applications, reading as much as I could of the resources, books, papers and articles. I remember almost viscerally the relief and excitement of feeling at home for the first time.

From the perspective of Perry's stages (1970), I was developing on two fronts: as an educator and as an educational developer. I had moved from multiplicity to relativism in my teaching, but I was still in the stage of dualism to multiplicity as an educational developer. Perry's scheme describes the learner moving to a position of relativism when they realize that knowledge is contextual. There are few absolutes in terms of right vs wrong answers. Instead, something that is wrong in one context might be right in another. Lectures provide a good example. Early in my career, I learnt that lectures were wrong. However, as I expanded my experience, I found situations where lectures could offer the best solution.

As a teacher, I had learnt that no two classes are ever the same. Teaching is not a pure science; the emotions, energy and motivation of all involved can have a huge impact. I was beginning to recognize that not only are there multiple answers, but that one must exercise judgement and recognize context in evaluating one approach compared to another. As an educational developer, though, I was in the foothills of knowledge. To use the journey/map metaphor: I had found a set of maps for teaching but was still clinging to the one map for my educational development role. SEDA and the colleagues I met at conferences and workshops helped me build my confidence, and they gave me a sense of belonging. This camaraderie and professional support enabled me to develop and build my expertise.

3. Department Manager in HE in the UK: Improving the Map

As the head of a teaching support centre, it was the first time since my days leading a team in the training company that I found myself in a formal position of seniority. The move to a new institution in some ways masked the transition I had to make in my role. As I learnt about the culture and values of the new institution, teaching led in contrast to the research focus of my previous employers. I also had to work out my leadership style and strategies for success.

I was helped enormously by a generous mentor. By mutual agreement we held monthly offsite meetings which helped me to reflect on my progress: I was able to hear my thoughts and opinions mirrored back to me. My mentor listened carefully to both what I was and was not saying; advice was offered in a thoughtful way; and I was led to reach conclusions for myself. This skilful mentorship guided me through Perry's stages, as I moved towards a position of commitment in my managerial style. As a new manager seeking to lead a centre, I also had to learn how to deal with a group of very diverse individuals with varying degrees of commitment and engagement. I learnt to tread the path between being overly friendly or distant and aloof while remaining true to my core beliefs and values.

4. Department Manager in HE in Canada: Creating a New Map

In 2011 I moved to Canada. I was diagnosed with cancer in 2008; I had been told I had limited life expectancy. (I am pleased to report that thirteen years later I have exceeded the five to ten years I was led to expect, and my doctors seem to have reset the clock for me.) As clichéd as this observation has become, this experience does make one re-evaluate life choices. In our case, my husband and I decided to live for the day and take on challenges and adventures we might previously have put off as something to do in the future. Moving to Canada might not be on everyone's list but, after attending Glastonbury and Wimbledon, it was certainly on ours. So, when the opportunity came: we took it.

Moving to a new city can be challenging, moving to another country even more so. For me, the move presented a wholly unexpected chapter in my life. I seized it with energy and enthusiasm. That energy and enthusiasm was vital in propelling me through the next eight years, during which I worked with inspirational colleagues to build a teaching support centre offering resources, guidance, courses and leadership for all who teach. Building on my experience in the UK, I reached out first to those most likely to listen. Having established my credibility with them by sharing my beliefs and knowledge about teaching, they became part of my wider circle, encouraging others to attend workshops, running events themselves and engaging in action research projects with me and my team. An early project was to introduce an annual teaching and learning conference. I did this within the first year of my appointment, and I am pleased to say it is now a highly regarded fixture in the university calendar. Rather than preach to my new colleagues, I recognized the power of listening to them, encouraging them to share their practice, their innovations and their challenges with peers.

As someone who likes speaking their mind, I tried very hard to listen as much if not more than I spoke. Aside from being good practice as a developer, it proved to be good practice as an immigrant leader. As a native English speaker, I did not anticipate language being one of the challenges in this role. How wrong can a person be? I rapidly learnt not to make assumptions about language, but of course it is easy to say that and much harder to do it when you do not know which words are shared and which are not. After being asked for some help from another professor, I was taken aback when she e-mailed to say my suggestions had been 'quite helpful'. To my British ears, 'quite helpful' meant 'virtually no help at all', whereas to a Canadian, it means 'extremely helpful'. The list of synonyms are anything but – and the opportunities to offend and be offended – legion. So not only did I have to learn how to avoid offending, I had to learn not to be offended – at least until the case was proven beyond doubt.

There was one incident that stands out for me. A head of department asked me to arrange a workshop for his colleagues, but because, according to him, they were too busy to attend the scheduled workshop provided for all lecturers on the topic, we should cover the material in half the time. I explained that this would have consequences, but he was adamant. Not surprisingly, the workshop was not a resounding success, at least in his view, although the evaluations suggested otherwise, and several of the participants attended further workshops and individual consultations with the team. I was summoned to his office the following day. I turned up expecting to discuss the needs for the department and how we might improve our support. Instead, the head told me that I was exemplifying the Peter principle in which people are promoted to their level of incompetence. I treasure this as the single most stinging insult I've received in my career! He may have been right, but I did not feel the meeting was the appropriate time to tell me. I smiled, observed there was little point in continuing the conversation and left.

What did that incident teach me? It taught me that there are some people who need to insult others to reassure themselves of their own importance. It also taught me that it is possible to behave graciously and with dignity in the face of outright rudeness while getting a great dinner party story out of what could be a deeply humiliating experience. I am not sure why I delight in this story so much, but I suspect it is in part to do with confidence and maturity. I did not believe I was incompetent, all evidence suggested otherwise, I was not vulnerable to the sting of the insult, and I did not need to allow that one negative incident to cloud all the positive exchanges with other people. I rather wished my younger, more self-conscious self could have known the time would come when I could deal with other people's negative behaviour.

Sadly, it is not unusual to face rudeness, bullying or aggression in any workplace, and universities are no exception (McKay et al., 2008). The nature of educational development may attract more than the average since the work taps into potential insecurities. Some professors are so wedded to the notion of their identity as expert that any suggestion of lack of expertise can be experienced as an existential threat. I was confident in my team and my own performance, but had I not been, I might have reacted much more aggressively to the perceived threat posed by the head. For some lecturers, regardless of how many years they have taught, the suggestion that there might be better ways to teach can present a threat – just as it may have done to the doctor in the UK, mentioned earlier. I see this as evidence of having reached a position of commitment (Perry, 1970) in my professional life.

It is not sufficient to offer suggestions, to provide resources or run workshops; we must take people on board with us, rather than trying to change them. With the polarizing of politics in many countries, I am fascinated by the apparent pointlessness of trying to change the mind of someone who holds opposing views by telling them why they are wrong and why the speaker is right. It is highly unlikely that anyone faced with this will change their mind. Instead they stick in their heels and either shut down or state their own views ever louder. To win an argument, if winning means changing someone else's point of view, we have to understand their perspective, to see life from their context and then find a way to reframe the argument in a way that makes sense to that person. I believe the same is true when working with some lecturers. It is counterproductive to present teaching and learning approaches as best practice if that flies in the face of their experience. It is for this reason that I put a great deal of store in encouraging research into teaching and learning. The Scholarship of Teaching and Learning (SoTL) drawing on Boyer's (1990) seminal work encourages faculty to take the same scholarly approach to their teaching as they do to their research. Boyer's work is seminal both because it has had a transformative effect on the way research into teaching is viewed and also because this was the first time that such research had been treated as scholarly activity.

If I could change one thing in HE, it would be the strange (to my eyes and ears) denigration of research into teaching in HE (SoTL) beneath that of research into virtually anything else (Chen, 2015). If we could value the prodigious research that has been published, particularly in recent years, and encourage our HE teachers to research their teaching practice, alone and with each other, we would find it easier to encourage practices such as experiential SCL. The combination of experience, support from my community and growing confidence enabled me to move – in Perry's terms – to a position of commitment in my work both as an educational developer and as a manager. I was now able to state with conviction my stance on learning, on management and on educational development. There is synthesis in all three areas, as I recognize the need to continuously learn and develop, but that recognition that this is a journey and not a destination does not prevent me from acknowledging my expertise and the validity of my views.

5. Professor in HE in Canada: New Map Made by Others

Two years ago, I moved once more into another chapter of my career. Having completed all that I had sought to do with the teaching support centre, I recognized that it was time for new voices and new ideas. I had given my all to the centre, and it felt like my 'baby', but just as with my human babies, there came a time to move on. I was sad to leave the team, but I did not leave the university. My team now became my source of support. I was appointed as a faculty member when I joined the university, but the nature of the role meant that I was not really viewed as one, not least by myself. My identity has always been that of an 'educational developer'. Now I was expected to take up my place as a tenured professor in the Faculty of Education. After eight years at the institution, I was a newbie again.

The transition from director to associate professor has been further complicated by a year's sabbatical during which the entire world changed, owing to COVID-19. This has given me plenty of time for reflection, for recovery and for planning. The move from the centre to the faculty is not as drastic in geographical terms as the move from the UK to Canada: I moved from one building to another rather than 3,000 miles, but in other ways it is just as unsettling. I am in the Faculty of Education because that is the closest fit to my research and publication field. Fortunately for me, there is a thriving body of scholars engaged in PSE research, so I do have a home. There are courses that I am qualified and (more importantly) confident to teach. But I am not automatically 'one of the crew'. I was not selected for a post in the faculty; I am known in that people recognize my name and my face, but I am not known in terms of faculty identity. I have not sat on committees in the faculty; I have not taken part in debates or formed personal connections for good or ill; I am not known to the support staff. I do not have a faculty-based history. So, I am starting over. In this likely final chapter of my working life, I am learning to understand the microculture of a faculty within a large university that I had thought I knew well. I am charting my course as someone with an extensive career history who is regarded as a newcomer. I am learning first hand about the challenges and joys of being a professor – lessons that would have been priceless when I was in the centre, particularly in the early days.

When my husband and I decided to embark on this adventure, we thought it would be for a few years, that we would return to the UK. However, as time has progressed, we have found ourselves increasingly at home here and two years ago became dual British/Canadian citizens. I am sure UK friends notice the odd turn of phrase or choice of words that have changed, but to most ears we remain faithful to the accent we learnt to use for our first fifty years. Despite Canada, and Toronto in particular, having high proportions of first- and second-generation immigrants, I do wonder if colleagues ever see past my identity as a Brit. Others have commented on the curse of the immigrant, that you can find yourself an outsider in your new home, but also in your old one: we all move on; it is impossible to go back.

So, finally, I find myself back at the start in some ways, but ultimately in a position that Perry would describe as commitment. I may have lingering moments of imposter syndrome (Wilkinson, 2020), wondering if I will ever fit in and feel authentically at home, but underlying this is an understanding that I am competent, that I have a nuanced understanding of the knowledge, skills and attitudes required as educator and leader, and that this is enough!

Conclusion

As I reflect on my career and think about leadership, lessons learnt, challenges overcome, I notice recurring themes. I see myself as an outsider, whether that is as an academic or not, as a native or not, as a professional or not, as a leader with credibility or not. I suspect it is this sense of being an outsider looking in that influenced my choice of career. Sometimes we confuse cause and effect: did I choose educational development because I enjoyed the sense of separateness, or did I feel an outsider because I was an educational developer? In terms of learning, I have followed a path of learning in action, but I have sought out professional development at every turn. Some courses and books have proved to be inspirational and others less so. As I take on the identity of 'elder', which I see as another form of leader, and reflect on my career, I find patterns in my journey that at the time seemed to be disjointed and haphazard, but – from this vantage I can see – were all necessary steps to where I am now. I am excited to see where the next chapter leads me. Wherever that path goes, I know who I am; my values are clear to me; I am hungry always to learn, but that learning is now, in Perry's terms, from a position of commitment. If I were to meet my younger self, knowing what I know now, I would tell myself to trust my instincts, to identify my values and make them explicit to myself as well as to others, and to be true to myself. A leader is only a leader if others follow.

However, leadership does not have to take place from the front; leading from the side and valuing other peoples' voices can be far more effective than being the loudest voice in the room. At times my own lack of confidence, a feeling of being an imposter, may have held me back from a conventional leadership stance, but ultimately, I brought about change by being true to myself, to my values, and by growing into a position of what Perry would term commitment. My advice to those considering leadership positions in learning and teaching is to adopt a nurturing approach, to approach those initially who are willing to listen and establish credibility by sharing your values and beliefs about teaching and making them part of your wider circle. It is important that we listen to these individuals and encourage them to share their practice and appreciate their challenges. We need to recognize that irrespective of years of experience, the suggestion that there might be better ways to teach can present a threat to individuals. It is not sufficient to offer suggestions, to provide resources or run workshops; it is important to take people on board rather than trying to change them.

References

Baume, D. and Popovic, C. (2016), *Advancing Practice in Academic Development*, London: Routledge.

Becher, T. and Trowler, P. (2001), *Academic Tribes and Territories: Intellectual Enquiry and the Cultures of Disciplines*, 2nd edn, Buckingham: Open University Press/SRHE.

Boyer, E. (1990), *Scholarship Reconsidered: Priorities of the Professoriate*, Princeton, NJ: Carnegie Foundation for the Advancement of Teaching.

Chen, C. Y. (2015), 'A Study Showing Research Has Been Valued over Teaching', *Higher Education Journal of the Scholarship of Teaching and Learning*, 15 (3): 15–32.

Little, D., Green, D. and Felton, P. (2019), 'Identity, Intersectionality and Educational Development', *New Directions for Teaching and Learning*, 158: 11–23.

McKay, R., Arnold, D., Fratzl, J. and Thomas, R. (2008), 'Workplace Bullying in Academia: A Canadian Study', *Employee Responsibilities and Rights Journal*, 20: 77–100.

Perry, W. G., Jr. (1981), 'Cognitive and Ethical Growth: The Making of Meaning', in A. W. Chickering (ed.), *The Modern American College*, 76–116, San Francisco, CA: Jossey-Bass.

Perry, W. G., Jr. ([1970] 1998), *Forms of Intellectual and Ethical Development in the College Years: A Scheme*, San Francisco, CA: Jossey-Bass.

Veblen, T. ([1899] 2009), *Theory of the Leisure Class: An Economic Study of Institutions*, Oxford: Oxford University Press.

Wilkinson, C. (2020), 'Imposter Syndrome and the Accidental Academic: An Autoethnographic Account', *International Journal for Academic Development*, 25 (4): 363–74.

Zou, T. and Felten, P. (2019), 'Being and Becoming in Academic Development: Enduring Questions, New Contexts', *International Journal for Academic Development*, 24 (4): 301–4.

4

Examining a Leadership Journey through a Lens of 'Integrated Scholarship'

Mike McLinden

Introduction

While the paths navigated by academics seeking research leadership within higher education (HE) are relatively well-defined and recognized, the leadership journeys in learning and teaching (L&T) are often less widely discussed and/or acknowledged. Indeed, the criteria of what constitutes L&T 'leadership' can be vague and the journeys of how individuals enter into universities as academics with expertise in particular disciplines and then develop as leaders in L&T have not been widely researched. Thus, as academics progress into senior L&T leadership roles, they can potentially feel increasingly separated from their original discipline communities and networks given they may no longer be contributing to developments in their respective fields. This separation may cause them to question their sense of belonging to a discipline-focused academic community as their 'contributions' may be more aligned to administration and broader pedagogically focused activities. In short, their perception of themselves as discipline-focused 'scholars' who entered HE in order to contribute to the discovery and application of new knowledge through research and teaching within a discipline community may shift or, indeed, instil a sense of not belonging to a particular discipline community at all.

In this chapter, I explore this under-researched area through examining my own leadership journey as a senior academic at a large research-intensive university in the UK. I start by mapping out the context of my journey and draw attention to the distinctive ways in which academic activities have been captured with respect to, for example, workload and promotion. I introduce what I term a profile of 'integrated scholarship' and, through reference to the work of Ernest

Boyer (e.g. Boyer, 1990), seek to show how I have engaged with the 'practice and praxis of scholarship as a conscious engagement' as well as 'with the act of being a scholar' (Boyd, 2013, p. 6). Through such conscious engagement, I draw on the four types of scholarship outlined in the report by the Boyer Commission as a conceptual lens to examine my leadership journey. I offer insights into some of the challenges and issues I have faced in undertaking senior leadership roles in L&T and examine how I have sought to navigate these. I end with some reflections on my leadership journey and offer suggestions for how we might work towards creating a more integrated view of our academic endeavours within HE.

Mapping Out the Context of My Leadership Journey

When starting work as an academic in HE, I recall being continually frustrated and, to some extent, surprised by the clear divide I witnessed between what were commonly described as the 'core' activities of the university at the time – 'research' and 'teaching'. Administration roles, workload models and promotion pathways tended to divide these activities into discrete activities, thereby reinforcing their distinctiveness. Further, there were few explicit rewards or incentives offered, nor time allocated for trying to promote synergies between these activities. This frustration has continued, to some extent, throughout my time in HE, despite efforts within the sector to develop and indeed promote greater *integrated* academic practice (e.g. Barnet, 2005; Brew, 2006; Cleaver, Lintern and McLinden, 2018; Elton, 2005).

In the UK, the drivers for creating distinctive academic activities include national 'excellence frameworks' that have a focus on either 'research' (i.e. the Research Excellence Framework, REF) or 'teaching (i.e. the Teaching Excellence Framework). Indeed, there appears to be an irony in introducing such frameworks while, at the same time, higher education institutions (HEIs) are increasingly seeking to ensure that from the students' perspective, research and teaching activities are viewed as being more closely aligned (e.g. Cleaver et al. 2018; Edwards and McLinden, 2017; Healey, 2005).

In a co-authored text on L&T in HE (Cleaver, Lintern and McLinden, 2018), we argued in our final chapter that rather than separating these activities into discrete categories, universities should be seeking to develop closer synergies in academic activities guided by a commitment to promoting more integrated 'critical enquiry'. This reflected our own experiences as senior academics and managers in our respective institutions and was an attempt to create a more integrated approach to academic work within the sector more generally. We proposed that such an approach would help to remind us about what is distinctive about the nature of our work as academics engaged in HE and, where possible, trying to see the more integrated nature of our activities as 'scholars'. This point is worthy of emphasis (and indeed I revisit it in the final section) given that in the UK the term 'scholarship' has, in some contexts, been relegated into activities that are akin to writing dictionaries and producing databases. As an example, in the context of the UK, the definition drawn upon in the guidance for the most recent REF (2019) makes reference to research as being 'defined as a process of investigation leading to new insights, effectively shared' (p. 90). In comparison, the term 'scholarship' for the purpose of the REF guidance is defined as 'the creation, development and maintenance of the intellectual infrastructure of subjects and disciplines, in forms such as dictionaries, scholarly editions, catalogues and contributions to major research databases' (p. 90). This chapter therefore is an attempt to illustrate how a profile of 'integrated scholarship' can be usefully drawn upon as a lens through which to review academic activities and support the planning of individual L&T leadership pathways.

Promoting My Own Profile of Integrated Scholarship

For many years in my various academic roles, I became resigned to accepting the distinction I have outlined earlier as a way of academic life, with an acceptance that teaching and research activities 'need' to be situated in very different places, run by different academic groups, and therefore result in very distinctive leadership roles (and journeys), depending on the selected route. While teaching committees, not surprisingly, have a focus primarily on activities that relate to teaching (and similarly with research-focused committees), I could find no space in my early years as an academic for promoting the synergies between the two in either forum. As I discuss later, part of my L&T leadership role therefore has involved finding ways of creating such a space through developing communities of like-minded colleagues and promoting a more integrated view of our 'pedagogical scholarship' that focused on applying extensive scholarship skills to our L&T activities (e.g. Cleaver, Lintern and McLinden, 2018; Healey, 2000, 2003). When I started as an academic, the notion of pedagogical scholarship was very much in its infancy, however, and did not appear to have penetrated through the thick walls of university systems. Finding out about the work of Ernest Boyer and his colleagues when reading the report of the Boyer Commission (1998) as a relatively new academic (but an experienced schoolteacher) was therefore a revelation to me. Although the findings of this report focused on HE in the context of the United States (and, in particular, on undergraduates studying in research-intensive institutions), the key messages it sought to convey, and in particular the alignment between research and teaching through scholarship, had clear resonance with my own view of how we should be seeking to promote a more integrated approach to our academic activities, particularly if we were to lead and inspire future academics.

As an example, a key conclusion of the report produced by the Boyer Commission was that research should be the basis of all learning at university and that the *production* of knowledge should be viewed not as being an exclusive activity, but rather as one that all members of an institution can participate in (Boyer, 1990). Further, the report recommended that undergraduates who enter research-intensive universities should engage in discovery-based activities as 'active' participants within a student-centred approach to teaching, with students provided with scope for intellectual and creative development, including opportunities to learn through inquiry as researchers rather than simple knowledge transmission (Boyer, 1990). This recommendation for promoting student-centred approaches to teaching aligned with my own training as a teacher in school-based education and was very much in keeping with how I approached HE teaching as a new academic. It was also argued in the report that 'scholarship' should be viewed as a central tenet of promoting such an approach through four distinctive but overlapping 'types' of scholarship:

- *The Scholarship of Discovery* (the undertaking of original research);
- *The Scholarship of Integration* (connecting new knowledge to existing knowledge, across disciplines, in order to solve real-life issues faced by society);
- *The Scholarship of Application* (also described as the scholarship of 'engagement' in seeking to close the gap between values in the academy and the needs of the larger world);
- *The Scholarship of Teaching* (involving the reflective analysis of the knowledge about teaching and learning).

An important conclusion of the Boyer Commission therefore was that these four types of scholarship should align and overlap (see Figure 4.1).

Since the publication of the Boyer Commission's report, there has been an extensive body of literature outlining the complex and multifaceted nature of the relationships between teaching, research and scholarship (e.g. Blackmore, 2016;

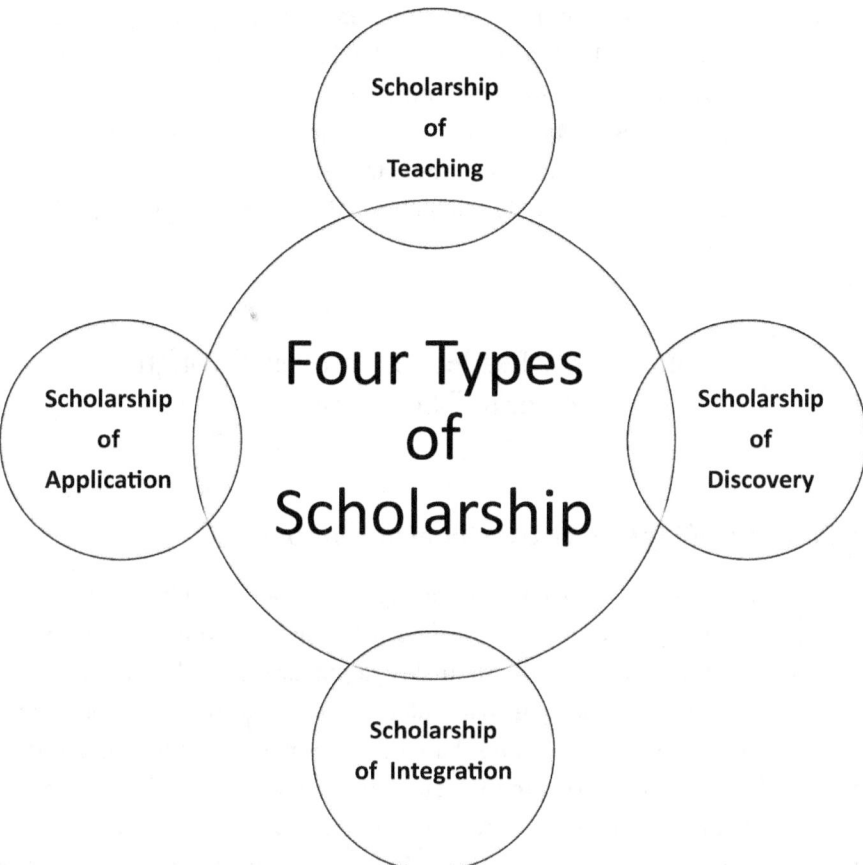

Figure 4.1 A summary of the four types of 'integrated scholarship' outlined in the report of the Boyer Commission (Boyer, 1990; Boyer Commission, 1998). Figure adapted from McLinden et al. (2015).

Brew, 2006; Cleaver, Lintern and McLinden, 2018; Edwards and McLinden, 2017), which has provided an impetus for promoting what is broadly now referred to as the 'Scholarship of L&T', or variants of this theme (e.g. Cleaver, Lintern and McLinden, 2018; Fanghanel et al., 2016; Healey, 2005). While the notion of a more integrated scholarship that draws on the four distinctive but overlapping types of scholarship introduced by the Boyer Commission is not designed specifically for individual academics to review a career pathway, with some modification it can offer a useful vehicle to allow for such an examination (e.g. Boyd, 2013).

For the purpose of this chapter, therefore, I incorporated the four types of scholarship outlined in Figure 4.1 into a proforma to allow me to review my own leadership journey that includes an introduction to myself as an academic working in HE, the nature of my own integrated scholarship through reference to the four types of scholarship outlined in the Boyer Commission's report and reflections on my leadership journey. I provide a summary of this proforma in Appendix 1 should readers wish to undertake a similar review to my own.

I present an overview of my review next through reference to this proforma and illustrate this with examples of published outputs that reflect aligned scholarship activities.

Exploring My Leadership Journey through Integrated Scholarship

A Timeline of My Career Development within HE

My substantive discipline area when starting work as a full-time academic over twenty-five years ago could broadly be described as being about the professional development of teachers to promote inclusive practice for children and young people with disabilities (and, in particular, vision impairment). Prior to this I had worked as a teacher in school-based education and was now involved in training the teachers. I start with this statement as it offers a helpful benchmark from which to consider my future journey from this point. My role at this time was therefore very much concerned with teaching alongside my studies for a PhD. Since completing my doctorate, I pursued two broad (and at times interconnected) strands of research activity – one with a broad focus on the 'inclusive education' of learners with disabilities (e.g. Douglas et al., 2012; McLinden et al., 2018b) and the other on 'HE pedagogy' with a particular focus on student learning in HE (e.g. McLinden et al., 2006, 2007, 2015). Alongside my research, I have been involved in a range of teaching leadership activities (including my current role as programme director for a large postgraduate course and co-director of a teaching and research centre) and undertaken several senior teaching leadership roles at faculty and institutional levels (including the role of director of L&T in the School of Education). I have also worked closely with senior colleagues in the institutional centre for academic practice on a range of funded pedagogical research projects (e.g. McLinden, 2013, McLinden et al., 2019) and have been involved in the development of pedagogical resources for academics working in HE at a national level (e.g. Cleaver et al., 2020; McLinden, 2013; McLinden et al., 2019).

A Description of My Current Areas of Interest in Terms of 'Scholarship' and a Short Description of How I See Myself as a Scholar

My current scholarship activities can be broadly described as having a focus on facilitating 'equitable' participation in education to ensure that *all* learners receive a high-quality educational experience, which fosters personal agency and independent learning, enhances employability and prepares them for life in a global world. This focus is very much aligned with recent international drivers promoting inclusive education (including, for example, United Nations Sustainable Development Goal 4), which seek to ensure inclusive and equitable quality education for all children and young people (e.g. McLinden et al., 2018b). I seek to promote this focus in the design of courses I teach, as well as in the research, knowledge exchange and impact activities I am engaged with.

While this summary would have been broadly aligned with my areas of interest when I first entered HE as an academic, a key distinction over two decades later is the breadth and depth of the activities I now engage in. As an example, in the earlier stages of my academic career, my activities were very much concerned with preparing teachers to support children and young people in inclusive school settings (e.g. McLinden et al., 2006, 2007). My interests and expertise have since evolved not just into thinking about learners, learning and, indeed, inclusive education as discrete entities which are taught in separate modules, but rather into looking at the nature of the relationships between the learner and the complex ecosystem in which learning and education takes place. In my teaching I draw on a systems-based approach as a lens through which to view the development of learners in different educational systems and through which we can examine the potential influences (including identifying facilitators and barriers) for ensuring equitable participation in education throughout a given educational pathway (e.g. McLinden, 2013; McLinden et al., 2019).

An Overview of Challenges/Issues I Have Faced in My L&T Leadership Journey in HE and Strategies Developed to Overcome These Challenges

As I have indicated above, a key challenge I have faced in my L&T leadership journey has been the clear divide I have encountered between research and teaching activities with respect to, for example, administration, workload modelling and promotion pathways. This has created clear boundaries, which to some extent have helped to define career progression routes (e.g. 'teaching/teaching leadership-focused' or 'research-focused' contracts). To address this challenge, I have sought, where possible, to promote the more integrated nature of my activities in various dissemination outlets (including recent applications for promotion). As an example, despite institutional drivers at the time which sought to promote 'research' centres, with two like-minded colleagues in the faculty we created a new centre (VICTAR) in 2001. This centre had the explicit mission of integrating original research and high-quality teaching through which to help reduce barriers to learning and participation experienced by learners with vision impairment. As a co-founder and co-director, I take pride therefore in promoting the work of the centre with our stakeholders and talk about how we have explicitly badged it as a teaching *and* research centre to emphasize the synergies between our various activities, through which we seek to promote 'equitable access' for people with vision impairment.

Similarly, in mentoring colleagues, I have found that encouraging them to think about their activities through a lens of integrated scholarship is helpful in moving the emphasis away from engagement in *either* teaching, research or administration (which tends to reflect the broad headings used in annual appraisal proformas). Making a reference to the 'Scholarship of Teaching' in particular offers a helpful way of illustrating this and helps ensure that they feel it is a legitimate activity for an academic to keep abreast of pedagogical developments in their discipline area.

Other Issues of Relevance to Shaping My L&T Leadership Journey

Of particular relevance to my review is that my leadership journey can only be based on working in only one HEI in the UK, giving me no other first-hand experiences to draw upon. My experience is therefore restricted and may have been quite different if I had been able to draw on working practice in more than one HEI. On one level, my L&T leadership journey within this HEI can be described as consisting of parallel pathways – the first relating to my discipline 'home' (inclusive education of learners with disabilities) and the second more focused on pedagogy and pedagogical research in the context of HE (and laterally with a focus on inclusive education more generally). As I consider in the second part of my overview, a reference to Boyer's four types of scholarship enables an examination of my journey in a more integrated way.

Exploring the Nature of My Integrated Scholarship within this Journey

I start this section by briefly examining the nature of how I have engaged in the *Scholarship of Discovery* (i.e. discovering new knowledge) in my leadership journey. On starting my role in HE, I embraced a career as an academic who was to be involved in the discovery of 'new' knowledge through disciplinary investigation; and through my mentoring and the promotion routes at the time, I was of the view that such an engagement was essential in order to progress. As an experienced teacher arriving from school-based education, I found it somewhat depressing to find that teaching was under-represented in academic promotion routes, with my appraisals very much about focusing on research 'inputs' (e.g. number and quality of funded projects) and 'outputs' (e.g. number and quality of peer-reviewed articles and research-focused books). As noted above, my role was made easier through the alignment of my activities within an innovative centre for teaching and research in the field of vision impairment education. Working in partnership with two close colleagues of a similar mindset, and who were similarly committed to ensuring that teaching (and indeed 'teachers'!) should not be separated from the research we were to undertake, we sought to promote closer synergies between our respective teaching and research activities in line with our common focus. In many respects, this successful synergy was the beginning of my own attempts at creating a more integrated scholarship in order to ensure that new knowledge arising from our research activities could be suitably disseminated through our own teaching activities. I have since been involved in a wide range of externally funded projects that through various outputs have contributed new knowledge to the field of vision impairment education, both in the courses we run in the centre and as outputs in the public domain (e.g. Douglas et al., 2012; McLinden et al., 2020a, 2020b), as well as being actively engaged in pedagogical research with a focus on improving student engagement within HE (e.g. Edwards and McLinden, 2017; McLinden, 2016; McLinden et al., 2019).

The second type of scholarship, the *Scholarship of Integration* (i.e. synthesizing knowledge across disciplines), would have been quite new to me when commencing my academic career. As I recall, activities were very much embedded in discipline communities, with limited opportunities for synthesizing knowledge across disciplines (even within the context of education). On reflection, however, I can see how my broader interests in L&T within HE can be framed within this type of scholarship – essentially synthesizing my engagement in vision impairment education and interests in pedagogical research to find out the most effective ways of engaging students in meaningful learning experiences (e.g. McLinden et al., 2006, 2007). This then developed into a broader interest in enquiry/problem-based learning and the opportunity of a secondment within the institutional centre for academic practice to research and develop innovative resources for use in the sector (e.g. McLinden and Edwards, 2011).

With respect to the *Scholarship of Application* (applying knowledge to consequential problems), as with the previous type of scholarship this was not a strand of work I would have consciously engaged with when first entering university. However, on reflection I can see how helpful it is to reflect on this type of scholarship in examining a given leadership journey. Many academics come into HE in order to 'make a difference' (even if it is not always clear what difference we plan to make!), and our work will increasingly be designed to address complex 'real world' problems. In terms of my own leadership journey, my work has directly been engaged in applying 'knowledge' to consequential problems in a range of ways, including, for example, with respect to the UK HE sector (e.g. McLinden, 2013), as well as globally through my more recent work on promoting inclusive education for learners with disabilities in sub-Saharan Africa (e.g. McLinden et al., 2020a). This journey reflects my increasing interest in addressing consequential problems beyond my own national boundaries and, as indicated above, is part of an increasing desire to promote equality of opportunity for learners with disabilities, not only in well-resourced countries but also in relatively low-resource educational systems (e.g. McLinden, Cleaver and Lintern, 2018a).

As indicated above, the fourth type of scholarship, the *Scholarship of Teaching* (i.e. sharing knowledge to transform teaching), is perhaps the one that I found most refreshing when I first found out about the work of the Boyer Commission. In terms of my leadership journey, it is possible for me to map out a distinctive journey that shows how I sought initially to share knowledge to transform teaching in education, with a focus initially on the programmes I was involved with as a programme director (e.g. McLinden et al., 2006), through to broader activities in my teaching leadership roles (including, for example, director of L&T for the School of Education) to help transform teaching at a broader level. Outputs in this role include funded pedagogical research projects (e.g. McLinden and Edwards, 2011) and the co-authoring of publications on L&T in HE (e.g. Cleaver, Lintern and McLinden, 2018; Edwards and McLinden, 2017).

Through the lens of integrated scholarship, I have been able to establish the more joined-up nature of my work and, in particular, how my interest in student learning more generally aligns with my discipline focus. Through this analysis I can also see clearer alignment between my academic outputs, which have been drawn upon to illustrate this more integrated scholarship. Indeed, in recent applications for promotion to senior academic roles, I have been able to make a successful case for the synergies I have promoted between my various activities, drawing on integrated scholarship as a vehicle in which to place these.

Reflections on My Leadership Journey to Date and Next Steps

As indicated above, a significant challenge when starting out as a new academic was that I was not always aware of the possible links between the various activities I was involved with, and as such these could at times feel very disjointed. My teaching and research activities fell into very discrete categories, which were then reflected in my workload planning. When mentoring new colleagues now, I often ask them to think about how they might describe their own scholarship *aspirations* within HE. Using Boyer's four types of scholarship, I find it is helpful to examine where they are in their own scholarship journey and where they would like to focus their activities as they progress. This is helpful for career planning purposes as it offers an opportunity to review and then plan in a more integrated way within a framework that has direct relevance to their work within HE.

A valuable lesson I have learnt from mentoring colleagues engaged in senior leadership roles is that it is important for them to take clear ownership of their own profile as they review and map out their career pathway. While activities within HE will no doubt still be divided into broad categories that reflect research, teaching and administration (or variants thereof), we should also be considering the links between these own activities in relation to our roles and ensure the synergies are suitably promoted. As an example, if I had been asked to list my interests as a scholar when I started my role, I would probably have described the *activities* I was involved in (the modules I am teaching, the papers I am writing, the research projects I am working on, etc.). If I am asked now, or if I have to provide an introduction to myself as a guest speaker, I usually seek to demonstrate the distinctive nature of my activities as a more integrated 'whole' and illustrate this profile through reference to my work in relation to each of Boyer's types of scholarship (Figure 4.1). With respect to my teaching and teaching leadership roles, I can elaborate by talking about how this profile helps guide my activities – for example, how an investigation on a particular aspect of student learning in an administrative role can then feed in to the 'scholarship of teaching' through writing it up as an article for publication (e.g. Cleaver et al., 2020; McLinden et al., 2015); how an institutional survey to find out how academics within the university view particular teaching and learning approaches can be written up into an article for a global audience (e.g. McLinden and Edwards, 2011). I find that such an approach helps colleagues appreciate the complex landscape in which HE is situated, and rather than feeling despondent about the rigid divisions, they can begin to work within these to identify and promote their own distinctive profiles within a more integrated analysis of their academic activities. As I consider in the final section, for academics engaged in HE, this profile should also reflect, and be underpinned by, what I would argue is at the very core of our various roles – namely a commitment to building in opportunities for 'critical enquiry'.

Final Reflections: Building in Opportunities for Critical Enquiry

Undertaking this review has reinforced my view that if integrated scholarship is viewed as being a 'vehicle', then the fuel that helps it to 'drive' reminds us that what is distinctive about our L&T leadership roles in HE is a commitment to 'critical enquiry' (e.g. McLinden, Cleaver and Lintern, 2018a). While such enquiry is normally associated with undertaking research, it is not necessarily linked with L&T or L&T leadership roles. As I indicated in mapping out the landscape for my journey, however, it is helpful to conclude this review by examining about what is distinctive about our work in HE.

Having been involved in HE for almost three decades, I am aware that introducing major changes in institutional systems and processes is not always feasible (an analogy of a super tanker changing its direction is often used to describe these frustrations by colleagues), and to a large extent there may be an inevitability that in some HEIs research will always 'trump' teaching (Blackmore, 2016, p. 4). I would argue, therefore, that it is important that we seek to define and describe our own distinctive profiles of activities within these systems. It is clear that despite the emphasis in the Boyer Commission's report on synergies rather than divisions between activities, the reality can be a sense of navigating quite disparate activities that are not always aligned, let alone 'integrated'. If

I had known in the early stages of my academic career what I know now, my sense is that I would have sought to have crafted a more integrated trajectory in my academic career profile from an earlier stage. Indeed, in revising a text on the role of educational enquiry in HE (Cleaver, Lintern and McLinden, 2018), we were struck as co-authors by the fact that since the first edition some four years earlier, important themes had emerged that we felt would feature in the future landscape of HE. We argued that these themes included an increasing emphasis on:

- articulating the characteristics and value of HE in a context increasingly populated by new providers and differing routes towards knowledge and skills;
- promoting aligned career progression routes for academics on teaching- and/or research-focused contracts.

Within this landscape we reported that it will be increasingly important for academics, as well as students, to showcase their abilities and to be able to articulate and draw on skills that can be broadly captured through use of the term 'critical enquiry'. We argued that these skills will sit at the heart of an HEI's possible answer to two important questions, namely:

- What is 'higher' about the HE we offer?
- How might our institution demonstrate evidence of its teaching excellence?

Further, we proposed that critical enquiry should sit very much 'at the heart of the twenty-first century academic endeavour' (McLinden, Cleaver and Lintern, 2018, p. 270), in that it underpins our students' and our own abilities to navigate and contribute to the post-industrial or knowledge economy; and, as such, an important task of an HEI will be 'to develop and promote an ethos of critical enquiry that permeates throughout its institutional "culture"' (McLinden, Cleaver and Lintern, 2018, p. 270). We ended the text by mapping out a vision for institutional learning cultures within HE that are founded on critical enquiry, proposing a conceptual model that serves to illustrate how different forms of critical enquiry within HE can align. Within this model, we proposed that there are key elements of our academic activities that have the potential to differentiate us from non-academic sectors while bringing together aspects of our academic practice that may have diverged in recent years: the higher-order skill of critical thinking and the associated activity of critical enquiry. As such, we concluded that a 'conscious acknowledgment and development of an institutional ethos of critical enquiry, that imbues all relevant activities, has the potential to facilitate and promote a unique yet unified institutional learning culture in higher education' (McLinden, Cleaver and Lintern, 2018, p. 270).

As well as the work of Boyer, we drew on the ideas of other academics who had influenced our thinking, including Rowland (2006) and his notion of the 'enquiring tutor' and the 'enquiring university' (Rowland, 2000), and in the work by Fung (2017) in which she stresses the importance of ensuring 'that scholarship, research and education, *all rooted in enquiry* [emphasis added] and expressed through engagement, can enrich one another' (p. 108). It is in this spirit, as a senior academic committed to promoting critical enquiry in my own profile of integrated scholarship, that I present lessons learnt from my own experiences in the hope that others can learn from these as they seek to develop their own distinctive academic profiles and can draw upon them to help shape the next steps in their own leadership journey. To support such an endeavour, I present a proforma in Appendix 1 that can be drawn upon to review a leadership profile through a lens of integrated scholarship.

Appendix 4.1 A Proforma to Review a Leadership Profile through a Lens of Integrated Scholarship

Reviewing Your Leadership Journey

Introduction

- A short timeline of your career development within HE (select milestones with key dates, discipline area, focus of your postgraduate studies, etc.).
- A description of your current areas of interest in terms of 'scholarship' (to include discipline or pedagogical scholarship). How might you portray a description of how you see yourself as a scholar in under twenty words? You can list examples of your outputs to show how these are aligned with your description.
- Reflect on when you first came into HE. How similar or different would your description be of your area/s of interest?
- Outline a short overview of up to three challenges/issues you have faced in your L&T leadership journeys in HE (e.g. from an academic entering

HE with a discipline focus to your role now as a leader in L&T) and examples of strategies you have developed to overcome these.
- Any other issues that might be relevant to shaping your L&T leadership journey (e.g. educational/cultural systems; other contextual factors such as discipline, country context, etc.).

Exploring the Nature of Your Scholarship within This Journey

With reference to Boyer's four types of scholarship, consider how each type can be drawn upon to describe the nature of your journey, starting with your current L&T leadership practices and reflecting on the journey to this point. You can list examples of your outputs to show how they are aligned with each type of scholarship.

The Scholarship of Discovery: discovering 'new' knowledge through disciplined investigation

- How would you describe this type of scholarship with respect to your leadership journey? For example, what were you doing then that you are not doing now – what are you doing now that you were not doing then?

The Scholarship of Integration: synthesizing knowledge across disciplines

- How would you describe this type of scholarship with respect to your leadership journey? For example, what were you doing then that you are not doing now – what are you doing now that you were not doing then?

The Scholarship of Application: applying knowledge to consequential problems

- How would you describe this type of scholarship with respect to your leadership journey? For example, what were you doing then that you are not doing now – what are you doing now that you were not doing then?

The Scholarship of Teaching: sharing knowledge to transform teaching

- How would you describe this type of scholarship with respect to your leadership journey? For example, what were you doing then that you are not doing now – what are you doing now that you were not doing then?

> ### Reflections on Your Leadership Journey to Date and Next Steps
>
> - Provide a short summary of your reflections on your leadership journey, having undertaken this review.
> - Consider how you might be able to draw upon this review in planning the next steps of this journey.

References

Barnett, R. (2005), *Reshaping the University: New Relationships between Research, Scholarship and Teaching*, Maidenhead: McGraw-Hill/Open University Press.

Blackmore, P. (2016), 'Why Research Trumps Teaching and What Can Be Done about It', in P. Blackmore, R. Blackwell and M. Edmondson (eds), *Tackling Wicked Issues: Prestige, Employment Outcomes and the Teaching Excellence Framework*, HEPI Occasional Paper 14, 4–37, Oxford: Higher Education Policy Institute. http://www.hepi.ac.uk/wp-content/uploads/2016/09/Hepi_TTWI-Web.pdf.

Boyd, W. E. (2013), 'Does Boyer's Integrated Scholarships Model Work on the Ground? An Adaption of Boyer's Model for Scholarly Professional Development', *International Journal for the Scholarship of Teaching and Learning*, 7 (2): article 25. https://digitalcommons.georgiasouthern.edu/cgi/viewcontent.cgi?article=1413&context=ij-sotl.

Boyer, E. (1990), *Scholarship Reconsidered: Priorities of the Professoriate*, San Francisco, CA: Jossey Bass.

Boyer Commission on Educating Undergraduates in the Research University (1998), *Reinventing Undergraduate Education: A Blueprint for America's Research Universities*, New York: Stony Brook. https://eric.ed.gov/?id=ED424840.

Brew, A. (2006), *Research and Teaching: Beyond the Divide*, Basingstoke: Palgrave Macmillan.

Cleaver, E., Lintern, M. and McLinden, M., eds (2018), *Teaching and Learning in Higher Education: Disciplinary Approaches to Educational Enquiry*, 2nd edn, London: Sage.

Cleaver, E., McLinden, M., Lintern, M. and Birch, A. (2020), 'The Enquiring University: The Scholarship of Teaching and Learning as a Foundation for Strategic Educational Transformation', in R. C. Plews and M. L. Amos (eds), *Evidence-Based Faculty Development through the Scholarship of Teaching and Learning (SoTL)*, 20–41, Hershey, PA: IGI Global. https://doi.org/10.4018/978-1-7998-2212-7.

Douglas, G., Travers, J., McLinden, M., Robertson, C., Smith, E., Macnab, N., Powers, S., Guldberg, K., McGough, A., O'Donnell, M. and Lacey, P. (2012), *Measuring Educational Engagement, Progress and Outcomes for Children with Special Educational Needs: A Review*, Meath: National Council for Special Education. http://ncse.ie/wp-content/uploads/2014/10/Outcomes26_11_12Acc.pdf.

Edwards, C. and McLinden, M. (2017), 'Cultivating Student Expectations of a Research-Informed Curriculum: Developing and Promoting Pedagogic Resonance in the Undergraduate Student Learning Pathway', in C. Brent and D. Fung (eds), *Developing the Higher Education Curriculum: Research-Based Education in Practice*, 14–30, London: UCL Press.

Elton, L. (2005), 'Scholarship and the Research and Teaching Nexus', in R. Barnett (ed.), *Reshaping the University: New Relationships between Research, Scholarship and Teaching*, 108–18, Maidenhead: McGraw-Hill/Open University Press.

Fanghanel, J., Prichard, J., Potter, J. and Wisker, G. (2016), *Defining and Supporting the Scholarship of Teaching and Learning (SoTL): A Sector-Wide Study – Executive Summary*, York: Higher Education Academy. https://www.advance-he.ac.uk/knowledge-hub/defining-and-supporting-scholarship-teaching-and-learning-sotl-sector-wide-study.

Fung, D. (2017), 'Strength-Based Scholarship and Good Education: The Scholarship Circle', *Innovations in Education and Teaching International*, 54 (2): 101–10. https://doi.org/10.1080/14703297.2016.1257951.

Healey, M. (2000), 'Developing the Scholarship of Teaching in Higher Education: A Discipline-Based Approach', *Higher Education Research and Development*, 19 (2): 169–89. https://doi.org/10.1080/072943600445637.

Healey, M. (2003), 'The Scholarship of Teaching: Issues around an Evolving Concept', *Journal on Excellence in College Teaching*, 14 (2/3): 5–26.

Healey, M. (2005), 'Linking Research and Teaching: Exploring Disciplinary Spaces and the Role of Inquiry-Based Learning', in R. Barnett (ed.), *Reshaping the University: New Relationships between Research, Scholarship and Teaching*, 67–78, Maidenhead: McGraw-Hill/Open University Press.

McLinden, M. (2013), *Flexible Pedagogies: Part Time Learning and Learners – Final Report*, York: Higher Education Academy.

McLinden, M. (2016), 'Examining Proximal and Distal Influences on the Part-Time Student Experience through an Ecological Systems Theory', *Teaching in Higher Education*, 22 (3): 373–88. http://www.tandfonline.com/doi/full/10.1080/13562517.2016.1248391.

McLinden, M., Cleaver, E. and Lintern, M. (2018a), 'Developing and Promoting a Culture of Critical Enquiry within Higher Education: Some Final Reflections', in E. Cleaver, M. Lintern and M. McLinden (eds), *Teaching and Learning in Higher Education: Disciplinary Approaches to Educational Enquiry*, 2nd edn, 269–76, London: Sage.

McLinden, M. and Edwards, C. (2011), 'Developing a Culture of Enquiry-Based, Independent Learning in a Research-Led Institution: Findings from a Survey of Pedagogic Practice', *International Journal for Academic Development*, 16 (2): 147–62. https://doi.org/10.1080/1360144x.2011.568699.

McLinden, M., Edwards, C., Garfield, J. and Moron-Garcia, S. (2015), 'Strengthening the Links between Research and Teaching: Cultivating Student Expectations of Research-Informed Teaching', *Education in Practice*, 2 (1): 24–9.

McLinden, M., Grove, M., Green, J. and Birch, A. (2019), 'Developing and Embedding Inclusive Policy and Practice within Higher-Education Institutions', in K. Krčmář (ed.), *The Inclusivity Gap: Expectations and Delivery in Higher Education*, 160–76, Aberdeen: Inspired by Learning.

McLinden, M., Lynch, P., Mbukwa-Ngwira, J., Mankhwazi, M. and Soni, A. (2020a), 'Inclusive, Equitable, Quality Education for Children with Disabilities: A Country Study of Malawi', in L. Glickman (ed.), *Malawi: Its History, Culture, Environment, Education and Healthcare*, 90–114, New York: Nova Science.

McLinden, M., Lynch, P., Soni, A., Artiles, A., Kholowa, F., Kamchedzera, E., Mbukwa, J. and Mankhwazi, M. (2018b), 'Supporting Children with Disabilities in Low- and Middle-Income Countries: Promoting Inclusive Practice within Community-Based Childcare Centres in Malawi through a Bioecological Systems Perspective', *International Journal of Early Childhood*, 50: 1–16. https://doi.org/10.1007/s13158-018-0223-y.

McLinden, M., McCall, S., Hinton, D. and Weston, A. (2007), 'Embedding Online Problem-Based Learning Case Scenarios in a Distance Education Programme for Specialist Teachers of Children with Visual Impairment', *European Journal of Special Needs Education*, 22 (3): 275–93.

McLinden, M., McCall, S., Hinton, D., Weston, A. and Douglas, G. (2006), 'Developing Online Problem-Based Resources for the Professional Development of Teachers of Children with Visual Impairment', *Open Learning*, 21 (3): 235–49.

McLinden, M., Ravenscroft, J., Douglas, G., Hewett, R., McCann, E. and Roe, J. (2020b), 'Promoting a Balanced Early Years Curriculum for Young Children with Vision Impairment: Developing and Sustaining Personal Agency through a Bioecological Systems Perspective', *British Journal of Visual Impairment*, 38 (2): 248–64. https://doi.org/10.1177/0264619619901036.

REF (2019), *Guidance on Submissions*, no. 19/01, Bristol: REF. https://www.ref.ac.uk/media/1092/ref-2019_01-guidance-on-submissions.pdf.

Rowland, S. (2000), *The Enquiring University Teacher*, Milton Keynes: Open University Press.

Rowland, S. (2006), *The Enquiring University: Compliance and Contestation in Higher Education*, Milton Keynes: Open University Press.

Part 2

Becoming Leaders in the Discipline

5

Finding the Space for Disciplinary Leadership in Biological Sciences

Amalia Hosein

Introduction

Back in 2001, I first dipped my toes into teaching as a demonstrator in life sciences laboratories. While doing my MPhil in microbiology, teaching was something I did both equally for its monetary value and to gain the valuable teaching experience, which was desirable for future employment, just like other graduate teaching assistants (Rao, Hosein and Raaper, 2021). Although I never explicitly thought about it at the time, I envied the flexible lifestyle of academics and the perceived prestige that came with the position (Coate and Howson, 2016). As a female, South Asian, Caribbean researcher in the field of biological sciences, sitting here as an assistant professor, some twenty years later, I realize that my leadership journey in learning and teaching has been long and circuitous. It involved a number of small steps that did not always realize the vision of an academic I had back in 2001. In this chapter, I will explore how the governance and social structures of both my university and discipline affected my agency in developing my learning and teaching in the biological sciences. I will also specifically focus on one story of leadership where I implemented technology within my teaching and how the structures and my agency influenced the process.

Starting as a postgraduate researcher, I was very aware that to realize my desire to be an academic in biological sciences, I would have to undertake both teaching and research. Over the past twenty years, my research profile has paved the way for my expertise in the fields of food microbiology (Hosein et al., 1999), environmental pollution and microbiology (Hosein et al., 2008) and the epidemiology of non-communicable diseases (Hosein et al., 2020; Samaroo et al.,

2021). In teaching, however, I took great delight in developing my academic discipline, particularly in technology-aided and enhanced teaching. However, living in the small developing island state (SIDS) of Trinidad and Tobago meant my opportunities were dictated by geographical constraints, changing government policies, the restructuring of university systems and limited vertical growth (Briguglio, 1995; Crossley and Sprague, 2014). Coupled with this, I was navigating a postcolonial system situated within a patriarchal society which the university settings mimicked (Reddock, 2019). These social structures affected my agency in my leadership journey.

In a small island state like Trinidad and Tobago, one of the highly subscribed science, technology, engineering and mathematics (STEM) postgraduate research areas is biological sciences. This creates a ceiling for young academics aspiring to leadership positions. For example, as a postgraduate researcher, I was given the opportunity to moderate and tutor undergraduate laboratory sessions, a position that was respected, comfortable and easy, and for some of my fellow postgraduate researchers, it was their career. In such a microcosm, leadership opportunities were limited and, dare I say, somewhat stunted.

In the microcosm of Trinidad and Tobago, writing this chapter is challenging because of the very close networks. Although I have taken an autoethnographic approach, I have to be conscious about maintaining the privacy of individuals and consider the ethics of preserving confidentiality as well as the possible implications for me from a backlash (Chang, 2008; Ellis, 2007; Lapadat, 2017). Hence, I must be cautious in sharing my experience so that I do not inadvertently identify or cause defamation to anyone. Hence, throughout this chapter I may create 'stories' that may mimic what happened to me – or amalgamate different people in order to make a constructed persona (Chang, 2008).

Structure and Agency

For this chapter, I have used the theoretical lens of structure and agency to help make sense of my leadership journey so far. My leadership journey is still one of becoming rather than being, and my agency is limited by both the governance and social structures of my university. Structure is considered to be the recurrent and patterned arrangements which influence and limit choices and opportunities available (Archer, 1995), while agency is considered to be the ability of individuals to act independently and make their own free choices (Archer, 1995). According to Amundsen (2019), the debate of structure versus agency strengthens the concept of socialization versus autonomy in determining if a person can act as a free agent or if their actions are dictated by social structure.

Agency

My agency was influenced in a large part by my upbringing and sense of self-worth. My primary school motto of 'Where there is a Will, there is a Way' became my personal motto, and it instilled in me a sense of determination. I wanted to succeed academically, initially to make my parents proud and later to establish my self-worth in academia. I wrote my national primary school exam where I secured a place in one of the low-tier secondary schools. As an eleven-year-old, I was devastated, ashamed and afraid (Sheldrake, 2019). Of course, I did not understand the structure of the system and how my attendance at a low-ranking primary school could influence my outcomes. It was my first experience of privilege which was imposed due to the structure I was part of. It is also how I understood that the school you go to matters, and networks and influence play a great deal in one's success (Stadtfeld et al., 2019). Lesson learnt – life is not fair.

After this, it was an uphill battle to restore my self-esteem and confidence. However, I kept getting by, failing and struggling all the way to university. Around the penultimate year of my undergraduate degree, I began to regain confidence, trusting once again my academic ability and realizing how I could probably help others learn and achieve their academic ambitions. I led the development of a magazine called *Nature Zone* as part of the university's Botany Club, and although I did most of the work, I was voted vice president, an outcome which again emphasized to me the constraints posed by the societal structures which I existed within. During elections, as a female, I thought I should be coy and self-sacrificing (Gündemir, Carton and Homan, 2019): so much so that I lost the presidency, while a male with a more dominant personality became the president. I was angry at myself, for not speaking up and saying that I wanted to be considered for the presidency! Lesson learnt – assert your authority.

In graduate school, having already learnt some life lessons from these experiences, I was more focused and became better at leading students, learning alongside the craft of teaching. As a teaching assistant, I was managing students, demonstrators (other postgraduate students) and lecturers to ensure the course outcomes were achieved. It is here I was in my element. I enjoyed the autonomy of individual courses and the ability to lead the learning experience of students. I enjoyed teaching the students and sharing my vision with the demonstrators I coordinated. It was reminiscent of something my father shared: 'A really good teacher is able to take the most complex concepts and make even a primary school student understand the said concept.' I looked for mentors with this philosophy while also practising this approach in my own teaching. I found using real-life examples really helpful in simplifying complex concepts – for example, explaining the concept of human genetics on how different we all look, yet we all share a universal genetic code. Seeing that ah-ha moment on student faces continues to be my incentive and almost an addiction (Meyer and Land, 2003; Perkins, 2006), so that I am always working my way trying to identify what other concepts can be made simple. Lesson learnt – teaching is my calling.

Structure

In order to understand my leadership journey, it is important to understand the structures within which I existed and undertook all this work. According to Crossley (2011, p. 111), tertiary education providers among SIDS are noted for having 'their intellectual origins in small state contexts, where the politics of research, the potential of diverse forms of knowledge and modes of knowledge generation reflect the views of the marginalized, the disadvantaged, and the "other"'.

I have observed that the structure of tertiary education institutions in Trinidad and Tobago is similar to many British postcolonial educational institutions, deeply affected by the past and present socioeconomic challenges. Colonization has suppressed indigenous learning systems and the social structures that supported the development and creation of indigenous knowledge. For example, the *ustad-chela* (mentor–mentee) tradition of apprenticeship, brought by the South Asians to Trinidad and Tobago, was a rich relationship based on ethics, knowledge and capacity building (Ubhaykar, 2019). This has now become almost obsolete. Further, there is also a lack of local content in the curriculum/course materials, thus finding relevant local content is a real challenge.

In general, SIDS over the years have experienced significant brain drain, dearth of specializations, small population, low student numbers, competing universities, competing areas of specializations and micromanagement by the government and other entities (Martin and Bray, 2011). Due to the limited layers between university and government, there can be a direct influence of governmental decisions and other external agencies on the university programme or course. In my experience, the major players in any influential networks appear to be related by alumni, family, close networks, and so on, and such influential leadership positions are often inaccessible without such networks. It is a balancing act to ensure individuals in such influential structures are not upset, as it can impact significantly on my ability to create change/innovate. For example, within the university at this time, there were internal pressures from other engineering fields, where biomedical engineering was being led by a mainly biological sciences team who are often not considered real engineers. This eventually led to its demise. Within our unit, some individuals were friends with senior management. This created an atmosphere of bias and allowed the exposure of minor departmental issues to the board in an informal setting. This created turbulence, which affected the programme in the small microcosm of the university. This uneasiness and slow collapse of the programme made me question my leadership, purpose and ability to create change or innovate. It also seemed that my leadership would not be able to break the ceiling, and I questioned my ability to secure a leadership position.

Benedict (1967) observed that just as it is possible to have a small society in a large territory, it also possible to have part of a large society in a small territory. In my academic world, the latter allowed for academics, who were varied in their disciplinary specializations, to occupy the same physical space. During my many moves as a biomedical engineering academic in the past ten years, I have been housed with administrative staff responsible for entrepreneurship at the university, senior administrative staff from the provost and postgraduate offices, procurement and human resource staff, criminology academic staff, internal audit and quality assurance staff, sports academic staff and health sciences academic staff. The university at this time was made up of more than fourteen different campuses located throughout Trinidad and Tobago. This has allowed me to work with a diverse network of individuals, which has been an asset in my leadership journey. It especially became interesting in a small lunchroom, where some of the most important happenings at the university were informally discussed. However, to me, the plights of janitors, office clerks, junior academics, senior academics, finance staff, human resource personnel, information technology technicians, and so on, were all shared. A common theme among most staff was adherence to and respect for approved procedural processes. This has impacted my leadership, in ensuring that whatever activity is undertaken at the university, those conversations are held with administrative staff, especially those who are aware of procedures and processes. As an academic at a fairly young university (just fifteen years old), sometimes processes are not even present. For this reason, I would usually create a process where none may otherwise exist. For instance, when dealing with my MPhil/PhD students, I have adopted the use of a student–supervisor agreement, so that the student is aware of their responsibilities and those of their supervisors. This has been very useful in successfully leading my supervision and providing accountability between my students and myself.

My Leadership Journey in Embedding Technology within Biological Sciences

My teaching philosophy stems from my passion for imparting knowledge along with a fundamental belief that each student has the potential to master any subject. I believe that facilitating learning and knowledge creation is the main role of a university lecturer. Utilizing a combination of current and emerging technologies, I can relate and advocate the ideas/knowledge in a manner that enhances student learning as well as fosters a passion for lifelong learning.

In a SIDS such as Trinidad and Tobago, just about 6,000 students per year will be eligible for undergraduate studies. This has placed the three main universities plus many other tertiary education institutions competing for the same pool of students under severe strain. My university has, as a consequence of dwindling student numbers and interest in programmes, undertaken restructuring of programmes on a regular basis. This suspension and discontinuation of programmes is a constant albatross on our programme's viability and job stability. One of the challenges of being in a SIDS is that there is not much lateral movement in jobs, and hence if I wanted to stay in higher education, I had to make my opportunities within my organization. In such an environment, with the pressure to bring in more students, I saw the opportunity to attract students from outside Trinidad and Tobago as a viable option, considering the constraints of the small population within Trinidad and Tobago.

The Idea

Back in 2016, face-to-face teaching was the accepted and preferred mode of instruction at the university. I thought I would not be able to attract international students into the face-to-face environment and hence wanted to consider online instruction. However, this idea was fairly farfetched for instructors, as the focus always seemed to be on recruiting students from Trinidad and Tobago who would not have devices to undertake online instruction. I proposed the idea, and although management approved that I could work on it, when I invited members to collaborate with me, there was no buy-in; most people indicated they were too busy. I recognized that I had an uphill battle. If this idea was to take off, I would have to have a strong proposal based on facts and evidence as this is the best-recognized currency for change in my institution. It is in this setting that I led the development of an online biomedical engineering degree. Bringing this idea to my team, it was considered a non-priority as an option to recruit students and cut cost. Further, I was informed by our programme leader that the university was not in a position to fund the development of any online/virtual degree. However, I was given the approval by my programme leader to develop the proposal and find funding for the idea, though it was made clear this would have to be pursued in my own time and would be very much an individual endeavour.

Armed with this information, I began researching and developing the proposal for online teaching. I thought if I could develop a framework for taking face-to-face instructional material and transfer it to an online mode of teaching; it would benefit not only my programme but all programmes using face-to-face instructional materials. It was also important to measure student gains in problem-solving and critical thinking skills, so employing different quantitative and qualitative data collection methods was critical for continuous updates and enhancement. I also wanted to ensure that the quality of teaching was high-end by helping staff to incorporate critical thinking and problem-solving skills through reflective practice into their existing teaching practice. From this, I hoped to produce teaching toolkits in collaboration with other teaching staff, which would be adapted to the local context and used for their teaching as open educational resources.

At this juncture, I recognized from conversations with international colleagues the importance and distinctiveness of the local teaching and learning strategies that were being utilized by different departments at my university, which were unique for our population (Kinchin et al., 2018). I was keen to develop content that the students could relate to using the local language, otherwise known as the Trinidad dialect, and relatable local current events. This was done in many creative ways; for example, one of my colleagues used animation software to create an avatar of himself that spoke in the local parlance. His students loved it whenever 'Soca Teach' appeared on the screen; it meant it was a joke, an activity, some fun fact or a local example about some part of their country. I thought developing toolkits to create your own avatar and having it mimic a lecturer would give the online teaching experience an added boost.

My Approach and Leadership Journey

While the idea of taking the programme online was the vision, it still had to go through the hoops and balances. This meant trying to get senior management to take up my idea as important and bringing it to the Academic Council. The Academic Council is a body comprising the leads for each programme/department, and they meet with the provost to make decisions on academic matters. While an Academic Council is an excellent way to prioritize university activities, it was a forum where you needed a driver for your idea to be prioritized. Thus, I invested in strategically walking near the offices of senior management/academics and informally starting the conversation so that they would not be in shock when they heard of it nor shoot down the idea when it was introduced in the Academic Council for approval. Tacitly, I knew that if the idea was too new and unknown, it would be critically examined and possibly be discarded at this stage before even getting a chance to be evaluated properly. There were no structures in place for evaluating new ideas and establishing their viability based on any particular rubric or scale. It was based on opinion and personal knowledge. Therefore, in this situation, I tried to educate senior management/academics informally about the idea. I developed a structure for evaluation and asked for their feedback, which would be incorporated. My strategy at this point was that I hoped they would be invested enough to drive the idea with other senior management/academics in the formal setting. I also provided them with some foundation which could be modified, a structure that could be used for evaluation rather than opinion. However, I did find this technology-based idea more difficult to sell in an environment that was just only starting to incorporate and understand online teaching. Hence, my approach was getting one or two senior drivers invested in the idea. I chose these individuals based on availability and their ability to offer time for informal conversations. I especially tried to meet them around lunchtime at the university cafeteria. For me, the meeting of two personalities is like the contact of two chemical substances: if there is any reaction, both are transformed.

I then continued having informal conversations with colleagues and anecdotally collecting information from both students and staff by asking them questions such as: What are their thoughts on an online programme? What would they like to see in such a programme? How do they think we should approach such a programme? Some of the feedback from colleagues on this idea was to emulate the MIT open course, where each course is available as a pdf and as a video with transcription and associated activities in a pdf. Others liked the Coursera format, where the course was built as modules with questions and material presented as activities. Some colleagues thought it would involve too much commitment from the university to develop this idea, and I should abandon it for now until funding could be sourced. All the students were on board, and some even told me that they had cousins and friends who would do the programme if it was offered online, which was encouraging. An important component of my agency is my belief that there is a solution to every problem, better yet every challenge. So, the critiques for me were challenges that needed to be addressed and did not hinder the development of my idea at this stage. Rather, I considered all the ideas and developed the proposal, in which the activities were expected to lay the foundation for the development of a community of practice (Wenger, 1999). This was also the point of evolution of my leadership method, which involved finding out the needs of the clients (lecturer and students) in an informal setting. What I learnt from this was to listen, learn and grow.

If the vision for the online platform was to be impactful for all tertiary teaching staff in Trinidad and Tobago, so that it could contribute to a better-quality education for students entering the tertiary education sector, it needed to meet their personal needs, the requirements of the employment market and the government goals for its young people. Further, I really wanted to enhance local content and develop autonomy in teaching and learning pedagogies that would be impactful in our country's education journey. I also wanted to measure this by the learning gains for students in problem-solving and critical thinking skills by enabling teaching staff with the appropriate skills and tools to reflect on their practice and develop more sophisticated, learner-centred approaches to teaching. From my background research on online platforms for tertiary education in Trinidad and Tobago, I knew a wide range of courses that students could take online, but there was no local content. Our competitor university also had a few degree offerings online; however, none were science and technology based. While my current university excelled in some programmes, one of the weaknesses identified was the perception that my university was a second choice for academic excellence. I saw this as an opportunity to be ahead of the curve in implementing innovative and high-demand training in biomedical engineering readily available to all students. I knew that biomedical engineers worldwide were in high demand at that time, with the occupational growth rate expected in 2018 at 72 per cent (US Bureau of Labor Statistics, 2016). With the relatively low fees at my university, the hope was to attract foreign and geographically distant local students using an online platform. Thus, it was imperative that I do extensive background preparation, looking at similar structures for online delivery and evaluating their structures and effectiveness. I felt that success is where preparation and opportunity meet.

It is important to realize that while biomedical engineering worldwide was in high demand, in Trinidad and Tobago it was a new word and concept. As the only biomedical engineering undergraduate programme in the country, and by extension the Caribbean at that time, it was not highly subscribed. Student numbers for this programme remained low, and we were facing discontinuation due to the high cost of running the programme. The increasing pressure to justify supporting this particular programme with low student numbers drove our need to access information on the factors affecting student applications and retention. Data showed that 80 per cent of the potential students for this programme never registered largely due to the current geographic distance of the campus, so I was hoping to bring online delivery to make the running of the programme viable and affordable both for the university and for the students. Consultation with stakeholders further suggested that this was a problem felt across the board for many other programmes such as environmental sciences, marine sciences and aviation, to name a few. I had meetings with key individuals in these units, and they indicated online delivery and face-to-face delivery of their degree could be a viable option. They would be interested to see the cost and how senior management would receive this proposal. At this point, I felt I had some support from departments facing similar restructuring issues; however, their support would be covert until the viability of this approach could be proven. The idea again would be to offer a fully online undergraduate degree in biomedical engineering for access by local, regional and international students. Consequently, I found it was very valuable to identify other programmes that would benefit from a similar approach and get buy-in from these departments. I felt that unity was our strength, and diversity was our power.

The biggest challenge in any online STEM degree would be the practical aspect, which I hoped to address using virtual labs specially designed for each course and their respective learning outcomes. From my preparation, I found virtual laboratories are considered cheaper to operate and, when designed congruently, are able to promote student understanding (Bose, 2013; Rutten, van Joolingen and van der Veen, 2012). However, developing these online labs/practical components would involve investment and lecturers sharing lab content, working closely with developers and evaluating the product. Besides getting buy-in from management, I would have to get support from the learning centre, quality control, undergraduate studies and, of course, get the lecturers all on board. My approach to this was to approach a lecturer first. I did a pilot run using an existing online free virtual lab to evaluate any hiccups. I reached out to one of my close colleagues, who did laboratory practicals every week for an electronics course, and asked him if I could use his course to start building online practicals. He was excited and posed no opposition. He was also quite a committed lecturer, keen to create new content to enhance the students' learning experience. During all this time, the idea still had not gone to senior academics. All that was known by the individuals I had informally spoken to about the project was that I was working on this project, but the finer details had not been shared as yet. So, the pilot was undertaken to see if there was anything else that I needed to consider. The first session was very successful; however, the editing of the transcription was tedious and time-consuming. Therefore, I began looking at the possibility of getting professional transcribers. The students were quite excited to see the product, especially how their question-and-answer sessions would be transcribed and used to help other students. This brought up issues around the intellectual property of students, so I developed a release form they would have to sign so I could share their question-and-answer sessions more publicly. Recording and transcribing lectures and lab sessions made for a better learning environment. The lecturer indicated that during these recording sessions, his work was of better quality, and the students 'performed' better all around. Generally, he came better prepared for class and the students were more interactive during the session. The lecturer and the corresponding cohort of students really enjoyed the process of interacting with the online labs and receiving the course content online. His experience, I hoped, could be used to convince other lecturers and their classes. Thus, I was trying to build a team and a product to endorse and promote the idea. Hence, it was crucial to identify and work with lecturers and students who believed in the idea and were supportive of it. I firmly believe that anything is possible when you have the right people to support you.

Consequently, I went to my programme leader and requested the use of some junior staff to do transcribing, which was met with little opposition as long as it did not affect their work. However, when it came to directing the junior staff, they complained of excessive work, which resulted in delays. Hence, the production of the first pilot video of the lecture session was never completed by these staff members. The hierarchical structures allowed junior staff to have little accountability to any person other than the programme leader. So, leading them was difficult, and their lack of buy-in on this idea was not encouraging. I could not wait for the transcription to be completed, nor did I want to create tension by reporting their non-performance, which would involve reports and creation of an inhospitable working environment. I still needed to work with the junior staff to get other work done in the department. I guess I expected junior staff to see what a great idea this was and assumed that they would be excited to do the transcription, which would help everyone in the department keep their jobs. To overcome this, I employed a graduate student from my personal funds to transcribe and to achieve my targets and produce a prototype product. Therefore, my approach involved personal investment into the idea. For me, it's not just about the ideas, it's about making ideas happen.

At this point, I think I really realized the importance of these sessions being done in consultation with the course lead. Now while some lecturers were quite happy to take part in the experiment, some lecturers refused outright. It had to be a university policy, or a mandate from the provost, to ensure buy-in from all staff. Not even the programme leader in my unit had the kind of influence to ensure compliance. Hence, the vision for this online learning and teaching emerged, where I wanted my programme, and by extension my university, to stand out as the premier institution for biomedical engineering at a national, regional and international scale. Therefore, I made an appointment to see the provost for an informal conversation. During our conversation, the provost indicated that, while it was a good idea, the university did not have any money to invest in the idea, nor could they force lecturers to take part in it. I asked him if I found funds/grants, would the university then be willing to endorse the programme? To this he agreed. This was the way in; get the money and the university would enforce, through a policy, lecturers recording and publishing their content, or so I hoped. I just had the provost's word to go on; however, the situation was slightly complex, in that he was an international academic whose contract as the provost was coming to an end. Therefore, to ensure something was on paper, I wrote up the idea as a grant application to the European Development Fund and got our research and grant funding department to sign off the idea, endorsed by the provost's office. This approach was of significance because it involved endorsement from senior management. I felt that the written word endures, the spoken word disappears.

With all of these guarantees, I was able to persist in developing virtual laboratories. This undoubtedly made the transition to online learning – when the Covid-19 pandemic hit – easier. However, the biomedical engineering degree has since closed, and I have moved departments.

Conclusions, Lessons Learnt and Implications for People on the Journey

My journey is not finished and is continuing. What I have learnt from the introspection required for this chapter is that in my leadership approach,

I am risk-averse. If you are risk-adverse, then, like me, you may prefer to have evidence and data to back up ideas before attempting to navigate such an idea through the power structures. My agency allows me to network at the lower levels to build support. I do recognize the importance of having my ideas endorsed by the highest power structures at the university both informally and formally. However, before attempting to convince the highest power structures, you may, like me, want to ensure that you have a strong grounding in evidence and support.

The lessons that others can learn from my leadership journey are to recognize that your agency is your strength, and you should use your agency to construct lower-level networks and to collect evidence to promote ideas amongst the power structures. These lower-level networks can include choosing individuals based on their availability for informal conversations, finding out the needs of stakeholders (lecturers and students) in an informal setting and selecting and working with other departments with similar agendas.

To navigate vertically within the power structures of the university, the collection of evidence for an innovative teaching idea can allow you to speak from a position of knowledge. Evidence collection can include extensive background preparation, looking at similar structures of an innovative teaching idea, evaluating these structures, investing time and finances to produce a prototype and, finally, getting a written endorsement from upper management in support of the idea. I have also learnt that my agency is influenced by my fear of failure and rejection, which prevents me from taking risks in navigating the power structures. Writing this chapter has opened my eyes about who I am and what my strengths are. I do not plan on changing my approach to leadership; however, the realization of what I do for leadership has made me more confident in my approach. My journey continues …

References

Amundsen, D. (2019), 'Student Voice and Agency for Indigenous Maori Students in Higher Education Transitions', *Australian Journal of Adult Learning*, 59 (3): 405–34.

Archer, M. S. (1995), *Realist Social Theory: The Morphogenetic Approach*, Cambridge: Cambridge University Press.

Benedict, B., ed. (1967), *Problems of Smaller Territories*, Institute of Commonwealth Studies, vol. 10, London: Athlone Press.

Bose, R. (2013), 'Virtual Labs Project: A Paradigm Shift in Internet-Based Remote Experimentation', *IEEE Access*, 1: 718–25. https://doi.org/10.1109/ACC ESS.2013.2286202.

Briguglio, L. (1995), 'Small Island Developing States and Their Economic Vulnerabilities', *World Development*, 23 (9): 1615–32. https://doi.org/10.1016/0305-750X(95)00065-K.

Chang, H. (2008), *Autoethnography as Method*, Abingdon: Routledge.

Coate, K. and Howson, C. K. (2016), 'Indicators of Esteem: Gender and Prestige in Academic Work', *British Journal of Sociology of Education*, 37 (4): 567–85. https://doi.org/10.1080/01425692.2014.955082.

Crossley, M. (2011), 'Strengthening Educational Research Capacity in Small States', in M. Martin and M. Bray (eds), *Tertiary Education in Small States: Planning in the Context of Globalization*, 101–18, Paris: UNESCO/IIEP.

Crossley, M. and Sprague, T. (2014), 'Education for Sustainable Development: Implications for Small Island Developing States (SIDS)', *International Journal of Educational Development*, 35: 86–95. https://doi.org/10.1016/j.ijedudev.2013.03.002.

Ellis, C. (2007), 'Telling Secrets, Revealing Lives', *Qualitative Inquiry*, 13 (1): 3–29. https://doi.org/10.1177/1077800406294947.

Gündemir, S., Carton, A. M. and Homan, A. C. (2019), 'The Impact of Organizational Performance on the Emergence of Asian American Leaders', *Journal of Applied Psychology*, 104 (1): 107–22. https://doi.org/10.1037/apl0000347.

Hosein, A., Ramsaroop, R. and Siegel, D. (1999), 'Developing a Protocol for Increasing the Shelf-Life of Coconut Water', paper presented at the *10th Annual General Meeting and Conference of the Caribbean Academy of Sciences*, 7–9 October, Paramaribo, Suriname.

Hosein, A., Ramsubhag, A., Mohammed, A. and Umaharan, P. (2008), 'Pyrene and Naturally Occurring Pyrene Degrading Bacteria Adjacent to the La Brea Pitch Lake in Trinidad', paper presented at the *16th Caribbean Academy of Sciences Biennial Conference on Science and Technology*, 11–13 October, St Georges, Grenada.

Hosein, A., Stoute, V., Chadee, S. and Singh, N. R. (2020), 'Evaluating Cardiovascular Disease (CVD) Risk Scores for Participants with Known CVD and Non-CVD in a Multiracial/Ethnic Caribbean Sample', *PeerJ*, 8: e8232. https://doi.org/10.7717/peerj.8232.

Kinchin, I. M., Rao, N., Hosein, A. and Mace, W. (2018), *Migrant Academics and Professional Learning Gains: Perspectives of the Native Academic: Research Report*, London: Society for Research into Higher Education. https://srhe.ac.uk/wp-content/uploads/2020/03/Kinchin-Rao-Hosein-Research-Report.pdf.

Lapadat, J. C. (2017), 'Ethics in Autoethnography and Collaborative Autoethnography', *Qualitative Inquiry*, 23 (8): 589–603. https://doi.org/10.1177/1077800417704462.

Martin, M. and Bray, M., eds (2011), *Tertiary Education in Small States: Planning in the Context of Globalization*, Paris: UNESCO/IIEP.

Meyer, J. and Land, R. (2003), *Threshold Concepts and Troublesome Knowledge: Linkages to Ways of Thinking and Practising within the Disciplines*, Enhancing Teaching-Learning Environments in Undergraduate Courses Project, Occasional Report 4, Edinburgh: University of Edinburgh School of Education. https://www.etl.tla.ed.ac.uk/docs/ETLreport4.pdf.

Perkins, D. (2006), 'Constructivism and Troublesome Knowledge', in J. Meyer and R. Land (eds), *Overcoming Barriers to Student Understanding*, 57–71, Abingdon: Routledge.

Rao, N., Hosein, A. and Raaper, R. (2021), 'Doctoral Students Navigating the Borderlands of Academic Teaching in an Era of Precarity', *Teaching in Higher Education*, 26 (3): 454–70. https://doi.org/10.1080/13562517.2021.1892058.

Reddock, R. (2019), 'Competing Victimhoods: A Framework for the Analysis of Post-Colonial Multi-ethnic Societies', *Social Identities*, 25 (6): 809–27. https://doi.org/10.1080/13504630.2019.1572503.

Rutten, N., van Joolingen, W. R and van der Veen, J. T. (2012), 'The Learning Effects of Computer Simulations in Science Education', *Computers & Education*, 58 (1): 136–53. https://doi.org/10.1016/j.compedu.2011.07.017.

Samaroo, K., Hosein, A., Olivier, L. K. and Ali, J. (2021), 'Breast Cancer in the Caribbean', *Cureus*, 13 (8): e17042. https://doi.org/10.7759/cureus.17042.

Sheldrake, J. L. (2019), 'An Examination of the Lived Experience of Students Passing through the Eleven-Plus Grammar School Selection Process: An Interpretation through a Bourdieuian Lens', PhD diss., University of Chester. http://hdl.handle.net/10034/623530.

Stadtfeld, C., Vörös, A., Elmer, T., Boda, Z. and Raabe, I. J. (2019), 'Integration in Emerging Social Networks Explains Academic Failure and Success', *Proceedings of the National Academy of Sciences*, 116 (3): 792–7. https://doi.org/10.1073/pnas.1811388115.

Ubhaykar, R. (2019), *Truck de India! A Hitchhiker's Guide to Hindustan*, London: Simon & Schuster.

US Bureau of Labor Statistics (2016), *Occupational Outlook Handbook, 2016–17*, Washington, DC: US Bureau of Labor Statistics.

Wenger, E. (1999), *Communities of Practice: Learning, Meaning, and Identity*, Cambridge: Cambridge University Press.

6

Developing a Learning and Teaching Leadership Profile in a Specialist Arts Institution

Louise H. Jackson

Introduction

How do you 'lead' artist/performer-educators who, in the main, operate in a system that reinforces an always-already notion that they are excellent? How do you earn trust with individuals and collectives who are known as international musicians (thereby 'excellent') and have been given a teaching role based on this? How do you lead performer-educators who value a system of prestige based on who they themselves have studied with and, in turn, where that lineage may take you in musical history (i.e. back to Mendelssohn or Chopin, or …)? How do you work with performer-educators who, because of the 'ineffability of the art form', resist routine operational matters such as evaluation reports, writing feedback on assessed work or module amendment forms!?

This chapter will explore my learning and teaching leadership within the performing arts, specifically music. The locations of my leadership development that I document in this chapter include a small university, a conservatoire (a specialist higher education [HE] institution focused on the vocational training of performing artists) and, most recently, a small alternative HE institution delivering popular music education. Across all three locations, performer-educators (Gaunt, 2007), employed because of their musical or artistic reputation, have formed the largest demographic of teaching staff, employed on a part-time basis and usually paid hourly. This chapter charts my journey in developing as a leader of learning and teaching in this area; behaviours and values that have emerged and, I believe, supported my success in leadership; and, finally, suggestions for what might be usefully extrapolated from reflections and observations on my experience. I conclude with ideas regarding leadership in this context, which suggest it doesn't mean focusing on how to lead but rather on understanding the complexities of the individuals, the departments and the nature of knowledge itself that operate across these institutions of performing arts in order to establish 'slow-burning' but effective communities of practice built on trust and artistic and educational inquisitiveness.

The context for this chapter focuses on the so-called specialist sector and challenges that arise when learning and teaching can be perceived to be subordinate to the perception of prestige of artistic reputation or 'creative industries readiness', rather than, perhaps, the more common hierarchical relationship between research and learning and teaching. I will detail these challenges in a critically reflective manner, whereby I identify how my leadership identity and ability has developed. This is leadership grounded in collaborative professionalism (Hargreaves and O'Connor, 2018), and I will explore this later in the chapter.

In preparing for writing this chapter, I asked colleagues past and present if they could identify aspects of my leadership that they felt were important or thought would be important to share within this chapter (the outcomes of which are discussed below). Following this exchange, one of my colleagues asked me what would change in my subsequent approach to leadership (or rather what change they might perceive) when I had completed this project. I was struck by this question. I identified two aspects of my thinking that had emerged from the composing of this chapter, and I wish to share these at the start.

The first point is: I have never wanted power over people. This is an idea of leadership that is commonly the focus (conscious or not), in my experience, of poor leaders who exert power over those they work with. I have never wanted power over people; rather I wanted to have the power to affect change, to create more equitable educational environments, experiences and processes. The second point is that part of my leadership identity values, recognizes and is open about my own vulnerability. I have found that my colleagues and I are able to build trusting relationships, and I believe this to be due to the way in which I approach openness to vulnerability. These combine to underpin a collaborative approach to leadership in learning and teaching.

One final point: I have not included personal context, but informing this writing is an awareness of the barriers that women face to leadership generally and in HE, the personal sacrifices I have made (and the sacrifices of those closest to me) and the mental health challenges that have been a constant underpinning of my experience. Although I haven't written about these explicitly, they have informed my approach and my understanding.

The Journey to Leadership and Initial Challenges

Formative professional experiences have very much informed the way in which I have developed as a leader in both positive and not-so-helpful ways, so I begin with a summary of those that stand out to me. I became a senior lecturer in 2007 aged twenty-six, teaching music and musical theatre in a small university on the south coast of the UK. I was fortunate in that I was mentored by a very engaging deputy dean who involved me in faculty quality committees – modelling rigorous committee behaviour, always asking if something was not clear and, most importantly, having a sense of humour, especially when dealing with more 'combative' colleagues. I don't really know why he decided to help me, other than he was a kind and generous academic leader. This was a formative experience of academic leadership that I still keep in mind.

In addition to my lecturing responsibilities, I became the department's academic development coordinator – ostensibly to organize developmental activity for the growing number of music tutors. At the same time, I developed an interest in widening access to HE and the arts and to set up a variety of activities, including a popular music summer school. I also established and ran community engagement activities using music as a facilitating approach. This became the focus of my doctoral study, which I eventually completed in 2015.

As can happen to many young academics and junior members of departments, the work I was doing started to become overwhelming, which was described as me being a victim of my own success. I had no research profile; kept restarting my doctorate as I couldn't find the right topic, institution or supervisor; and was the 'fixer' – any problematic modules were given to me to revive, lead and then teach. I became unhappy at the teaching load and the outreach work that was important to me but did not appear to be respected by others. I really wanted to develop expertise in educational research but had very little idea how to make that happen, not knowing what development opportunities to look for or request, or how to seek any formal mentoring to work out how to develop research in my educational practices. I had excellent mentoring in the ways of quality assurance and the management of an institution (which is why I was able to make the subsequent jump into a more senior role), but I felt as if I lost quite a lot of ground in developing research confidence and expertise through my professional practice.

I think about how these formative experiences affected my subsequent approach to leadership. For example, I could have more proactively explored different approaches to linking my professional practice to developing research, so I have tried to make opportunities for this readily available to colleagues. I could have attended more professional development activities focused on my aspirations rather than what I did, which was undertaking project management and professional leadership qualifications, so I have curated professional development activities that respond to conversations with individuals and groups of tutors and their own anxieties in order that they might recognize themselves in the types of sessions on offer.

Moving into Leadership

I identify the start of my learning and teaching leadership when I left the lecturing position and took up a role within a conservatoire (a specialist HE arts institution) in London, which focused on music, musical theatre and contemporary dance. There, I became the first head of learning enhancement – a role I would occupy for just over seven years. During that time, I went from being head of a non-existent department to having a large team with a portfolio that included academic staff development, digitally enhanced learning and management of the virtual learning environment, the learning support/advisory service, and pedagogic and education research. I was responsible for the development and implementation of the institutional Learning and Teaching Plan, of which I wrote three iterative versions. I was also involved with a host of other activities, including responding to institutional reviews and being part of the project management team for the application for taught degree awarding powers (which I did alongside completing, finally, my doctorate). During this time, I was also awarded a National Teaching Fellowship, the highest award for teaching in HE in the UK, and I additionally became a senior fellow of the Higher Education Academy (now Advance HE). This is a professional recognition of achievement in coordinating, managing, innovating and supporting those in learning and teaching by the leading professional membership organization for HE in the UK. Within the conservatoire context, however, there were several issues that may be useful to explore here:

Sole responsibility: When I started in this leadership role, enhancement to the provision was seen as my job – not everyone's role to continually enhance the provision across the institution.

Academic development as customer service: There was a perception that I was part of a customer service provision, particularly in academic development for teaching staff, responding to demands of what other people wanted, rather than being able to set the agenda based on evidence and institutional needs. In leadership terms this would eventually become a 'people-pleasing' problem for me.

It's historical: The institution was the result of the merger between two long-standing arts institutions, which had occurred seven years or so prior to my joining. Entrenched thinking can occur in any institution, between departments, faculties, academics and professional services, and makes it difficult to create meaningful change.

Respect for learning and teaching: People not accepting or recognizing expertise in learning and teaching is a significant challenge regardless of institution or discipline (see, for example, Cleaver, Lintern and McLinden, 2018; Cotton, Miller and Kneale, 2018). As is described in the rationale for this collection, research is commonly perceived as the more prestigious aspect of a role in HE, whereas learning and teaching and associated expertise are not as meaningful or don't belong to the same prestige economy (Blackmore, 2018). There is *also the assumption that everyone has expertise in teaching* because they are employed to teach. Those words in italics have probably been the biggest barrier in my developing as a leader in learning and teaching and may be explained by Wieman (2019), who suggests that part of this is caused by the positioning of teaching as an 'art' where an individual style is privileged, as opposed to academic research that has defined standards and expectations of endeavour.

These issues led to the following challenges:

- Establishing a vision for learning and teaching that connected the artistic practice of individuals but would lead to essential changes, especially relating to diversity and inclusive practice, was exceptionally difficult – and I know I didn't succeed in many ways;
- Economic considerations over pedagogy and curriculum, which is, of course, an ongoing issue for most HE institutions;
- Difficulty in challenging behaviours not commensurate with a contemporary understanding of learning and teaching because of the

excellence or prestige promoted by the individuals and their status within the creative industries;
- Decisions were largely based on embedded institutional practices rather than evidence or research, and this is largely, I believe, due to the way in which conservatoires conserve knowledges and practices rather than produce new ways of seeing, understanding and undertaking those knowledges and practices, which I explore later in this chapter.

There are two points that I think are worth highlighting here. The first relates to my own readiness for leadership. It is common for leaders in education to learn 'on the job' as Hopkin et al. (2011, p. 1) identified in their study of deans of education. Experts in educational practice are often promoted because of their subject expertise, not necessarily because of their leadership skills. This was certainly my experience. When I first moved into a leadership role, there was an expectation that I was entering with the experience and knowledge ready to undertake the job. This was compounded by two further issues, the first being my underestimating the differences of institutional culture between a music department within a newer university and a cross-institutional role within a conservatoire; and the second being the significant number of hourly paid teaching staff who had little expectation to inhabit a HE teaching role. By this, I mean no evaluation of teaching, no peer observation, little engagement with academic curriculum and little interest in programme or continuing professional development. This, of course, was not a universal experience, and I met many wonderful individuals who did engage enthusiastically. The dominant identity of this pool of teachers, however, was musician/artist first, and this meant that their HE teaching role was not a major part of how they saw themselves. This 'dual identity' has been variously explored in teacher and nursing education (e.g. Lopes et al., 2014), within the exploration of the concept of the 'pracademic', that is, those who are 'dually recognised as experts in both academic and professional practice' (Dickfos, 2019, p. 243) and, within the arts education specifically, as the artist-teacher or performer-educator (e.g. Gaunt, 2007; Jordan, 2015). Regardless of the lens through which this dual identity is explored, the tension between practitioner-academic identities is present. In my own context and experience, the building became an extension to the individual tutor's own private practice, which was closely guarded and protected from the centralized function that I was occupying.

There are many ways of understanding challenges that leaders in learning and teaching face – what is institutionally specific, subject-specific or due to individual personality and behaviour. I now explore the contextual and subject-specific factors before moving into an identification of my personal leadership traits that have developed through engaging with the issues identified.

Cultural and Subject Contextual Factors

There are two specific contextual concerns I wish to explore here. The first is the way in which the arts and conservatoires are positioned within HE, and the second is about how the arts are managed in professional venues in ways that may impact artists working as teachers within specialist HE institutions.

'It is not an easy ask to bring about learning and teaching changes in creative arts disciplines', stated de la Harpe and Mason (2014, p. 140), and I would concur. To encourage the consideration of different or efficient approaches to teaching means – in many cases – confronting the dominance of practice found in studio teaching, which is made more difficult by it being held as a 'sacred space' (Cox, 2014, p. 47) or as the long-standing 'zeitgeist of the creative arts that is resistant to change' (de la Harpe and Mason, 2014, p. 138).

Cox (2014) described affecting change in a conservatoire is difficult, where most changes are not to the core delivery or instrumental or vocal teaching, but rather to aspects of perceived non-essential topics, most commonly in academic-type modules. This metaphor of glacial movement certainly resonated with my experience, but had I thought more carefully about this earlier in my leadership journey, I may have developed more successful strategies. So I take the opportunity to understand this now.

If we understand professions to be occupational groups that 'possess autonomous control over a restricted domain of specialized knowledge' and 'as reproducing the values and interests of expert occupations' (Racko, Oborn and Barrett, 2019, p. 459), then we can understand artistic professions, such as musician or dancer, to likewise propagate specialized knowledge. This knowledge is embodied in physical, technical and musical expression. These knowledges are codified in the training of young artists. Within the conservatoire setting, the focus is on replication of existing knowledge or conserving artistic practices, rather than the development of new or original ideas (see, for example, Clark and Jackson, 2017). In classical music in the conservatoire, this knowledge reproduction is tied to a prestige economy both commercially and socially, and this is reflected in the reification of an individual's own prestigious lineage. Cox (2014) described this as apostolic succession, where a musician's prestige is linked to the lineage of musicians they themselves can trace, the most notable being able to trace a line back to Chopin or Mendelssohn, for example. In some ways this can be viewed as a variation of 'Freemasonry' or 'Old Boy Network'. And although the artistic professions exert the same will to maintain control over knowledge production as traditional academic subjects, the knowledge production is different because the knowledge is to be *conserved* or *reproduced* rather than contributing to the production of *new* knowledge. This, I would suggest, places conservatoires in constant tension with typical HE practices.

I do think, however, that there is a thread of commonality between the specialist elite and prestigious research institutions – where 'in skewing the distribution of funding increasingly towards the "best" research, the UK government has deliberately encouraged the growth of a research elite' (Blackmore, 2018, p. 244) – and specialist institutions which have had a competitive funding process known as institution-specific funding. This was 'additional and discretionary funding currently provided by HEFCE [Higher Education Funding Council of England] to a subset of HEFCE-funded higher education institutions. It is intended to recognize the higher cost and distinctive nature of specialist higher education providers' (HEFCE, 2015, p. 1), with HEFCE being responsible for the distribution of funding to universities in England until 2018, when it was replaced by the Office for Students and Research England. Both funding models position teaching as external to the prestige economy, but in different ways. In contrast to how Blackmore (2018) accurately describes the prestige/reputation hierarchy between research and teaching in universities, I think there is something different in specialist institutions. In some ways it makes sense that the apostolic succession (Cox, 2014) has remained so entrenched. The specialist institution, through the competitive but limited funding resource, can only maintain its prestige through demonstrating its 'world-classness', and much of that relies on teacher reputation. And, of course, if extra funding and position in the prestige economy is predicated on the reputation of teachers, it is almost impossible to make a structural change because of the potential threat to economic viability.

And so, we can perhaps start to see that the performer-educator in the conservatoire may view the imposition of HE practices as a turbulent force because it is disrupting the conservation of knowledge (practice). This can be a difficult aspect to counteract, particularly if you don't know it's happening! So, although I attempted to put in place collaborative structures, I hadn't identified this as being a potential challenge to confront and unpick. I was stuck in an attempt to resolve the disruption that I thought was being caused by colleagues not understanding the expectations of HE, rather than – what I do now – trying to understand the profession and how that is influencing expectations, behaviour and the definition of knowledge. Not understanding the problem was a significant barrier to my earlier leadership development!

So, if the artists/musicians are being employed because they are industry practitioners, I wondered whether their experience of other organizations and leadership might affect how they understand leadership within HE institutions. In arts organizations, such as theatres, music venues, opera houses and so on, it is quite typical to have leadership roles that are split between artistic and financial responsibilities, with an argument that this utilizes divergent and complementary skill sets (Reynolds, Tonks and MacNeill, 2017). I mention this because artist/performer-teachers, who make up the workforce in specialist institutions, will be familiar with this model. In particular, 'an artistic director assumes responsibility for artistic excellence and a managing director or general manager is responsible for organizational efficiency and financial sustainability' (Reynolds, Tonks and MacNeill, 2017, p. 91). Both types of leadership roles are vital to the arts organization, but generally the artistic director has a much closer link with the artists, having usually 'been one of them' at some time, whereas the general manager or the financial director is often perceived as restricting the artistic freedom of artists due to financial considerations. There are parallels with how I believe artists and musicians engage with academic and educational leadership, where many of the discussions the performer-educators wish to have relate to artistic leadership within the teaching organization, conflating a HE institution with a performance venue and then conflating educational leadership with the general manager's role, perceived as restricting their freedom to practice autonomously.

There are, however, two possible links with more widespread HE issues and the development of leadership roles in learning and teaching. The first is related to the nature of knowledge, as I have described above, being the focus of reproduction, and that conservation is part of what, I believe, the autonomy of the studio space is trying to preserve. This, as an authority, is a similar manifestation to the 'insulating against external influences used to describe academic professionals [who] have traditionally specialized in the development of "pure" research that is not tainted by the demands of knowledge users' (Racko, Oborn and Barrett, 2019, p. 460). The second is related to one of the external influences that may affect and challenge autonomy. In the creative arts, in HE at least, the situation has been described as being 'no longer sufficient for individuals in schools/programs/courses/subjects to independently implement learning and teaching initiatives' (de la Harpe and Mason, 2014, p. 129). As such, this has been part of what Jones et al. (2012) previously described as growing resentment by academic staff on the reduction of their autonomy through regulation and managerialism. I believe this was how my role was viewed. A perception, perhaps, was held that my role signified a reduction in the autonomy of teaching and offered a further example of how, for the conservatoire, music-educators were attempting to be repurposed away from the reproduction of the codified knowledges of the profession.

Strategies and Strengths

Having explored some of the challenges and the reasons why they may have occurred, I now explore strengths and strategies I have identified through reflection. I have developed some typical traits and behaviours that are suggested to be effective in leadership. These include 'silo busting', building trust, promoting diversity, continuing to develop soft skills (such as empathy and listening with empathy) and creating psychological safety (Goman, 2017). Cook (2016) has an extended list specific to the leadership context in HE and describes effective leadership being exhibited by individuals who are

> trusted and who has personal integrity; an individual who is supportive of their staff; a style which is inclusive and involves others in decision making; a style which is value driven and which involves others extensively in the creation of these values; a sense of direction, a vision; protection of staff ... assertiveness, competence, relatedness and morality ... a considered style which encompasses collaboration and equality rather than a top down managerialist style. (pp. 34–5)

Some of these traits have developed naturally, but it is only now that I can really articulate that these are part of my approach.

From a slightly different perspective, ethical leadership in education includes seven virtues: trust, wisdom, kindness, justice, service, courage and optimism, which reflect many of the traits identified above (Roberts, 2019). Roberts discusses these as being the basis of ethical leadership and decision-making – if decisions are not aligned with these 'virtues', then it is usually because of someone else's pressure. I would describe this as something that has become a mantra for me – I need to be able to look at myself in the mirror after every decision I make – that is, if my integrity is maintained and if my boundaries for ethical practice are clear and intact. But, as Roberts describes elsewhere, a dominant and rather toxic narrative of educational leadership relates to a strong, robust leadership that can lead to fast decision-making processes to prevent any perception of weakness (Speck, 2019). There is still a struggle to be had against leaders who adopt traditional modes of leadership and often exude a toxic confidence that do not betray any sign of weaknesses. This then also pertains to gender inequality (in the arts) – where less women are producing artistic outputs or being booked for performances and gigs (Bain, 2019) and are in less decision-making roles, mirroring HE. We have seen change begin to be called for, but in a specialist organization that uses industry professionals as the main source for teachers, you can begin to imagine how these issues of under-representation may start to compound. Therefore, the trend in expressing vulnerability, particularly by female leaders, is perhaps one that we should be embracing more to combat toxic behaviours. Great teaching often comes from spaces and places where the tutor has allowed vulnerability and humility into their practice, by decentring themselves and placing the student at the heart of the experience. It is often this approach that creates safe and engaging learning experiences, and I find it equally important to create that environment as a leader.

In preparing this chapter, I asked colleagues past and present what they thought were important features of my leadership that readers of this chapter might find useful to have identified. I was overwhelmed by the responses, and although there are obvious issues with asking for people's opinion of you, it taught me two things: (i) People you work with are willing to partner with you to understand your own 'sphere of influence', and (ii) when you are intent on building trusting communities of practice, you have to be willing to hear what they say. I have divided the strengths identified into the following categories – values, behaviours and abilities:

Values: professional; non-judgemental; understanding the wider context; commitment to dismantling barriers;

Behaviours: celebrating strengths of colleagues; appreciation of what has been achieved rather than what hasn't; kindness; personable; humorous; engaging critical friend; commitment to following up on actions; creative responses to setbacks; supportive and encouraging; approachable; communicative; open-minded; empathetic;

Abilities: Clarity of thought and articulating opinion; inquisitive listener; coaching to challenge; mentoring for research and professional practice; ability to get the best out of people; facilitating collaborative thinking; lateral thinking; validating what's working – and positively empowering to explore areas for development; sensitivity and skill in tuning in and critically appraising another's teaching style.

Through my colleagues' identification of my leadership behaviours, I was then able to position my leadership within the framework of collaborative professionalism (Hargreaves and O'Connor, 2018). For the first time in my career, I feel being able to locate my leadership practice, and I will explore this through various theoretical lenses.

Analysis of Leadership Approaches

I will now explore two ways in which I have come to understand my leadership practice. The first relates to understanding turbulence in educational institutions. The second relates to developing collaborative professionalism. Often, educational leaders are perceived as being brought in to an institution to 'shake the cage' or 'wake those teachers up' (Beabout, 2012, p. 16) as a way of formulating disruption to the status quo – disruption as the catalyst for change. As Beabout continues to outline, disruptive change rarely leads to a lasting and effective change because the focus is on resolving the disruption rather than on relationships, learning and context.

Disruption as change can be useful, but more often is a barrier to sustainable and meaningful change. Beabout describes two forms of disruption that may help further explain the barriers I encountered. The first, turbulence, 'can raise awareness, build commitment, and spawn imaginative thinking and practice' (Beabout, 2012, p. 26). As a disruptor, turbulence is energy-intensive and can be negative in its impact, and there is a threshold for how much an individual, team or organization can cope with. Perturbance, however, 'defined as a social process of examining its goals and practices, can be an important component in the process of sustainable educational change' (Beabout, 2012, p. 26). The difference between the two can be summarized as turbulence requiring a focus on speedy resolution (i.e. what now?), in contrast to the asking of 'what next' that occurs in a state of perturbance. This utilizes multiple perspectives and is 'characterized by a slow pace, collaborative trust, and solving shared problems' (Beabout, 2012, p. 26). It is in this space of perturbance that I attempt to focus my future leadership of change in learning and teaching.

The notion of slow pace and collaborative trust really resonates with my understanding of effective leadership in learning and teaching. It is also interesting when you reconsider how Cox (2014) described change within conservatoires. Cox described the slow shift in change within conservatoires and usually only on the periphery of the main activity of instrumental teaching because of how the sacred space of the teaching studio is maintained within these contexts.

The notion of slow pace also links with collaborative professionalism, whereby a key feature is 'build slowly, act fast' (Hargreaves and O'Connor, 2018, p. 14). The notion of collaborative professionalism (differentiated from professional collaboration), although more commonly found in research focused on leadership in schools, is starting to appear in more HE-related studies and has struck me as being a useful way of understanding my approach to leadership. Hargreaves and O'Connor (2018) describe collaborative professionalism as

> how teachers and other educators transform teaching and learning together to work with all students to develop fulfilling lives of meaning, purpose and success. It is evidence-informed, but not data-driven, and involves deep and sometimes demanding dialogue, candid but constructive feedback, and continuous collaborative inquiry. Finally, collaborative inquiry is embedded in the culture and life of the school, where educators actively care for and have solidarity with each other as fellow-professionals as they pursue their challenging work together in response to the cultures of their students, the society and themselves. (2018, p. 3)

Using collaborative professionalism as leadership requires utilizing high trust while maintaining high precision at the same time as developing strong relationships to facilitate risk-taking and mistake making (Hargreaves and O'Connor, 2018, p. 5). This is seen as a defining feature that also enables the overcoming of systemic educational inequalities through collective responsibilities and student and teacher empowerment (Washington and O'Connor, 2020).

Finally, collaborative professionalism can be viewed as a way of engaging and challenging the autonomous reproduction of authority and knowledge maintained by professions (Racko, Oborn and Barrett, 2019, p. 460). I need to do further work in implementing this in my new role, but I am interested in how collaborative professionalism can bring together different professional groups in order to cut across and transform 'the conventional concern of professionalism with the protection of occupational autonomy and enables innovative resolution of the emerging problems of a post-industrial society' (Racko, Oborn and Barrett, 2019, p. 476). I can say that I am beginning to implement the following, which are further characteristics of collaborative professionalism: emphasizing interdependence of different departments in non-hierarchical relationship building, developing rules with those different interdependent characters, building and promoting shared goals through interdependent contributions (after Racko, Oborn and Barrett, 2019, p. 459).

Conclusion

I wanted to end this chapter with some summary thoughts that have emerged during the process of its writing, which are contributing to my developing an approach to collaborative professionalism in the arts in HE:

What's the problem? Consider whether the challenge you face is sector-wide, institutional, departmental, team or individual or, as I have tried to describe here, caused by a dissonance between perceptions of two different groups, with different understandings of the role of knowledge and HE.

Invest in empathy and listening: HE is a complex context for us to navigate, and this can cloud our ability to empathize with the priorities and pressures of others – especially those we don't work with regularly. What is important to you may not be the most important or immediately pressing issue for someone else. This is particularly important when working with those who report to you and who need to trust that you are listening and taking action to enable them to undertake their roles. This approach has garnered a lot of goodwill with people I have worked with, and it mostly generates gratitude and positivity.

Mistakes will be made: So apologize! Sometimes I have apologized for things that were directly my mistake. Other times, I have apologized where the mistake was made elsewhere but someone in a senior position needed to show humility to move the narrative forward and to repair relationships. This does not mean, however, you become the scapegoat for all errors – when boundaries have been broken, it requires robust challenging.

Acknowledge and engage with your values: I have focused throughout this chapter on my collaborative approach. I knew I had a leadership role but hadn't really considered what makes me an effective leader – what I do within my role that actually makes me more successful than, perhaps, I would usually acknowledge. Ultimately, through this process, I can state that my mission is finding a balance between leading initiatives and fostering cooperative learning between adults in professional contexts who have diverse ideas and have had diverse life experiences.

Purpose of leadership: Leadership is often (mis)understood in relation to power over people – I never wanted power over people; I wanted power to affect change, to bring about social justice in the arts and, especially, to support those who are systematically excluded from or experiencing barriers to engaging with the arts in HE. This is reflective of my teaching ethos and will remain a guiding principle for my future leadership activity.

References

Bain, V. (2019), 'Counting the Music: The Gender Gap'. https://vbain.co.uk/research.

Beabout, B. R. (2012), 'Turbulence, Perturbance, and Educational Change', *Complicity: An International Journal of Complexity and Education*, 9 (2): 15–29.

Blackmore, P. (2018), 'What Can Policy-Makers Do with the Idea of Prestige, to Make Better Policy?', *Policy Reviews in Higher Education*, 2 (2): 227–54. https://doi.org/10.1080/23322969.2018.1498300.

Clark, J. O. and Jackson, L. H. (2017), 'Aesthetic Education, Critical Pedagogy and Specialist Institutions', in R. Hall and J. Winn (eds), *Mass Intellectuality, and Democratic Leadership in Higher Education*, 113–26, London: Bloomsbury.

Cleaver, E., Lintern, M. and McLinden, M., eds (2018), *Teaching and Learning in Higher Education: Disciplinary Approaches to Educational Enquiry*, 2nd edn, London: Sage.

Cook, C. C. (2016), 'Redefining Leadership in a Higher Education Context: Views from the Front Line', DBA diss., Edinburgh Napier University, Edinburgh. https://www.napier.ac.uk/~/media/worktribe/output-978802/redefining-leadership-in-a-higher-education-context-views-from-the-front-line.pdf.

Cotton, D. R. E., Miller, W. and Kneale, P. (2018), 'The Cinderella of Academia: Is Higher Education Pedagogic Research Undervalued in UK Research Assessment?', *Studies in Higher Education*, 43 (9): 1625–36. https://doi.org/10.1080/03075079.2016.1276549.

Cox, J. (2014), 'Encouraging and Training Conservatoire Students at Undergraduate and Taught-Postgraduate Level towards Fluency in the Thought-Processes and Methods of Artistic Research', in S. D. Harrison (ed.), *Research and Research Education in Music Performance and Pedagogy*, 45–64, Dordrecht: Springer.

Dickfos, J. (2019), 'Academic Professional Development: Benefits of a Pracademic Experience', *International Journal of Work-Integrated Learning*, 20 (3), 243–55. https://files.eric.ed.gov/fulltext/EJ1232894.pdf.

Gaunt, H. (2007). 'One-to-One Tuition in a Conservatoire: The Perceptions of Instrumental and Vocal Teachers', *Psychology of Music*, 36 (2): 215–45. https://doi.org/10.1177/0305735607080827.

Goman, C. K. (2017), 'Six Crucial Behaviors of Collaborative Leaders', *Forbes*, 11 July. https://www.forbes.com/sites/carolkinseygoman/2017/07/11/six-crucial-behaviors-of-collaborative-leaders/#5f2e35218cbe.

Hargreaves, A. and O'Connor, M. T. (2018), *Leading Collaborative Professionalism*, Seminar Series 274, Melbourne: Centre for Strategic Education. http://www.andyhargreaves.com/uploads/5/2/9/2/5292616/seminar_series_274-april2018.pdf.

de la Harpe, B. and Mason, T. (2014), 'Leadership of Learning and Teaching in the Creative Arts', *Higher Education Research & Development*, 33 (1): 129–43. https://doi.org/10.1080/07294360.2013.870982.

HEFCE (2015), 'Institution-Specific Funding: Circular Letter Outcomes and Invitation to Make a Submission', 10 June. https://dera.ioe.ac.uk/23356/1/HEFCE2015_10.pdf.

Hopkin, D., Johnson, V., Damico, S. and Wepner, S. (2011), 'Emerging Characteristics of Education Deans' Collaborative Leadership', *Academic Leadership: The Online Journal*, 9 (1): article 21. https://scholars.fhsu.edu/alj/vol9/iss1/21.

Jones, S., Lefoe, G., Harvey, M. and Ryland, K. (2012), 'Distributed Leadership: A Collaborative Framework for Academics, Executives and Professionals in Higher Education', *Journal of Higher Education Policy and Management*, 34 (1): 67–78. https://doi.org/10.1080/1360080X.2012.642334.

Jordan, D. (2015), 'The Dual Identity of the Artist-Teacher: What Does Teaching Do to the Artist-Teacher in the Contemporary Educational Context?', EdD diss., Dublin City University. http://doras.dcu.ie/22495/1/Dervil%20Jordan.pdf.

Lopes, A., Boyd, P., Andrew, N. and Pereira, F. (2014), 'The Research-Teaching Nexus in Nurse and Teacher Education: Contributions of an Ecological Approach to Academic Identities in Professional Fields', *Higher Education*, 68, 167–83. https://doi.org/10.1007/s10734-013-9700-2.

Racko, G., Oborn, E. and Barrett, M. (2019) 'Developing Collaborative Professionalism: An Investigation of Status Differentiation in Academic Organizations in Knowledge Transfer Partnerships', *International Journal of Human Resource Management*, 30 (3): 457–78. https://doi.org/10.1080/09585192.2017.1281830.

Reynolds, S., Tonks, A. and MacNeill, K. (2017), 'Collaborative Leadership in the Arts as a Unique Form of Dual Leadership', *Journal of Arts Management, Law and Society*, 47 (2): 89–104. https://doi.org/10.1080/10632921.2016.1241968.

Roberts, C. (2019), *Ethical Leadership for a Better Education System: What Kind of People Are We?*, Abingdon: Routledge.

Speck, D. (2019), 'Meet the Head Who Is Asking if "Strong" Leadership Is Enough', *TES*, 15 March. https://www.tes.com/news/meet-head-who-asking-if-strong-leadership-enough.

Washington, S. A. and O'Connor, M. T. (2020), 'Collaborative Professionalism across Cultures and Contexts: Cases of Professional Learning Networks Enhancing Teaching and Learning in Canada and Colombia', in L. Schnellert (ed.), *Professional Learning Networks: Facilitating Transformation in Diverse Contexts with Equity-Seeking Communities*, 17–47, Bingley: Emerald.

Wieman, C. E. (2019), 'Expertise in University Teaching and the Implications for Teaching Effectiveness, Evaluation and Training', *Daedalus*, 148 (4): 47–78. https://doi.org/10.1162/daed_a_01760.

7

Finding a Path to Leadership in Science by Choosing to Be Different: The Road Not Taken

Susan Rowland

Introduction

Robert Frost's beautiful 1916 poem 'The Road Not Taken' concludes with three lines: 'Two roads diverged in a wood, and I —; I took the one less traveled by; And that has made all the difference.' Frost's core idea is simple and profound – he says that making a choice has an impact.

A choice always has consequences; whether the choice is 'right' or the consequences are 'good' are complex questions without convenient answers. I am a teaching-focused science academic in a research-intensive Australian university. In my case, I made a choice to be different from the norm. As a consequence, I have become a leader in learning and teaching. In this chapter I explore the choice I made and the road I travel. I am not yet sure what is at the end of the road, because, as Frost (1916) says, 'way leads on to way'. No matter; the uncertainty and the opportunities for discovering a new destination are what make the journey interesting.

My Early Road in Science

I am a biochemist by training. My undergraduate degree, honours project and PhD degree are all in biochemistry. I used to be an expert in prokaryotic genetics, protein chemistry and the inner workings of how bacteria grow and divide. I published plenty of work in those areas and still find them fascinating in a 'New Scientist' sort of way – I'm an educated observer who marvels at the workings of nature and biological systems. Now, as a teaching-focused academic, I work alongside academic peers who run research laboratories and groups that address important questions in physics, chemistry, microbiology and many other facets of science. I respect them, and I hope they respect me.

When I completed my PhD in 1995, I obtained a postdoctoral fellowship and left Australia for the United States. At the time, this international foray was expected for Australian science graduates who wanted to forge an academic career. The Australian 'cultural cringe' (Phillips, 1950) was alive and well, and the only way to be legitimate as a scientist was to prove yourself by working in England, Europe or America. I intended to work in the United States for three years – the length of my fellowship funding – but that wasn't how things worked out. My husband came to do a sabbatical in the lab where I was working; the university recruited him as a full professor; and we ended up staying in the United States for eleven years.

This was a time of intense work, intense creativity and solid publication output, but I found myself frustrated with my career. My visa status tied me to one university, and there was no opportunity for professional development or promotion. My husband, who is a wonderful and appreciative collaborator, was a research group leader. I worked for him and for other group leaders on their projects. My visa status meant I could not apply for my own grant funding, so I was unable to drive independent research. Our two children were born in the United States. I love them passionately, but parenting as a laboratory scientist without family backup is not easy. I often had to make the choice between my children (who got sick like normal children do) and my protein. Of course, I stayed home with bronchial babies while the protein sat in the fridge and broke down into useless amino acids. I struggled mentally and emotionally around my self-worth as a scientist. I also wondered how I would ever make the jump from a postdoctoral researcher into a group leader academic. Despite my publication record, I worried about my lack of autonomy and scant funding. Academic science is a take-no-prisoners road race for grant money, papers and evidence of independent achievement. I felt my race plan was in serious trouble.

Various factors brought us home to Australia in late 2006. Certainly, my career frustration was one of them, so we chose an Australian university that seemed to understand the 'two body problem' (McNeil and Sher, 1998, p. 2) and was willing to employ both of us in academic positions. At our new university – The University of Queensland (UQ) – my husband's position was a full professorship, and mine was at a far lower academic level, part-time, on contract. At face value this didn't seem like a great deal, but I felt it was an improvement on my American situation, and I vowed to make the opportunity count.

Travelling towards the Fork in the Road

Our first year back in Australia was, for want of a better word, crazy. My academic teaching position was part-time (nominally 40 per cent), while I also held a 60 per cent research position in my husband's group. As we all know, 'part-time' work in academia doesn't really mean part-time, so to do both of my roles adequately, I needed to work about 175 per cent. I saw that as a given rather than as an unusual expectation.

For my teaching, my head of school gave me two masters-level courses and a large flagship undergraduate course to coordinate. I inherited these from previous staff who had retired or left the university. The available teaching material was relatively scanty. In my head's opinion, the undergraduate course was 'a mess', and he gave me carte blanche to rebuild it. Looking back, this was an extraordinary leap of faith on his part. Such unfettered ability to direct curriculum and learning modes was a gift; through it, I discovered my creativity and love of teaching.

I was a new teacher, with no prior training and no language or theory around pedagogy. I decided to complete a graduate certificate in education. My plan was to do it in one year, while working 175 per cent, and with two small children. My head of school financially supported my graduate certificate enrolment, and my husband supported the idea that my lab productivity would suffer. I was lucky on both counts. That year, I pulled extraordinarily long work weeks for ten months, caught real influenza, ended up in hospital with pneumonia, but managed to get enough medical certificates that I could hand all my assessments in and complete the programme.

I found the graduate certificate profoundly formative. The pedagogy in the programme was different to anything I had experienced in a transmission-style science lectures. The content was filled with ideas that were new to me – levels of cognition and Bloom's Revised Taxonomy (Anderson et al., 2001), the deficit model (Wallace, 2009), constructive alignment (Biggs and Tang, 2011) and backwards design (Wiggins and McTighe, 2005). In the classes, other students confidently said things that I considered unfounded opinions; they declared 'this resonates for me', and 'I'd like to amplify your comment'. These were terms that scientists didn't use in normal conversation. The science academics in the class bonded together, all offended (in a purist scientific way) by what we saw as the casual bastardization of physics.

Looking back, I was experiencing a culture shock that undermined my sense of self and my science-centric understanding of 'truth'. This was useful, but I can see why many science academics would (and do) reject education as a discipline they can comfortably adopt. During the graduate certificate we read a lot of education literature. To be honest, I still don't understand some of it, but at the time it was absolutely baffling to me. The structures were so different to anything I had read before. The arguments seemed so convoluted. In every paper I read, I was searching for a fact (any fact!) inside a maze of ideas and opinions. 'How do they know this is true?' I asked myself, my classmates and also my somewhat annoyed lecturers. I gradually came to the conclusion that, often, the authors don't know something is true. Instead, they propose ideas, and discuss them, and then somehow these ideas become educational dogma. I am still troubled by this, and I understand my scientific colleagues would also have great difficulty accepting it. The sense of needing to establish some evidenced truth around what works in teaching is a driver for my current research programme in science education.

Also, and very importantly, the graduate certificate made me a coursework student for the first time in fifteen years. I was transported back to a position of relative powerlessness. I was stressed about trying to juggle my life and job with study, confused by the assessment requirements and unenlightened by some of the feedback I got on my work. I learned that, even though I am an able student and an autodidact, I still struggled with the teachers' assumptions that I could speak discipline-specific language or absorb that language by osmosis. I was struck by my sense of being 'other' to the academy and offended that my lived experience and prior educational achievements didn't seem to count for anything in the eyes of my educators and assessors. It all made me think, very seriously, about how a less privileged and confident student would navigate (and stick with) their university experience.

I think every academic should try being a student. I hear colleagues dismissing student concerns as unimportant, or labelling students as 'disengaged' or somehow 'inadequate'. This is their form of educational dogma, but I think they are wrong, and I let them know! I remind my colleagues they cannot ignore the humanity of students; that's part of my role as a leader in science education.

The Fork Comes into View

The year I started working at UQ, the university defined a new academic track – the teaching-focused (TF) position. This was a revolutionary leap for the university, and indeed for Australian universities. UQ was the first Australian university to establish a TF pathway. Importantly, at our university TF is a bona fide academic category that people enter by choice. This is very different to the TF position that some other universities use to manage 'failed' or 'unproductive' researchers. TF academics at UQ do all the same things that more traditional academics do – they are expected to teach, to do service and to have a research programme. Importantly, this programme is in the Scholarship of Teaching and Learning (SoTL) (Hutchings and Shulman, 1999).

The TF model at our university involves embedding disciplinary experts with a teaching focus in the fabric of disciplinary schools. For example, a physics TF academic would work alongside (and have an office next to) the other physicists at the university. When this model was first proposed at UQ, my school's reaction was lukewarm. The school employed skilled chemists, biochemists, microbiologists and bioinformaticians who taught their disciplines. There did not seem to be any pressing need to add a TF academic into the mix.

My school decided, however, to create a TF position in 2009. I was not privy to the discussions around this new role, but I imagine the initiative had several drivers. The school teaches a large load, with first-year classes of around 1,100 students and second-year classes of 400 and more. A major review of higher education in Australia (Bradley, 2008) recommended uncapping the number of university places and moving to a 'demand-driven system'. The government was also moving to introduce new oversight of educational quality (this materialized in the form of the Tertiary Education Quality and Standards Agency, TEQSA). It seemed that classes were going to get larger, and the demands around quality were going to increase. The right TF academic colleague could help address these challenges. Again, I credit my head of school with foresight and vision, because I am sure he was a significant advocate for the TF position.

I got a phone call from a senior member of staff, asking 'Would you be interested in a TF position, should it be created?' There was no guarantee from the school about me being appointed to the role (and I would not have expected one) – the school was just canvassing interest. I imagine they spoke to more than one person about the position.

I took some time to think about the question and found myself standing at the fork of a career, 'sorry I could not travel both' roads (Frost, 1916). Frost's idea about grief here is important. My identity was firmly rooted in my work as a biochemist, and I felt that, once I started down the TF pathway, I could not come back to wet laboratory science. This was frightening, and I felt sad, thinking about what I would lose if I walked away from the bench. I wanted, however, to try something new. My wet lab research was proving very difficult – I had chosen an intractable experimental system, and I was exhausted by the struggle with my proteins. Like many biomedical researchers at the time (ASMR, 2016), I was concerned about funding and job security.

I wondered if I could make the transition to being an education researcher. I sensed it would be difficult to achieve, having read (and been so confused by) the education literature during my graduate certificate. I also wondered who I would talk to, and learn from, as I became a SoTL scholar in science. There was nobody in my school, or my university, or my country for that matter. The closest ones were in the United States. I realized I would be a trailblazer and, like many trailblazers, I would often find myself alone on an untravelled path. Still, that path seemed to have 'the better claim, because it was grassy and wanted wear' (Frost, 1916). I took stock of what I would need to survive and progress in this new type of role. I steeled myself for the struggle, relearning and constant sensemaking I knew I would encounter. The next day I wrote back to the school. 'Yes', I said. 'If the role were created, I would apply.'

The New Road

I was appointed as a continuing TF academic in 2010. My role as a teaching and learning leader really began at that point. The appointment (and the role itself) was a signal to the school that things were going to change. I was the embodiment of that change. I had chosen to be different. I was walking a road with no clear signposts, no accepted measures of 'success' and no precedent in the university system. Some of my colleagues probably considered me foolish, but I think they all appreciated the bravery in my decision. For my part, I felt the weight of responsibility; I needed to make the position work for myself, but also for everyone around me.

My head of school and I didn't discuss strategy, or quality measures, or anything particularly functional about how I should do my job. Instead, I had one directive – to 'change the teaching and learning culture in the school'. Here was another leap of faith on my head's part, and, through a potent mixture of naivety and self-belief, I assumed it was possible to achieve what he wanted.

My school and my colleagues had high expectations of me. In my opinion, high expectations and public scrutiny around TF appointments are essential. Academics are tribal, and they defend their intellectual and disciplinary territories (Becher and Trowler, 2001). When I started full time in the school, most of my colleagues were positive and welcoming. A few even venerated me as an icon of teaching excellence (that was odd, but I learnt to smile benevolently in a Mother Mary kind of way). Despite this sunny climate, there were some mutterings from colleagues who thought a TF academic was unnecessary, a weakness in the system or even a threat. I know some staff raised their eyebrows at my appointment.

My rigorous appointment process helped, however, to defuse this negative talk. The school had appointed me after an international search, an academic seminar and an interview with a large panel of senior academics. I was very glad of these hoops – I had jumped through them, just like any other academic staff member. It was difficult for colleagues to dismiss my legitimate intellectual and performative claim to membership of the academy.

My status as a practising, publishing biochemist also helped my colleagues accept me. My sixteen biochemistry papers were in high-quality journals like *Journal of Bacteriology*, *Molecular Cell*, *PNAS* and *Nature Structural Biology* (King et al., 2000; Rowland et al., 2004, 2010; Szeto et al., 2002). At the time, the culture in academic science – the 'sets of taken-for-granted values, attitudes and ways of behaving' (Becher and Troweler, 2001, p. 23) – prioritized research and publication. Since I was a biochemist, with a respectable publication record, I presented as something familiar. My colleagues felt they had a connection to me, and that I would understand their ways of being and of understanding science and science teaching.

At least one colleague looked up my publication record – he was probably wondering where this strange TF academic had come from. I know, because he stopped in my office door one day.

> 'You've published in *PNAS*, and the *Nature* journals', he stated.
>
> 'Yes', I replied.
>
> 'Huh', he said, then looked about thoughtfully, 'and you're teaching focused'.
>
> 'Yes', I confirmed.
>
> He nodded, still looking into the distance, then started off down the hall after a slightly bemused 'OK then'.
>
> Apparently, in his estimation I was odd, but all right.

I did other things to present myself as a normal part of the academic milieu. I participated in all the school's social events and meetings. I'm an introvert who finds parties tiring, but there were plenty of us in the school with the same social anxiety. We congregated in bashful flocks during functions. I was given the choice of two somewhat grim little offices. One was quiet – isolated from the staff foot traffic. Good for getting work done. Not good for meeting people.

The other office was in the main hall of our building, right next to the men's toilet and its wall-banging plumbing noise. I chose the second one. It was the size of a large cupboard, so I left my door open. I worked long hours and stayed in my office religiously. Every time my colleagues went to the bathroom, they saw me. Almost all the academic staff were male, so I was well positioned to catch them on a regular basis. Sometimes we waved hello. Sometimes they stopped in the door, hovering uncomfortably. I got a nice chair and put it directly inside the entrance. As people got more familiar with me, they came in and sat down.

Colleagues started talking to me about their teaching. They didn't usually make actual requests for help. Instead, they came with complaints, or niggling annoyances, or teaching issues they had tried to fix without success. They talked about their stress and their frustrations around unappreciated teaching effort. As a teacher of large classes (sometimes the same classes my colleagues taught), I was having the same issues, so I could empathize.

I certainly didn't feel like an expert teacher, and I didn't automatically have the solutions people sought. More than anything, I was a friendly face who legitimized the practice of talking about teaching. Having completed a graduate certificate in higher education, I knew more education language than many of my colleagues, and I had read more education literature. This knowledge helped unpack my colleagues' concerns, and we could form some ideas around how to examine the issues they described. Perhaps, more importantly, I knew enough to start framing my colleague's teaching issues as 'problems', as described by Randy Bass. Problems are things 'worth pursuing as an ongoing intellectual focus' that can drive 'creative and productive activity' (Bass, 1999, p. 1). That was something welcome to my colleagues! I'll return to the creative and productive activities later in this chapter.

Coming to Grips with Culture

From the conversations with my colleagues, it was clear that they wanted help with their teaching, and I found that very encouraging. As I noted earlier, my head wanted me to change the culture in the school. At the time, I didn't do any formal thinking about culture theory. Instead, I just dived in and started working to influence people by listening, talking, trying some new ideas and modelling practice. There is plenty of useful literature about culture, and it probably would have helped me to know it, so I will present a little of it here

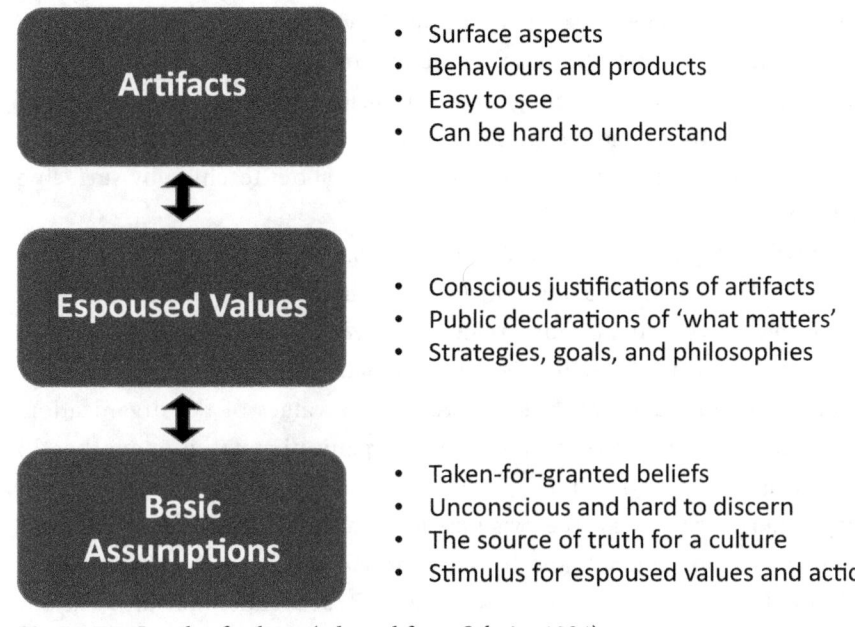

Figure 7.1 Levels of culture (adapted from Schein, 1984).

for the reader. I will also link it to the way I worked (and still work) to change the culture of teaching and learning in my school and, more broadly, at my university.

Edgar Schein's (1984) taxonomy is a good place to start. Schein conceptualized culture at three levels: Artifacts,[1] Espoused Values and Basic Assumptions (Figure 7.1).

Artefacts are the visible, tangible items and activities of an organization. At a university, cultural artefacts include the buildings, the staff, the website, the university governance structures and the strategic plan. Universities also display their culture in other ways. They organize and present educational offerings in a particular manner; they take an accepted approach to student interactions; and they privilege certain modes of learning and assessment.

When I first looked at the artefacts of our teaching culture, I was a bit disappointed in what I saw. The disciplinary teaching epistemology focused on research-derived content delivery. The student deficit model was alive and well and, for many of my colleagues, Piaget's concept of constructivism was still a distant haze on the horizon of awareness. There were isolated pockets of good practice – classes that used active learning, student-centred pedagogy and cognitively challenging work. These floated like rafts in a sea of more mediocre teaching – didactic 'sage on the stage' transmission lectures and assessment that focused on content memorization. When the students engaged poorly with this practice, my colleagues were mystified and disappointed. These feelings and confusions were the problems they brought to me. To change the artefacts of the culture – the way my colleagues taught – I worked to change the way they think about teaching by surfacing what they value.

Beneath Schein's Artifacts lie Espoused Values. Espoused Values are a declared set of norms, attitudes and ways of being. They can be expressed in multiple ways and at more than one level of the organization. At a university, public artefacts like the strategic plan, the mission statement and the published graduate attributes represent the values of the organization. These values can differ, however, from one organizational unit to another. In a large organization with internal tribes, the 'organizational' values are not always internalized by all the organizational units. Values affect how parts of an organization interact and how individuals represent the organization. As I noted earlier, when I started work as a TF academic, the values in our school seemed to include the idea that students were empty vessels and that teaching was a source of frustration rather than of joy. I also felt, however, that my colleagues cared deeply about their students' learning, and their distress around poor educational outcomes was an expression of the value they placed on education.

Basic Assumptions are deeply embedded beliefs and behaviours that form the essence of a culture. In a well-governed and high-functioning culture, the assumptions, espoused values and artefacts all operate in synergy. Because my university had created TF academic positions, I believed the university held a basic assumption about the high value of teaching and the student experience. As my colleagues came to talk to me about their teaching, I believed they had an assumption around the importance of improving their work. I also figured they must hold assumptions about my ability to listen and, maybe, even to help! They assumed I was trustworthy.

These assumptions form the bedrock of my relationships with my colleagues. In times of trouble and dissent, I have been able to call on them as a point of common understanding. When we disagree about the details (or the artefacts!), we can remind ourselves of our basic assumptions – that student learning is important, that good teaching practice is important and that I am going to work with them to help improve teaching and learning.

Trust has important implications for leadership and has been crucial in my context, so I will unpack it further below.

Coming to Grips with Trust

As I walk the new teaching and learning road at my university, I enjoy the companionship of my colleagues. They come and go on the path with me. Sometimes they arrive looking surprised – as if they have accidentally strayed out of a dark research thicket, or off the traditional academic track – and have suddenly found themselves in a patch of sun on the teaching road. Sometimes they arrive more purposefully, rushing to catch up with me and talk for a while, then tearing off ahead while they pursue an exciting teaching innovation that lies around the next bend. I figure they will come back and talk again when they need to. Others choose to walk with me, telling stories, sharing burdens and making plans that include us both. I see each of these travel experiences as a joy and as an opportunity to build understanding and trust.

There are plenty of podcasters and bloggers telling us how to gain others' trust. The source I trust, however, is the work of Shawn Burke and colleagues. In their literature synthesis, Burke et al. (2007) define three determinants of trust: Ability, Benevolence and Integrity. As a leader in teaching and learning, I must demonstrate all three consistently to earn the trust of my colleagues and to keep them walking the education road with me. Below I describe some of the ways I achieve this.

I have already noted the selection process my school has used to appoint me and my biochemistry publication record as things that helped establish my 'ability' – my 'group of skills, competencies, and characteristics that enable [my] influence' (Mayer et al., 1995, p. 717). As I demonstrate my ability as a teacher, my colleagues expect to see the usual academic marks of merit – my familiarity with appropriate literature, good teaching evaluations and engagement with teaching governance processes at my university.

In my opinion, the other key evidence of an academic's 'ability' is their research output. I no longer do any research in biochemistry, but I now have a busy SoTL research programme. I use varied SoTL approaches (Hutchings, 2000) to examine teaching and learning problems. SoTL often uses qualitative methodologies, and in becoming a SoTL researcher, I have transitioned from being a 'hard, pure' scientist (Becher, 1994) into a social scientist. It's been a difficult and humbling journey, but I have learned to appreciate new ways of being a researcher and a colleague.

SoTL publication has been a great way to engage my colleagues with their teaching. Publications are accepted academic currency, and they serve as tangible rewards for working with me and embarking on teaching innovations. The process of building and conducting a research project starts positive, creative and productive conversations about teaching. Importantly, collaborative research allows me to walk alongside my colleagues while we look at their teaching and their students' development. I'm not telling my colleagues what to do. Instead, I'm helping them evidence, understand and reflect on their practice.

Working on SoTL projects with my colleagues benefits me, but it is also a benevolent act (Burke et al., 2007). I support my colleagues with research expertise and discussion that helps their teaching-related sensemaking (DuToit, 2007). I am also genuinely interested in their teaching and professional advancement. I have a lot of mentees and I enjoy working with them; this relationship-building activity is a demonstrated contributor to perceptions of benevolence (Caldwell and Hayes, 2007). To help my colleagues advance, I coach them as they seek recognition for their teaching. This role includes sharing my own successful teaching award applications and acting as a critical friend and referee for their award submissions. Importantly, I have benefitted enormously from the mentoring of others, and I know it is important to pass the wisdom on.

The third determinant of trust is integrity, which Mayer et al. (1995) describe as 'the trustor's perception that the trustee adheres to a set of principles that the trustor finds acceptable' (p. 719). To me, this means I will never ask my colleagues to teach in a way that I myself would not do. It also means I test practices and tools for viability before making a recommendation to my colleagues. The Gartner Hype Cycle (Figure 7.2) is a helpful way to think about my 'integrity' role.

The Gartner Hype Cycle describes the stages people go through as they encounter and adopt an innovation. Naturally, innovations come with 'hype', a set of inflated expectations that the users adopt as they hope the innovation will deliver solutions to problems. Once the users develop a more realistic picture of the innovation, those expectations are usually shattered and the trough of disillusionment comes into view. Users then work through their disappointment, come to understand the opportunities the innovation affords and incorporate the innovation productively.

There are plenty of innovations in teaching and learning, but not all of them are practical or sustainable, and most of them don't deliver on their initial promise. Take MOOCs (massive open online courses) as an example. We all remember the hype around students learning online using self-paced activities, free worldwide access to education and the predicted MOOC-driven death of the university. Then, once we discovered that most MOOC enrolees don't finish their programme (Reich and Ruiperez-Valiente, 2019), we all became disillusioned with massified online instruction. However, in the face of a pandemic, we learnt

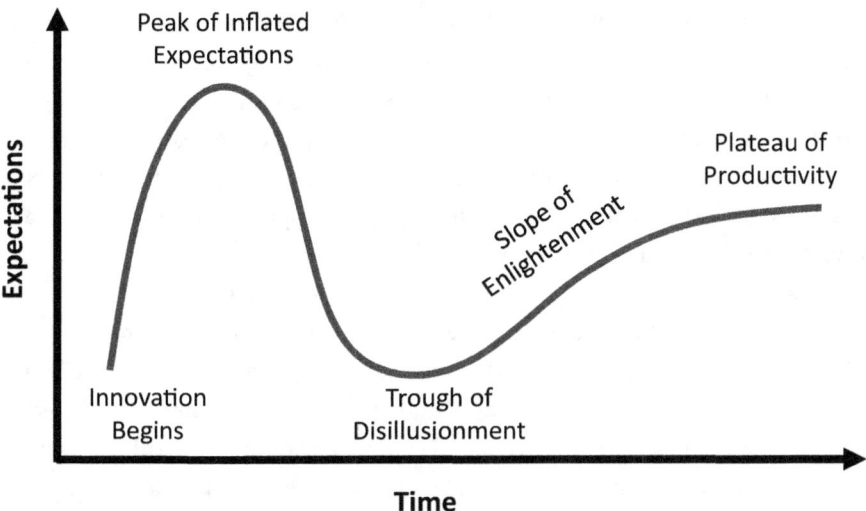

Figure 7.2 The Gartner Hype Cycle (adapted from Fenn and Blosch, 2018).

to productively incorporate online learning into our teaching *and* maintain connection with our students.

As a leader, I help shepherd my colleagues through the innovation trigger and peak of inflated expectation periods on the Gartner Hype Cycle. I gather information about new ideas or practices, and I share that information with colleagues. This tends to reduce the height of our peak excitement and the depth of our trough of disillusionment. It also tends to increase the speed at which we can reach a state of productivity. My integrity is essential to this process.

My Leadership Style

So far in this chapter I have spent plenty of time talking about how I lead and the touchstones I use in considering what will influence and support my colleagues as I work to create change. My approach doesn't really look like any of the classic executive leadership styles defined by Goleman (2000). These styles – Visionary, Coaching, Affiliative, Democratic, Commanding and Pacesetting – work well in industry, where a command-and-control culture exists. They don't work, however, in a university.

Universities are not top-down controlled, and like many academics, I am not in a position to command people to do anything different with their teaching or to implement programmes that they must complete. Although I have held (and do currently hold) positional leadership roles in my university, the university doesn't have a culture of requiring particular teaching approaches or standards from staff. As a result, my leadership roles aren't about monitoring my colleagues' practice and pushing them to conform to expectations. Instead, my roles and titles are very much about exemplifying good practice and influencing others to join in. My job is to enable others to improve and support them as they decide to invest their time and energy in their teaching work.

This type of leadership is very modern – it is about understanding what people need so they can change and then helping them find those resources or ways of being. It's what Heifetz calls adaptive leadership (Heifetz and Laurie, 2001; Heifetz et al., 2009). Adaptive leadership is focused on the idea that dispersed power (like the power in a university) requires a cooperative, problem-solving approach to leadership. Adaptive leaders need to be comfortable with opacity and complexity. They also need to look at the situation around them and understand it in depth, rather than looking for a quick technical solution to an issue. Adaptive leadership is also about helping an organization and its people adapt to change and embrace the new in a constructive way. This is what I do, and as universities struggle to stay afloat in a newly competitive digital age, my work will only get more important.

Challenges on the Road

The previous sections discussed the approaches I use and the theoretical frameworks I adopt to support my work. I can't claim, however, to be working without challenges! Like all academic roles, mine comes with its share of difficulties.

The biggest challenge has been the difficulty of learning how to be an SoTL researcher. Our SoTL community in Australia is relatively small, and the science SoTL community is a small proportion of that. We do suffer from the tyranny of distance, and learning in isolation is difficult. I have done a lot of professional development in this space, including the American Society for Microbiology Biology Scholars Program (Chang and Pribbenow, 2016) and two teaching fellowship programmes at my university, which gave me the opportunity to work with some skilled social scientists. I value the input of many amazing mentors, have read and reviewed a lot of papers and have written multiple manuscripts many of which faced rejections. Luckily, I'm a resilient person who is self-reliant, equanimous, perseverant and happy to be existentially alone (Wagnild and

Young, 1993). Also, I was trained as a biochemist, which is all about learning to fail with grace. When my SoTL papers get returned, I shrug my shoulders and move on to journal number two (or three). The referees always have something useful to say. There may be a better way to learn the SoTL craft, but I don't know what it is!

One of the best outcomes of my SoTL research stream is the students who work with me. They are scientists who love science, but who don't want to work in the lab. Getting my school to accept their research was initially problematic. There were questions from colleagues about who would mark my students' work, and one colleague even told me I couldn't have students because 'what you do is not research'. They were concerned for the students upon graduation, because scientists don't have a lot of experience of social science careers. I understood their reservations, but I was employed to teach and research, so I was not going to give up. I turned my frustration about student supervision into a research paper (Rowland, 2012) and worked to change the system.

Addressing the research students' issue entailed some legwork. I prepared detailed research plans for my prospective students and submitted them to programme directors so they could understand what the students were doing. I invited markers from other schools and other disciplines to look at my students' project plans and theses. I prepared my students very thoroughly for their oral defences, so they gave amazing presentations and got strong marks. In a couple of years, the school came to see the students as legitimate and skilled in their own research methodologies. The research programme convenors willingly included my students and their talks in the regular 'science' student presentation sessions. They also allowed the students to present science education papers in 'Science' journal clubs.

This change is really important for the culture of science academics and students. My group's work focuses on the learning experiences of students and staff in science, so it surfaces aspects of the learning process that my colleagues may not have considered. By presenting to staff and their student peers, my students help everyone understand that teaching and learning is not easy. My colleagues see they are not alone in their teaching struggles, and it also helps them to view their students as people who need nurturing. The student audience also get a richer perspective of the amount of work that staff put into teaching. Importantly, my colleagues and their students often participate in my group's studies. My students can help them evaluate an aspect of their course delivery. My students may also interview them about their work and learning. In our studies, students and staff get an opportunity to talk about their thoughts and emotions. Often our interviewees comment that it's the first time someone in science has asked them how they feel.

I'm very proud of my research students and the work they produce. I'm also proud to see them go on to interesting careers that use their science, but also use the skills they learn through SoTL research. I think the school has come to realize this too, and our research and student nurturing culture is better for it.

When I started working as a TF academic, I also wondered about promotion prospects. The university didn't have clear guidelines or metrics around being a TF or being promoted as a TF. One could see this as a problem, but I saw it as an opportunity to make the rules up as I went along. Because nobody knew what a 'successful' TF academic looked like at my university, I thought carefully about what my university would value. I had been employed to change the culture of teaching and learning, so I was careful to document the impact of my work. I was also careful to map my work against the metrics that universities normally value – grants, awards, publications, service, innovation, a public profile and good teaching evaluations. I applied for every grant, professional development opportunity and award I could find. A proportion of these came through, and I was able to build a portfolio of funding, fellowships and awards to go alongside my publications. I also pursue secondments to interesting units in my university, apply for election to university governance committees and sit on national boards for education-relevant organizations. I consistently look to hit traditional indicators of value and esteem. This is the same behaviour that all successful academics and leaders exhibit; there is no reason why a teaching and learning leader should be any different.

In 2019 I was promoted to full professor – the first TF to achieve this in science at my university. This was a relief and a source of enormous satisfaction. I felt pleased for myself (because I work really hard and have a lot of impact!) but also for all the other TFs who are now at my university. Promotion to professor for me meant that it was possible for other people too. The professorship also showed the university that teaching is valued at UQ and that teaching leadership is a valid academic pursuit.

Several people approached me after my promotion and thanked me for the hope I had just injected into their career plans. I'm very happy to say that several other TFs have also been promoted to professor now at UQ. As a leader, I willingly share my promotion paperwork with my colleagues, because it's useful to see how someone else has presented their teaching and service work for appraisal.

Promotion to professor meant recognition of my expertise at my university, which translates to kudos, invitations to participate in things like reviews and a sense that I can confidently and legitimately assert my ideas and opinions at the university. I didn't have to apologize or feel inadequate anymore.

Some Ideas That May Help You Travel and Lead

I have been teaching-focused for ten years now – and now it is not such an unusual career path. After swimming as a strange duck, however, I have learned some things that will help new TFs, so I will share them here. In particular, I'll point out how each item demonstrates that you are – and can be – a leader.

1. Publication is key to proving your legitimacy at a university, so make sure you publish your projects. Publicly and appropriately demonstrating your expertise is a leadership behaviour. Get ethics approval to do a study before you do it. You shouldn't be doing any studies without ethics approval from your university, and you definitely can't publish work that doesn't have ethics approval. Talk to your institutional ethics officers.
2. Don't try to think alone – asking for input is a leadership behaviour. My most productive coping mechanism is to talk about my ideas with others and test them in public. It turns out that two heads *are* better than one! Conversation sparks new thinking, and it saves time because it helps you discard unproductive approaches. Learn the phrase 'I would value your input'. Try saying: 'I have this idea', or 'I have an issue that's troubling me', then add 'I would value your input'. This conversation starter invites others to share their thoughts from a collegial perspective. That phrase changed my life. Try it.
3. Learn to say 'no' and give some of your work away – giving opportunities to others is a leadership behaviour. Don't accept every opportunity that comes your way. As a TF, you will get a lot of invitations to do things – particularly pastoral and community work – that can nibble away at your academic time. Ask yourself 'Can I demonstrate an impact from this?' and 'Is this in my area of expertise?' If you can't say 'yes' to these questions, say 'no' to the opportunity. Don't feel guilty about this. Instead, consider what you can hand off to someone else who would benefit from the opportunity (e.g. an early career researcher or a PhD student).
4. Actively curate and ask for roles that will give you an opportunity to lead – stepping up and looking for ways to be of service is a leadership behaviour. Don't assume someone will just offer roles to you. You must signal your intent.

5. Stay true to your values – working towards and demonstrating your values and strengths is a leadership behaviour. Don't behave in a way that's inauthentic just to 'get ahead'.

Where Is My Road Going?

Where to now? What is around the next corner? I'm not sure.

I do know that way has led on to way, just as Robert Frost suggested. I have a community of skilled TF academic colleagues, and I'm proud to be part of it. We continue to engage our academic colleagues in conversations about teaching, and we cheer them on as they innovate and explore in their teaching. Many of the TF academics now have positional leadership roles, which further raises the profile of teaching and teaching-focused work at the university.

My formal leadership role is for the Faculty of Science, where I hold the future students and employability portfolio. I work with a huge team of academic and non-academic colleagues on a variety of creative and administrative initiatives. I still teach. I still research. I still get to nurture people and projects. I still ask questions and learn. Right now, I'm learning the fine details of governance, strategic and operational planning, marketing and data management. I'm surrounded by smart people who are good at what they do and are generous in their attitudes. Once the level of challenge dies down, I will look for the next opportunity. Seeking out challenge – and growing to meet it – is a leadership behaviour.

I am happy with my road. I took the one less travelled by, and that has made all the difference.

Note

1 Schein uses the spelling 'artifacts'; throughout this chapter I have reverted to the spelling generally used, 'artefact', except when referring directly to Schein's work.

References

Anderson, L., Krathwohl, R., Airasian, P., Cruikshank, K., Mayer, R., Pintrich, P., Raths, J. and Wittrock, M., eds (2001), *Taxonomy for Learning, Teaching, and Assessing: A Revision of Bloom's Taxonomy*, New York: Longman.

ASMR (2016), *Building Knowledge, Supporting Innovation. 2016 ASMY Health and Medical Research Workforce Survey*, Sydney: Australian Society for Medical Research. https://asmr.org.au/wp-content/uploads/library/Workforce16.pdf.

Bass, R. (1999), 'The Scholarship of Teaching: What's the Problem?', *Inventio: Creative Thinking about Learning and Teaching*, 1 (1): 1–10.

Becher, T. (1994), 'The Significance of Disciplinary Differences', *Studies in Higher Education*, 19 (2): 151–61.

Becher, T. and Trowler, P. R. (2001), *Academic Tribes and Territories*, 2nd edn, Buckingham: Open University Press.

Biggs, J. B. and Tang, C. K. C. (2011), *Teaching for Quality Learning at University: What the Student Does*, Maidenhead: McGraw-Hill.

Bradley, D., Noonan, P., Nugent, H. and Scales, B. (2008), *Review of Australian Higher Education, Final Report*, Canberra: Department of Education, Employment and Workplace Relations. http://hdl.voced.edu.au/10707/44384.

Burke, C. S., Sims, D. E., Lazzara, E. H. and Salas, E. (2007), 'Trust in Leadership: A Multi-level Review and Integration', *Leadership Quarterly*, 18 (6): 606–32.

Caldwell, C. and Hayes, L. A. (2007), 'Leadership, Trustworthiness, and the Mediating Lens', *Journal of Management Development*, 26 (3): 261–81.

Chang, A. and Pribbenow, C. (2016), 'The ASM-NSF Biology Scholars Program: An Evidence-Based Model for Faculty Development', *Journal of Microbiology and Biology Education*, 17 (2): 197–203.

DuToit, A. (2007), 'Making Sense through Coaching', *Journal of Management Development*, 26 (3): 282–91.

Fenn, J. and Blosch, M. (2018), 'Understanding Gartner's Hype Cycles', *Gartner Research*, 20 August. https://www.gartner.com/en/documents/3887767.

Frost, R. (1916), 'The Road Not Taken', poem 1 in *Mountain Interval*, New York: Henry Holt.

Goleman, D. (2000), 'Leadership That Gets Results', *Harvard Business Review*, March–April. https://hbr.org/2000/03/leadership-that-gets-results.

Heifetz, R. A., Grashow, A. and Linsky, M. (2009), *The Practice of Adaptive Leadership: Tools and Tactics for Changing Your Organization and the World*, Cambridge, MA: Harvard Business Press.

Heifetz, R. A. and Laurie, D. L. (2001), 'The Work of Leadership', *Harvard Business Review*, 79 (11): 37–47.

Hutchings, P., ed. (2000), *Opening Lines: Approaches to the Scholarship of Teaching and Learning*, Princeton, NJ: Carnegie Foundation for the Advancement of Teaching.

Hutchings, P. and Shulman, L. S. (1999), 'The Scholarship of Teaching: New Elaborations, New Developments', *Change: The Magazine of Higher Learning*, 31 (5): 10–15. https://doi.org/10.1080/00091389909604218.

King, G., Shih, Y. L., Maciejewski, M., Bains, N., Pan, B., Rowland, S., Mullen, G. and Rothfield, L. (2000), 'Structural Basis for Topological Specificity Function of MinE', *Nature Structural Biology*, 7 (11): 1013–17.

Mayer, R. C., Davis, J. H. and Schoorman, F. D. (1995), 'An Integrative Model of Organization Trust', *Academy of Management Review*, 20 (3): 709–34.

McNeil, L. and Sher, M. (1998), 'Dual-Science-Career Couples: Survey Results'. http://www.physics.wm.edu/~sher/survey.pdf.

Phillips, A. A. ([1950] 2005), *On the Cultural Cringe*, Melbourne: Melbourne University Publishing.

Reich, J. and Ruipérez-Valiente, J. (2019), 'The MOOC Pivot', *Science*, 363 (6423): 130–1.

Rowland, S. (2012), 'Teaching-Focused Science Academics Supervising Research Students in Science Education: What's the Problem?', *Higher Education Research and Development*, 31 (5): 741–3.

Rowland, S. L., Burkholder, W. F., Cunningham, K. A., Maciejewski, M. W., Grossman, A. D. and King, G. F. (2004), 'Structure and Mechanism of Action of *Sda*, an Inhibitor of the Histidine Kinases That Regulate Initiation of Sporulation in *Bacillus subtilis*', *Molecular Cell*, 13 (5): 689–701.

Rowland, S. L., Wadsworth, K., Robson, S. A., Robichon, C., Beckwith, J. and King, G. F. (2010), 'Evidence from Artificial Septal Targeting and Site-Directed Mutagenesis That Residues in the Extracytoplasmic β Domain of DivIB Mediate Its Interaction with the Divisomal Transpeptidase PBP 2B', *Journal of Bacteriology*, 192 (23): 6116–25.

Schein, E. H. (1984), 'Coming to a New Awareness of Organizational Culture', *Sloan Management Review*, 25 (2): 3–16.

Szeto, T. H., Rowland, S. L., Rothfield, L. I. and King, G. F. (2002), 'Membrane Localization of MinD Is Mediated by a C-Terminal Motif That Is Conserved across Eubacteria, Archaea, and Chloroplasts', *Proceedings of the National Academy of Sciences USA*, 99 (24): 15693–8.

Wagnild, G. and Young, H. (1993), 'Development and Psychometric Evaluation of the Resilience Scale', *Journal of Nursing Measurement*, 1 (2):165–78.

Wallace, S. (2009), *Dictionary of Education*, Oxford: Oxford University Press.

Wiggins, G. and McTighe, J. (2005), *Understanding by Design*, Alexandra, VA: ASCD.

8

Building a Bridge from Chemistry to Educational Leadership: Overcoming the Valley between the Two Cultures

Paulo Rogério Miranda Correia

I and My Circumstance

This chapter is the result of self-reflection about my academic career. The construction of a bridge to cross the dark valley that separates chemistry from education is one of several metaphors I use so that the reader can understand the challenges and achievements that I identified in my journey. The starting point must contemplate the context where everything happened, and, therefore, I offer brief comments about my university and the school where I work. Identifying the circumstances and knowing how to utilize them to achieve daring projects is the first lesson I share with you. As José Ortega y Gasset (1963) says, 'I am I and my circumstance, and if I do not save it, I do not save myself.'

Founded in 1934, the University of São Paulo (USP) is one of the largest institutions of higher education in Latin America. Tuition-free, USP enrols 60,000 undergraduate and 30,000 graduate students distributed in forty-eight schools and specialized institutes. USP is also responsible for nineteen museums, five hospitals and supporting services, sixty-seven physical libraries and five digital libraries. A significant proportion of research papers published by Brazilian researchers are produced at USP. All these features justify the USP's position in international rankings and its prestige among Brazilians.

I was born in São Paulo city. I live here and all my academic life has been developed in USP. I enrolled in the Chemistry Institute in 1994, and I stayed there until finishing my PhD in 2004. Those years forged my scientific background and prepared me to become an academic. Luckily, in 2005 I started my career as a professor in the School of Arts, Sciences and Humanities (SASH), a new USP campus in São Paulo city. SASH was devised to foster interdisciplinary work among academics from different knowledge areas, overcoming the barriers imposed by departmentalization. It is worth mentioning that I have been at SASH since its foundation. In other words, my history and the history of SASH have been twined for fifteen years.

SASH has been fulfilling its vocation and has consolidated itself as a different space from other USP units. Being interdisciplinary, innovative, transformative and pluralist is the motto that guides teaching, research and interactions with the neighbouring community (Gomes, 2005). My entry into SASH marked a first shift from chemistry towards education. At the end of 2004, I was approved in the selection process for the hiring of a professor for the Licentiate on Natural Sciences course, which prepares undergraduate students to become teachers working in elementary and middle schools. The change in my work environment directed my research efforts towards the chemical education area, instead of continuing in analytical chemistry – a more comfortable choice which marked my master's dissertation and doctoral thesis. Without imagining the consequences that I will report in this chapter, I started building a bridge between chemistry and education.

'Two cultures' is the term coined by C. P. Snow (1959) in his legendary lecture at the University of Cambridge. In 1959, Snow already noticed the differences between the natural sciences and the humanities. In a nutshell, Snow condemned literary scholars for unfamiliarity with the second law of thermodynamics, the scientific equivalent of knowing Shakespeare's work, lamenting the chasm between literary intellectuals and scientists, as well as the distorted image that one group had of the other. The expression 'two cultures' suggests the distance that separates these worlds, each aimed at the production of knowledge to unveil reality. Ontological differences arise from the selection of study objects, research paradigms, methods of investigation and the language typically used to communicate the results achieved. These differences explain the chasm that isolates the natural sciences and the humanities at university. Knowledge specialization has produced a dark valley that needs to be overcome through interdisciplinary efforts which involve academics who barely recognize themselves as peers.

The dimension of the valley that separates chemistry and education can be seen from the excerpts below. The first is an excerpt from the summary of an article on the results of my doctoral thesis. Published in 2005, this was my first article as a professor at SASH (Correia and Oliveira, 2005).

The effectiveness of internal standardization for simultaneous atomic absorption spectrometry was investigated for arsenic and selenium determination in urine. Cobalt and tin were selected as internal standard candidates based on the evaluation of some physico-chemical parameters related to atomization. Correlation graphs, plotted from the normalized absorbance signals (n = 20) of internal standard (axis y) versus analyte (axis x), precision and accuracy of the analytical results were the supportive parameters to choose cobalt as the most appropriate internal standard.

In 2020, due to the social isolation imposed by the Covid-19 pandemic, I managed to develop a thesis (Correia, 2020) to become an associate professor (senior lecturer) in didactics. The thesis was part of a three-day examination in which a five-professor panel evaluated my career to confirm if I deserved the title, which can be considered as the first permanent position at my university after the entry-level position (assistant professor). The experiences I had accumulated in the past fifteen years as an assistant professor seemed to me to be sufficient to demonstrate my maturity and my intellectual independence. In other words, I recognized that it was time to show that the bridge under construction had arrived in education. The second excerpt is from the summary of my thesis that explores cognitive psychology to understand the use of concept maps. Although useful to represent knowledge, concept maps are not yet present in most classrooms. This intriguing situation, already pointed out by Kinchin (2001), deserved new contributions from Cognitive Load Theory (Correia, 2020; Correia and Aguiar, 2014).

This thesis aims to include instructional design as an additional obstacle to those already described in the literature. The theoretical framework that underlies concept mapping needs to be expanded to include new arguments that inform the effects of instructional design on teaching. The Cognitive Load Theory was associated with the Assimilation Theory in Meaningful Learning and Retention Processes to insert cognitive overload as a condition that prevents the manipulation and construction of conceptual schemes, which are mental activities closely related to meaningful learning.

The differences between the excerpts highlight the size of the bridge that was built between chemistry and education. The reflections I made about my transformation process considered the model of pedagogical fragility as a starting point.

Reflections on Teaching from the Pedagogic Frailty Model

Pedagogic frailty has been proposed as a concept that can help bring several critical ideas into simultaneous focus to enhance teaching in the university context. Frailty develops as a consequence of a decline in a range of factors which collectively result in an increased vulnerability to adverse actions that are triggered by relatively minor events (Kinchin et al., 2016, 2017). As highlighted by the authors:

> Frailty is not considered here as an internal quality or capacity of an individual academic per se, and indeed such a personal characterisation may be unhelpful in promoting openness to support academic faculty development. Rather we see frailty as resulting from the quality and degree of interaction with and between key elements of the professional environment. (2016, p. 2)

The pedagogical frailty model presents four domains with which to analyse my academic development. The regulative discourse and the pedagogy and discipline relationships are more under the individual's control. Perceptions about the research–teaching nexus and the locus of control are more under institutional control (Kinchin, 2016). My first movements towards chemical education occurred when I was approved as an assistant professor in SASH, which has an atmosphere fostering interdisciplinarity, innovation, transformation and pluralism. Given the opportunity offered by a school that still forged its identity in the practice of research, teaching and extension programmes, I realized that this change made sense to me and SASH. In addition to a bachelor's degree in chemistry, I completed a licentiate degree in chemistry during my master's degree, which enabled me to teach in middle school. Moreover, I published some articles during my PhD focusing on chemical education (Correia and Oliveira, 2004; Correia et al., 2004; Dazzani et al., 2003).

These seeds fell on fertile soil in 2005, when I joined SASH. The potential frailty that could be generated from this change did not occur. The alignment between my aspirations and institutional perspectives produced a favourable context for strengthening academic resilience. I found the right place to invest time in building the bridge towards education.

The changes in my career from chemistry to education exposed me to both cultures, transforming me into a good interlocutor in the interdisciplinary and pluralist SASH context. Presently, I see myself as a UN blue-helmeted peacemaker because I understand these two worlds better than would the majority of my counterparts. Being a mediator is an institutional reward for my transformation that reduced pedagogical frailty in the initial years, supporting the construction of the bridge for subsequent years.

The pedagogic frailty model was also used to compare the profiles of three academics who work at USP but have different backgrounds. A chemist and an educator served as references to characterize my trajectory as someone who is in transformation (Aguiar and Correia, 2019; Aguiar et al., 2020). This comparison was useful to recognize my hybrid identity since I have a transitory profile between the extremes represented by my chemistry and education peers.

Currently, I see myself as a science faculty with education specialties (SFES), that is, a scientist who takes on specialized roles within science education in their discipline (Bush et al., 2008). My previous licentiate degree in chemistry was convenient in sustaining the migration considering the teaching assignments I received. My classes are offered to students enrolled in the licentiate degree in natural sciences at SASH and, therefore, I could confidently reflect on my teaching practices. This fact helped me build a bridge between the two cultures. Education, which is on the other side of the valley, got closer and closer and contributed to the expansion of my understanding of teaching. The curriculum regulative discourse, the relationships between pedagogy and discipline and the scholarship of teaching and learning are examples of new knowledge that I learnt during my early years as an academic at SASH. From the knowledge about teaching I got during my licentiate degree in chemistry, I was able to find the meaning of relevant concepts in the educational field. In addition to improving my educational practice, this understanding was useful to explain the educational jargon to my peers who were settled in the natural sciences. The difficulties in understanding the language of education are worthy of mention here, and it is a fact not recognized by the natives of humanities. These possibilities are in line with my school's expectations, as SASH is an interdisciplinary, innovative, transformative and pluralist place. In this context, I did not feel any difficulties regarding teaching assignments. I cannot say the same when I reflect on my research activities.

Reflections on Research and the Methodological Shock

The need to produce knowledge in a different area from the one in which I developed my PhD was the most complex challenge I faced when crossing the valley between the two cultures. USP is a research-oriented university, and, therefore, professors are charged to do this. Beyond the teaching assignments, publications in specialized journals are desirable to prove the production of knowledge. Recognizing this circumstance in my institutional context, I endeavoured to keep my publications at an acceptable level during the construction of the bridge between chemistry and education. In the beginning, I published the latest results from my PhD in analytical chemistry and a few articles on chemical education. Over time, this proportion has been inverted, and papers on the use of concept maps in science education have become prevalent.

My accreditation as a graduate advisor was another important event that helped me maintain my scientific publications. Since 2005, I have been an advisor in USP's Interunit Graduate Programme in Science Education. In addition to the Faculty of Education, the institutes of natural sciences (biology, chemistry and physics) work together to offer master and doctoral programmes in science education. The interdisciplinary nature of this subject required a combination of efforts between several USP units, resulting in one of the few interunit graduate programmes at my university. Although SASH is not part of the programme, I develop most of my research with graduate students at USP's west campus in São Paulo city. It should be borne in mind that my school is at the USP campus in the east of the São Paulo city, forty kilometres away from the main USP campus. The price to pay to advise graduate students and maintain my scientific production was travel between these campuses, which can take more than two hours depending on the chaotic traffic that is common in a metropolitan region with more than 20 million inhabitants.

Unexpectedly, I discovered in 2005 the existence of an international conference on concept mapping. The first occurrence took place in 2004 while I was completing my PhD. The second, scheduled for 2006, would be an opportunity to develop research in the area of chemical education using a technique for representing knowledge that did not receive much attention from my peers. Little or almost nothing was discussed about concept maps in the research seminars organized by the Interunit Graduate Programme in Science Education. The identification of this gap led me to produce my first research results with concept maps, resulting in a poster presentation at the conference held in Costa Rica (Donner, Infante-Malachias and Correia, 2006). Two years later, the complete results of this investigation were published in the best journal on science education in Brazil (Correia, Donner and Infante-Malachias, 2008). At that point, I realized that I found a particular way to develop my research in science education using concept mapping to interrogate how students learn the fundamental chemical concepts. Once again, I found a path to act at the interface between the two cultures. This research topic helped to align me with the leading interests of my school (SASH) and the Interunit Graduate Programme in Science Education. Despite changing my trajectory as a researcher, leaving aside my past in analytical chemistry, the solution I found was suitable to manage the stress associated with the bridge I decided to build.

In 2008, during the third conference on concept mapping in Estonia and Finland, I foresaw the opportunity of choosing concept maps as the study object of my research. Instead of only applying concept maps to improve teaching and learning, I decided to investigate this knowledge representation technique in depth. This moment was decisive in determining how I would approach the educational field. The emphasis on chemical education lost space in favour of research projects centred on concept maps. This conscious option has moulded my identity, and since then, I identify myself as a researcher interested in concept mapping. The innovative feature of this investigative angle aligned perfectly with the institutional aims of my school. Therefore, this change minimized the stress of my journey between chemistry and education.

The methodological differences between the research developed in the natural sciences and in the humanities were the biggest obstacle to changing my research interests. I recognize that the methodological shock was more pronounced in my research activities than in my teaching assignments, as the licentiate degree in chemistry helped me understand the complexity of the classroom environment. On the other hand, my PhD in analytical chemistry did not contribute to my understanding of research methodologies usually used in science education.

Studying and learning new ways of producing knowledge required persistence on my part and the institution's patience. The background I brought from my PhD in analytical chemistry was useful only for the first foundations of the bridge. If initially the bridge was built with concrete and bricks, I started using glass and steel when I was over the dark valley between the two cultures. The change in raw materials represents a shift from the quantitative certainties that characterize chemistry to the polysemic definitions and communication challenges surrounding educational jargon of the qualitative research paradigm. The use of glass was a requirement that broadened my horizons because it was possible to appreciate the richness of the valley that appeared below my feet – there was no darkness anymore. In that instant, I realized that I was doing a kind of second doctorate, but without any formal advisor to help me. Between returning to the safe harbour of analytical chemistry and proceeding towards the unknown, I chose the option that enhanced SASH's institutional values.

The methodological tension was a source of stress that arises from an interdisciplinary discipline (Rowland and Myatt, 2014). The approach of cognitive psychology, which values the quantitative research paradigm and statistical methods to analyse the data, was a way to deal with this tension. At the same time as cognitive psychology informed my investigations on concept mapping, it offered a connection with the paradigmatic foundations I built in analytical chemistry. This helped me in the development of quantitative works in science education, which stood out among my peers in Brazil. In 2016, an article on the visual organization of concept maps in study materials was accepted in one of the best international journals in chemical education (Aguiar and Correia, 2016).

Although I have switched from research in chemistry to educational research, I feel that I am a foreigner in this new world. In other words, when I finished crossing the valley between the two cultures, I arrived transformed, but with an accent that characterizes me as a foreigner. Despite having completed the bridge with glass and steel – materials that broadened my academic horizons – my DNA is linked to the natural sciences. My transformation left me with a hybrid identity, partially disconnected from the two cultures. It can be a weakness or a virtue, depending on one's institutional circumstances. My institutional context values my new identity and all my efforts I put in to build the bridge. Even so, I recognize that the methodological tension in the research turned me into a foreigner, a researcher not native to the humanities.

My passport is always requested by my peers when I present the results of my investigations with an educational emphasis. They are reported in an unusual way, confirming that my origins belong to another culture. For example, my works present several tables and graphs to prove the differences between the control and experimental groups. This is so different from the usual that I can't go unnoticed. To paraphrase Kinchin et al. (2016, p. 2), 'The adoption of what he/she might consider a safe and sustainable research approach can eventually inhibit his/her capacity to change practice in response to an evolving researching environment', especially if he/she does not have an increased level of academic resilience (Bailey, 2014). Originally, this excerpt referred to teaching, and in my case, it adapts perfectly to the methodological tension that I found in research.

Currently, I have been exploring concept maps to mediate interviews with teachers and students. This way of using the concept mapping technique has brought me closer to qualitative research methods, increasing the range of methodological options that I can use to develop my investigations. In addition to cognitive psychology, having chosen concept maps as my study object contributed to the transit between the two cultures. Concept maps can be used to represent knowledge from any knowledge area, being useful in the natural sciences and the humanities.

One Valley, Two Cultures and Fifteen Years

The reflections I shared about my academic trajectory have broadened my understanding of everything that has happened in the past fifteen years. The need to use an autoethnographic approach generated original reflections for thoughts about me and my career. The pedagogical frailty model was a valuable starting point for analysing, interpreting and understanding my academic development in the particular context of a school that is interdisciplinary, innovative, transformative and pluralist.

After fifteen years, I realized that I had arrived in the humanities. The bridge was completed. Looking at it, I notice that its shape is not straight, and the materials used are mixed in different proportions along the way. In other words, my bridge does not present an optimal solution expected of scientists, nor of literary intellectuals. It looks more like Gaudí's work, full of colours and with seemingly unnecessary curves – see Bridge on Arcades at Park Güell in Barcelona. Without equating to Gaudí's genius, this comparison serves to show all the idiosyncrasy that the valley between the two cultures imposes on everyone who tries to cross it. The result pleases me so much that it seems that I have found a deeper meaning for academic life. I must serve everyone who works with me, teachers and students, from the privileged point of view of those who know both cultures.

Louis Lavelle (1955) tells us about those special moments in life marked by a deeper understanding of our existence. The universe opened up to me when I placed service as the guiding perspective of the actions that I develop at my university, helping others to better understand the challenges imposed by interdisciplinary practice.

> There are privileged moments in life when it seems that the Universe is enlightened, that our life reveals its meaning, that we want the destiny even if it was ours as if we had chosen it ourselves. Then the Universe closes, and we become lonely and miserable again. We no longer walk if we do not feel for an obscure path where everything becomes an obstacle to our steps. Wisdom consists in keeping the memory of those fleeting moments, in knowing how to make them revive, in making them the plot of our daily existence, and so to speak, the usual home of our spirit. (Lavelle, 1955, p. 281)

Rather than feeling like an exile, as mentioned previously, I see myself as an academic who has received the blue helmet from UN peacekeepers. My experience is at the service of dialogue between my peers in the natural sciences and in

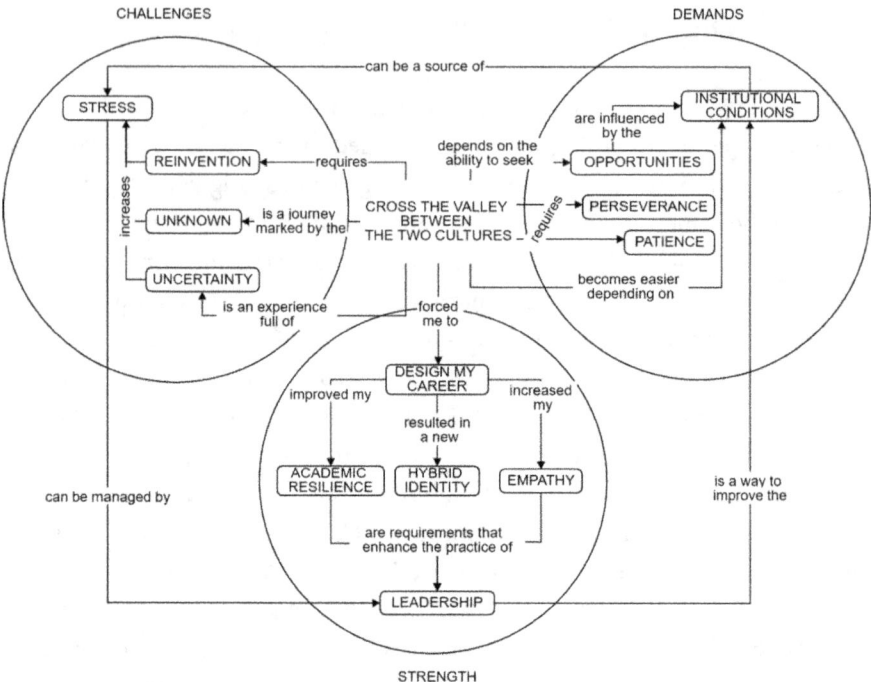

Figure 8.1 Concept map to highlight the main aspects of my journey.

the humanities, who otherwise experience severe difficulties in talking. Blue helmets are necessary for a school that aims to be interdisciplinary, innovative, transformative and pluralist. I am recognized at my institution for making this transition and having unique skills, developed during the appreciation of the valley that separates the two cultures.

Figure 8.1 presents a concept map that highlights the main features of my academic journey, based on my reflections when writing this text. The circles refer to the challenges, demands and strengths resulting from the process. An external cycle highlights the concepts of 'institutional conditions', 'stress' and 'leadership' and the relationships that exist between challenges, demands and personal development. The experience accumulated during the crossing of the valley separating the mountains of sciences and humanities gave me a distinctive view of the role of leaders in supporting teachers in the development of their academic careers.

I was forced to design my own career when I decided to cross the valley without having an exact dimension of the efforts that I would have to put in. As a result, I improved my academic resilience, developed a fluid identity and increased my empathy. Today, I can put myself in the place of other teachers more easily and naturally, due to the breadth of the experiences I have had. These combined characteristics allow me to act as a mediator of conflicts between scientists and literary intellectuals, which are frequent in the SASH environment. The following paragraphs illustrate how my experience helped SASH on administrative (bureaucratic) issues.

For example, I took part in the committee that supported SASH's dean to respond to the institutional assessment implemented in 2014. I acted to consolidate the report that was to be sent to the USP rectory. This was an eighteen-month endeavour that asked me to dialogue with scientists and literary intellectuals to understand and harmonize the academic diversity of my school into a coherent document.

Currently, I have been invited to join a committee responsible for identifying the professors who deserve to be promoted in their academic career. This delicate issue asks for experienced people who can recognize the intrinsic complexity of SASH, considering it has more than 250 academics from diverse knowledge fields. How to compare a musician's and a biochemist's research? This diversity is absent in all other USP units, and our committee must ask for clarifications and special instructions constantly because the USP rectory could not anticipate SASH idiosyncrasies beforehand.

Since 2021, I have been working more closely with the coordinator responsible for managing the Licentiate on Natural Science course. Frequently we need to harmonize the arguments presented by intellectuals (colleagues from education and psychology) and scientists (counterparts from astronomy and biology). They have different perspectives from which to discuss problems related to the curriculum, teaching practices and expectations about student development throughout the course. Being a mediator is key to finding compromise solutions and to keep all working to pursue the continuous improvement of the course.

Being able to design my career gives a high degree of autonomy and confidence for even bigger ventures. Taking on the role of academic leadership is a way of rewarding SASH for their patience in waiting for me to complete the bridge between chemistry and education. Improving the institutional conditions so that other academics are encouraged to carry out interdisciplinary practices is a plausible justification for me to assume responsibilities as an academic leader. However, this story will be told in another chapter, some years from now.

Finally, I share some lessons learnt after crossing the valley between the two cultures. The following items sum up the more relevant aspects that the reader can reflect upon.

- An academic career can be an original endeavour, with lots of space to create routes according to one's life purposes. On the other hand, it can also be marked by the go-with-the-flow approach, resulting in a more predictable outcome.
- Perseverance and patience are relevant aspects to be cultivated throughout the journey. A solid academic career is built up in years, not in bright single moments.
- Doubts and mistakes are part of the process. Reflection-on-the-action and reflection-in-the-action can help one learn during this process.
- The ability to capture and interpret the institutional context is key to identifying valuable opportunities. The alignment between the academic and the institution strengthens pedagogic resilience and reduces pedagogic frailty.
- Experienced mentors are a valuable source of advice and support, mainly when they understand one's purposes and the institutional expectations. Avoid being alone when you are crossing your academic valley.

Acknowledgements

I thank the University of São Paulo and the SASH for allowing me to complete the journey between the two cultures. I am thankful to São Paulo Research Foundation (FAPESP, grants #2016/24553-7 and #2012/22693-5) and the National Council for Scientific and Technological Development (CNPq) for funding my research group.

References

Aguiar, J. and Correia, P. R. M. (2016), 'Using Concept Maps as Instructional Materials to Foster the Understanding of the Atomic Model and Matter–Energy Interaction', *Chemistry Education Research and Practice*, 17 (4): 756–65.

Aguiar, J. and Correia, P. R. M. (2019), 'A New Look at Academic Life: A Case Study of Teachers' Conceptions, *Educação e Pesquisa*, 45: e193301.

Aguiar, J., Kinchin, I. M., Correia, P. R. M., Infante-Malachias, M. E. and Paixão, T. R. L. C. (2020), 'Uncovering and Comparing Academics' Views of Teaching Using the Pedagogic Frailty Model as a Tool: A Case Study in Science Education', *Educational Research*, 62 (4): 434–54.

Bailey, G. (2014), 'Accountability and the Rise of "Play Safe" Pedagogical Practices', *Education + Training*, 56 (7): 663–74.

Bush, S. D., Pelaez, N. J., Rudd, J. A., Stevens, M. T., Tanner, K. D. and Williams, K. S. (2008), 'Science Faculty with Education Specialties', *Science*, 322 (5909): 1795–6.

Correia, P. R. M. (2020), 'Reflections on the Use of Concept Maps in Higher Education from the Cognitive Load Theory', Associate Professor thesis, Universidade de São Paulo.

Correia, P. R. M. and Aguiar, J. G. (2014), 'Concept Mapping Informed by Cognitive Load Theory: Implications for Tasks Involving Learner-Generated Cmaps', in *Sixth International Conference on Concept Mapping*, 150–7, São Paulo: Escola de Artes, Ciências e Humanidades.

Correia, P. R. M., Donner Jr, J. W. A. and Infante-Malachias, M. E. (2008), 'Concept Mapping as a Tool to Break Disciplinary Boundaries: Isomerism in Biological Systems', *Ciência & Educação*, 14 (3): 483–95.

Correia, P. R. M. and Oliveira, P. V. (2004), 'Simultaneous Atomic Absorption Spectrometry for Cadmium and Lead Determination in Wastewater: A Laboratory Exercise', *Journal of Chemical Education*, 81 (8): 1174–6.

Correia, P. R. M. and Oliveira, P. V. (2005), 'Cobalt as Internal Standard for Arsenic and Selenium Determination in Urine by Simultaneous Atomic Absorption Spectrometry', *Talanta*, 67 (1): 46–53.

Correia, P. R. M., Siloto, R. C., Cavicchioli, A., Oliveira, P. V. and Rocha, F. R. P. (2004), 'Green Analytical Chemistry in Undergraduate Laboratories: Flow-Injection Determination of Creatinine in Urine with Photochemical Treatment of Waste', *Chemical Educator*, 9 (4): 242–6.

Dazzani, M., Correia, P. R. M., Oliveira, P. V. and Marcondes, M. E. R. (2003), 'Exploring Chemistry in the Determination of the Ethanol Content in Gasoline', *Química Nova na Escola*, 17: 41–5.

Donner Jr, J. W. A., Infante-Malachias, M. E. and Correia, P. R. M. (2006), 'Concept Maps as Tools for Assessing the Merge of Disciplinary Knowledge', in *Second International Conference on Concept Mapping*, 104–8, San Jose: Universidad de Costa Rica.

Gomes, C. B. (2005), *USP Leste: a expansão da Universidade do oeste para o leste*, São Paulo: EUSP.

Kinchin, I. M. (2001), 'If Concept Mapping Is So Helpful to Learning Biology, Why Aren't We All Doing It?', *International Journal of Science Education*, 23 (12): 1257–69.

Kinchin, I. M., Alpay, E., Curtis, K., Franklin, J., Rivers, C. and Winstone, N. E. (2016), 'Charting the Elements of Pedagogic Frailty', *Educational Research*, 58 (1): 1–23.

Kinchin, I. M. and Winstone, N. E. (2017), *Pedagogic Frailty and Resilience in the University*, Rotterdam: Sense Publishers.

Lavelle, L. (1955), *De l'Intimité spirituelle*, Paris: Aubier.

Ortega y Gasset, J. (1963), *Meditations on Quixote*, New York: W. W. Norton.
Rowland, S. L. and Myatt, P. M. (2014), 'Getting Started in the Scholarship of Teaching and Learning: A "How to" Guide for Science Academics', *Biochemistry and Molecular Biology Education*, 42 (1): 6–14.
Snow, C. P. (1959), *The Two Cultures*, Cambridge: Cambridge University Press.

Education and Leadership in Physics: Making Every Step of My Journey Count

Alison Voice

Introduction

I have never had a plan for my career. I just took everything one step at a time, taking on opportunities as they came. But with each step I gained valuable skills and experience, building a portfolio that has shaped each subsequent step. My career has thus developed around the themes of physics, education and leadership.

This chapter describes my career journey to senior leadership in a university physics department, documenting the choices I have made or that have come my way. My philosophy of leadership has followed that of Kotter (1996), who states that 'an effective leader must be both student and teacher', and using this framework I will reflect on each step of my career to showcase what I have learned about being a leader in different educational contexts.

I am unusual within physics academia in two respects – firstly that I am female, and secondly that I have a higher profile in education than in scientific research, both of which had the potential to limit my career progression due to strongly held traditional views in the discipline. Thankfully, the academic climate has changed much in recent years, with the creation of teaching and scholarship career pathways, but these changes came too late to plan my career in this vein. So, in the early years of my lectureship, I had to undertake my educational projects as a side-line to my 'day job' of teaching and scientific research, since these were the contractual outputs against which my career development would be evidenced.

Throughout the time I have worked in physics (the past thirty years), the percentage of female students nationally at degree level has remained steady between 20 and 25 despite many initiatives; however, in that time the number of female academics has risen from almost zero to around 25 per cent, with many women now holding senior leadership roles. I was proud to be the first female academic in the School of Physics and Astronomy at the University of Leeds, and even prouder to see that number grow, with many of these newly appointed women saying that I have been a role model for them.

My journey has seen me progress from high school teaching, through PhD and postdoctoral research to lecturer, with leadership roles as director of learning and teaching and head of a physics education research group. Below I describe each of these steps, discussing what I have learned about leadership at each stage.

Step 1: Teacher Training

Having graduated in physics from Exeter University (1984), it was time to make my first career decision. Combining the things that I appear to be good at – physics, study and explaining – teacher training seemed to be a sensible first step. I thus headed off to the Liverpool Institute of Higher Education (Saint Katherine's and Christ's & Notre Dame College, now Hope University) to undertake a PGCE (Postgraduate Certificate in Education). Liverpool is a fantastic city with amazing cultural heritage, and it was exciting to undertake teaching practice in schools such as The Holt in Childwall, Plessington on the Wirral, and Notre Dame in Everton.

What Did I Learn?

Although physics and maths are intimately intertwined as disciplines, they are completely different departments in a high school. With a long-standing national shortage of physics teachers (French, 2015), I have often wondered if it might be prudent to readdress this to attract more physics graduates into the teaching profession.

I again encountered the under-representation of females in physics. I was the only female of four training to teach physics in my college that year. The three schools in which I undertook my teaching practice were very different: one all-boys, one all-girls and one co-education. And, while I very much believe all children are individuals, there was a different atmosphere in each of the three schools. A class of boys appeared competitive, and many were keen to answer questions (even if they were unsure of the answer). In a mixed class, many of the boys still exhibited this behaviour, leaving most of the girls too shy to respond.

In a class of all girls, the dynamic was very different; while still shy to speak up if they were unsure of an answer, they responded to encouragement and grew in confidence, without a feeling they had to compete with the boys. Even with today's important focus on diversity and on removing stereotypes, some of these factors are still at play (Eisenkopf et al., 2015; Pennington et al., 2021).

Thus, it was here that I first began to formulate my ideas about leadership in education. At this stage of my career, my responsibilities were for students, rather than staff, and as such my views of leadership (as detailed in the five paragraphs below) focused on teaching and pastoral care. My emerging view of leadership strongly resonated with research collated by Marzano (2003), and I found Leithwood's (2010) analysis of the effect that different leadership 'pathways' (rational, emotions, family and organization) have on students' learning to be very insightful.

As leaders in education we should be facilitators of learning. We are not the 'sage on the stage'; rather we are the 'guide on the side' (King, 1993). Our role is to provide information and semi-structured activities to allow learners to explore and develop their knowledge and understanding. This has become increasingly true with the development of the internet, where information is readily to hand, and education should be about empowering students to research, evaluate and apply the information they have access to. This approach has remained the foundation of all my teaching, whatever the level of my students.

We should create an environment where learners feel empowered to work and question without fear of making mistakes. I believe that the best learning takes place when students venture into the unknown, but that is a scary place for students who lack confidence, or who feel they may be ridiculed by others. Boaler (2015) discusses this fear in the context of maths, showing how the pressure to get the right answer causes widespread fear in adults as well as children. Providing less pressured environments, such as multiple-choice quizzes with electronic voting or allowing students to post anonymous questions, are ways to address this. And rewarding effort, bravery and partial answers is another way I have encouraged 'fearless' learning.

Proactively encourage and value participation from all members of the class, not just those who 'shout loudest' or demand more attention. For me, this speaks to supporting the diversity of learners, to give equal voice to all. When teaching mixed-gender classes, I make particular efforts to garner responses from both males and females at all points. And asking for responses in different ways (group response, anonymous voting, etc.) can provide a safe environment for all to contribute.

Praise and thanks are the best motivators. This allows learners to know they are making progress and that their efforts are valued, building satisfaction and confidence to keep trying. This is particularly important not just for students but for adults as well. Sometimes I have found a quiet word, or even just a smile is enough to convey this appreciation, in agreement with Burnett (2001), who finds that pupils often prefer praise to be a private thing. But on other occasions, it is public celebration that provides the needed recognition.

Pupils may have a lot going on in their lives that detracts from learning, which they can't just 'switch off' when they enter the classroom. It is not our role to solve their problems, but to be empathetic, finding ways to support and motivate them. The COVID-19 pandemic particularly highlighted the disadvantages many suffer in terms of access to Wi-Fi, quiet places to study and difficult home situations. I have found that just asking if students are okay, and showing empathy for what they reveal, can provide tremendous support, over and above any practical solutions that can be offered.

It was also during my PGCE that I first developed my philosophy of education:

1. *Framework of the discipline:* Learning does not take place in a vacuum. Material is best understood and remembered when new ideas build on prior learning. To develop this cognitive understanding requires students to have a mental framework of the discipline and for new knowledge to link to that framework. Thus, before teaching a topic, it is important to determine where the learners are at, as this informs both the teacher and the students what they may need to revisit. This idea is well researched and follows the work of giants such as Piaget and Inhelder (1969) and Ausubel (1968). This principle is so fundamental to learning that it is also central to artificial intelligence (Aksoy, Schoeler and Wörgötter, 2014).
2. *Spiral curriculum:* Learning in many situations requires a cyclical process of experience, reflection and adaptation (Bruner, 1971; Kolb, 1975). While in some disciplines the reliance on specific prior learning may be problematic, in science and maths it is necessary to allow fundamentals to be securely mastered before more complex aspects can be tackled. Topics studied at age sixteen are revisited at age eighteen and then again at university, but in greater depth and complexity each time. This poses the challenge to simplify a complex topic to be manageable at a lower level without being incorrect or confusing when students meet it again at a higher level.
3. *Practice make perfect:* Discipline-based skills and conceptual understanding are best developed by probing new knowledge in a variety

of situations (Alant, 2004) and thus problem-solving and problem-based learning are key tools (Raine and Symonds, 2012; Van Heuvelen, 1991).
4. *Engagement is crucial:* In education, students are provided with expert knowledge, tuition and facilities, but in order to achieve and succeed, they need to engage in a personal way (Pace, 1984). This can be likened to paying for gym membership, where it is not only the personal trainers and facilities provided that enable the user to achieve fitness, but it is the combination of this with hard work and repeated practice.

These four 'principles' have underpinned all my teaching and interaction with students in high school and higher education (HE) throughout my career and have informed the way I encourage and advise staff to develop their planning, teaching, assessment and support of students.

Step 2: School Physics Teacher

At the end of my PGCE, the natural next step was to find a job in a school. This is where I first consciously realized the shortage of physics teachers. I had plenty of job vacancies to choose from, and having submitted my application to one school, I was approached by the head of another school in the locality asking me to consider their school. However, I took the first job at All Hallows School in Farnham, and I loved my time there with friendly and supportive staff and children who in the main were respectful and wanted to learn.

What Did I Learn?

I learnt that teaching in a high school is a full-time job! I always knew my first year in teaching would be hard, with so many new things to get to grips with, but I had inadvertently managed to time my NQT year (first year as a newly qualified teacher) with a UK government review of high school qualifications at age sixteen (changing the syllabus and examination system from 'O Level' to 'GCSE'). I realized the influence we have on young lives and the responsibility we have as role models, even when 'off-duty'. It's amazing how much of a role model you can be just by being yourself and doing your job. As a female physics teacher, I was aware of being a role model for women in physics. I had long hair, I often wore skirts, and I had a good collection of earrings. I wanted to show (to both girls and boys) that it is perfectly acceptable for women in science to exhibit feminine qualities. So, I had to develop fast, in many different directions all at once, to find the most effective methods to support the rich diversity of learners I met every day. Whether such skills are considered 'leadership' or 'teaching' can be debated, but being in charge of a class of lively children requires strong leadership over and above the education that is being delivered.

Step 3: PhD

While I really enjoyed teaching in high school, I think I probably burned out after two years due to the relentless workload in and beyond school hours and, at age twenty-four, needed more variety in my life, so it was good to step away. However, this experience of teaching would turn out to be the key to opening many new doors throughout my career.

This forced me to reflect on my career pathway much earlier than expected. I was unsure what to do next and applied for a few jobs in physics-related industries as this seemed a sensible thing to do with a physics degree. I was unsuccessful in attaining any of these, probably due to the three-year gap since I graduated and the lack of any industry-related experience developed while teaching. With hindsight, I was glad I did not move into industry, but at the time, it left me no obvious choice but to return to my own education. I thus decided to study for a PhD and build up the physics side of my profile. And so, I came to the University of Leeds to undertake a PhD in soft matter physics, which immersed me in laboratory work and analysis.

What Did I Learn?

Women are still under-represented in physics. I was the only female postgraduate student out of about forty in the department, with no female academic staff. Being in a small minority has many challenges, but being the only one has advantages. When I looked around the department, I saw only males and thus, in a strange way, did not notice any difference between myself and my colleagues. And to my colleagues, I was the only female they were working with, so they took me at face value, for who I am, rather than as a stereotype. In this way, I have stayed strong and felt able to be myself. But I am very aware it is quite a different experience for many women working in physics. Skibba (2019) reported that physicists are usually expected to be male, geeky and socially isolated.

I quickly realized that my prior teaching experience was very valuable, and I was frequently asked to undertake demonstrating and tutoring. These teaching duties in HE were a nice way to earn extra money but also to extend my portfolio of teaching experience, in particular working with university students from the viewpoint of an educator rather than that of a fellow student.

Step 4: Postdoctoral Researcher

On finishing my PhD, the next step was obvious, to find a postdoctoral research assistant (PDRA) contract. I was successful in staying at the University of Leeds and spent two years in the School of Textile Industries researching high-performance synthetic fibres, before undertaking another three-year PDRA contract in the School of Physics and Astronomy working on gel electrolytes for lithium batteries. All of this was building my academic profile and allowed me to apply for and achieve the Chartered Physicist (CPhys) status. My leadership role took more of a back seat during this time, but I was quietly observing and learning, and my experiences would inform my future work.

What Did I Learn?

With my PGCE and two years of teaching in high school, I quickly appreciated that I had more teaching experience than any of the postgraduate demonstrators, and indeed more than quite a few of the academic staff in physics, and this meant that even as a PDRA I was invited to run an undergraduate laboratory and to sit on the school teaching committee. Both these roles enhanced my experience and leadership skills. At the time I just saw them as interesting extensions of my role, but in reality, they were massively preparing me for the next step, which I hadn't seen coming. Specific leadership training was not given during my PDRA role, although plenty of useful advice and support was available. However, this is something I have addressed later in my career when I had a formal responsibility for learning and teaching in the school.

Step 5: University Lecturer

Life on the temporary contract regime of a PDRA is not a sustainable career route, and when my PhD supervisor retired and the post of lecturer was advertised, it seemed natural for me to apply. At interview, all my previous physics, education and leadership experiences came together, and I was appointed as the first female lecturer in the School of Physics and Astronomy at the University of Leeds in 1995.

All new appointees were enrolled on a university training course as an introduction to teaching in HE, but with my PGCE and prior teaching experience, it was decided that I only needed to attend specific sessions. At the same time, I was also invited to mentor an early career staff member taking the course, so I was both an attendee and a mentor at the same time. It was a valuable experience to see the process from both sides, which further developed my education philosophy and leadership skills by bringing the two together in teaching someone else to teach.

This was a key step in my academic leadership development and one from which I would draw upon many times in the future.

I was quick to attend teaching conferences for HE and became inspired by the Recording and Reviewing Movement (Department of Education and Science, 1987) to help students to reflect on their learning and to plan for their future employability. I thus developed Progress Files with my own tutor group, and student feedback on this gave me the confidence to inspire other tutors to try it, and soon it became embedded as school practice. My dissemination at conferences saw my Progress Files adopted by other departments around the UK, with the Universities of St Andrews, York; Queen's Belfast; and Queen Mary excited to use my materials with their physics students.

This was the first example of my vision for good education being taken up more widely and where my fledgling leadership in HE was first recognized. This gave me confidence to apply for my first teaching development grant from the Learning and Teaching Subject Network in Physical Sciences (LTSN-PS) under the leadership of Professor Tina Overton, allowing me to undertake research and development in this area which was widely disseminated.

This work gained me recognition nationally, and I was invited to be a member of the Quality Assurance Agency (QAA) committee to write the Benchmark Statement for Physics from scratch in 2002 and then extend it to master's qualifications in 2008 (QAA, 2008). This Benchmark statement is a policy document that describes the nature and outcomes of a physics degree and is used as the national regulatory requirement. Further recognition of my leadership in pedagogy in physics saw me invited to act as a national accreditation assessor for our professional body, The Institute of Physics (IOP). This was a wonderful opportunity to learn as well as to give back, and it afforded me experience and status to expand my profile in leadership, to work as an external examiner and to build up a profile suitable for promotion.

I was delighted to achieve promotion as a senior lecturer (more often termed associate professor these days) on the merits of teaching and leadership. This was very unusual in a school of physics in the early 2000s. Tradition dictated that a long list of scientific publications was the only way to be promoted in physics, or so I was led to believe by my colleagues. But thankfully, my experience and profile were recognized by leaders in the wider university.

I continued to be a role model for women in physics, and the number of female staff in the School of Physics and Astronomy at Leeds increased from one to eight and has remained at around 25 per cent female staff to this day. I have taken maternity leave twice, showing that it is possible to combine an academic career and have a family. My experience has taught me that it is important to view someone's career as a whole and to accept that there may be times when family duties require flexibility with no prior warning (as when kids become ill overnight). And, of course, this flexibility extends much more widely than issues with children. As a leader, it is important to value people for what they bring to the role, and not what they can't deliver.

Step 6: Director of Student Education in Physics

On returning from my second maternity leave, I was asked to chair the school teaching committee, which I saw as a massive opportunity to extend my leadership experience. These duties rapidly expanded to encompass leadership in all aspects of education for the school as director of learning and teaching, with the role later revised institutionally to have the title director of student education. This put me in one of the three senior leadership roles in the school and was the culmination of all my previous experiences in teaching and leadership. There was still much to learn, but now I had a title to recognize my skills, and I was part of a wider university network with training and colleagues to share and bounce ideas off.

With this formalization of my role, I was better empowered to make changes. For example, to raise the visibility of our female and other minority staff, I asked a diverse range of staff to take on core first-year modules. To further build a sense of belonging with all our students, I instigated a system of small group allocations where I 'paired' students from minority groups (gender, mature, international, etc.) with at least one other similar student in the group. This was not overtly done, but it allowed students within the group to find 'someone else like them' to build their confidence and support network. I also created training for postgraduate teaching assistants on unconscious bias to ensure they acted fairly to all students.

Leadership of staff is different from leadership of students. With students (in high school or undergraduates), I felt I was guiding them on a path which was already well-trodden – to prepare for specific qualifications and develop skills for their future. While many of these paths could be new to me, the skills I required to navigate the landscape were very familiar. Whereas with staff in HE, my leadership was about how we could chart a way into the unknown, and this required collaboration. I needed to invite and evaluate ideas from everyone, to establish common goals and to agree how we might reach them together. While I may need to take ultimate responsibility for the decisions, or may have to set the ground rules, it was this leadership 'from within' that was most effective, along with helping others develop their own leadership skills by inviting them to take responsibility for different strands of a project.

A particular example of this was when I led a full curriculum review in the School of Physics and Astronomy. To get buy-in from staff and help them appreciate the bigger picture which academics often struggle with (Pepper et al., 2018), I commenced with a school-away day to consider the drivers, incorporating students' views, professional body developments and staff insights. From a more theoretical standpoint, helping staff to understand the interrelation between external drivers and internal processes is key: 'Transformational change occurs as a response to the external environment and directly affects organizational mission and strategy' (Burke and Litwin, 1992, p. 523).

Step 7: Head of a Physics Education Research Group

In recent years, universities have increasingly recognized the crucial importance of their staff demonstrating excellent teaching skills and have developed teaching and scholarship career promotion routes (Fanghanel, 2016). And although many developments along this route have come a little later than I would have liked for my own career, eventually the time was right for me to push for my educational work to be centre stage. So in 2016, in discussion with my head of school, I was given the green light to switch from science and start up a research group in physics education.

Finally, the skills I had developed throughout my varied career roles all came together. I was able to combine my vision and philosophy of good pedagogy, my knowledge of the physics curriculum (from high school to undergraduate degree), my research skills (in science and education) and my leadership in many different contexts. But leading a research group is different again from leading staff in learning and teaching roles. In a research group, leading is about helping others achieve their dreams. Here, my leadership was not so much to help everyone reach a common goal, but to help staff to progress in ways that inspired them, albeit by bringing a coherence to our activities.

Figure 9.1 shows the 'life cycle' of HE that our group developed to represent our diverse yet intertwined research activities. Starting with effective Outreach to attract and inspire young people to study (physics, in this case), and following with Engagement to ensure diverse students feel they belong, provides a sound foundation for students to benefit from HE. Research into Learning and Assessment techniques investigates core HE skills. Understanding how students engage with Employability comes full circle to link with Outreach. These two areas are so closely related, both showcasing what the discipline has to offer and enabling students to follow their dreams.

Being able to focus my full academic efforts on physics education has allowed me to develop my own research in several of these areas. In outreach, I have supervised a PhD student looking at the narrative around increasing the diversity in physics (Crilly, Voice and Pugh, 2021). In learning, I have researched the technique of spaced repetition in university physics classes (Voice and Stirton, 2020). And in employability, I have evaluated the effect of work-based

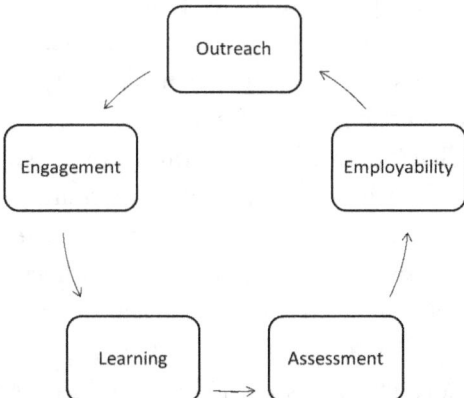

Figure 9.1 Schematic showing the life cycle of students in higher education, developed by my research group to represent our diverse yet intertwined research activities.

placements on student employability (Voice et al., 2020) and created a Physics Exploration Careers Tool (Voice and Vaughan, 2021) to help students tailor their employment planning according to their skills and preferences.

As a research group leader, there was an increased national focus on my work. Due to the very low number of similar research groups within physics departments in the UK, a significant element of my work became persuasion and trailblazing. I was invited to blog on the IOP website about the founding of my research group, and I was elected to the committee of the IOP Higher Education Group (a national group running events in support of physics education). And to address the urgent requirement for remote teaching due to the pandemic, I co-founded a national network in physics (PHYSICS-LTHE) in summer 2020 to support physics staff in the UK and beyond to share ideas and best practices. My own thoughts on the essential elements of remote teaching are captured in Sands et al. (2020). In all these activities, I have been able to present a positive and supportive environment and showcase the similarity of education research to scientific research (Wieman 2014) in order to inspire other physicists to develop physics education research in their own institutions.

Conclusion

I have enjoyed every step of my career. The fact that my career was not at all planned is a testament to the benefits of building a portfolio. I have had the freedom to explore different areas of interest, to take opportunities as they arise, to accommodate maternity leave, to develop new skills and to attain positions and recognition to be able to make a difference to others.

Starting out, my passion was to deliver high-quality pedagogy in schools and universities. Leadership positions have allowed me to work alongside staff and enabled me to build a shared vision for delivering high-quality education. Through this, I have been able to provide opportunities for staff to build their own leadership skills and hence create the next generation of leaders in education. And the research skills I learnt through my laboratory-based physics provided a solid foundation from which to lead an educational research group.

There have been challenges along the way. The numbers of women studying or working in any area of physics are still low, and I have been conscious of having to be a role model and ambassador for my gender, and for minorities in general, within the discipline.

In a discipline where the main success criteria have traditionally been large research grants for laboratory work and papers in high-profile scientific journals, establishing a career focused on education has been difficult. The advent of teaching and scholarship promotion routes in recent years shows that institutions now recognize and value staff who have time to develop and research good pedagogy, and I am excited that new staff can now plan their career to have this focus. But this needs to be underpinned with available funding for their endeavours. A specific funding stream for physics education research urgently needs to be established in the UK to allow physics in HE to deliver on both elements of its mission (science and education).

From all the different roles I have undertaken, I now have a more rounded view of leadership. As exemplified by Black (2015) and Kouzes and Posner (2013), I summarize my philosophy of leadership in the following principles:

- Care about those you lead, listen to them, empathize and motivate.
- Establish vision (theirs, yours, the institution's – as appropriate).
- Appreciate the challenges, barriers and fears. Meet people 'halfway' to set manageable, agreed targets.
- Allow for 'silly questions' and failures; these are normal. Increase or decrease the challenge as required over time.
- Celebrate every small success along the way. Attribute praise to everyone.

Finally, to reflect on Kotter's view (1996) that all leaders must be both a student and a teacher, I can affirm that I have never stopped learning through all my different teaching roles: as a high school teacher, a postgraduate demonstrator, a lecturer and a research group leader. This learning comes informally from the multitude of experiences faced every day as I interact with the students and staff for whom I have a leadership responsibility. In this way, I learn directly from those I am teaching. This combines with the more formal learning from training courses, literature and conferences, resulting in an iterative method of enhancing my leadership qualities, and I am excited for what I will learn next.

References

Aksoy, E. E., Schoeler, M. and Wörgötter, F. (2014), 'Testing Piaget's Ideas on Robots: Assimilation and Accommodation Using the Semantics of Actions', in *Fourth Joint IEEE International Conference on Development and Learning and* on *Epigenetic Robotics*, 107–8, New York: IEEE, https://doi.org/10.1109/DEV LRN.2014.6982962.

Alant, B. (2004), 'Researching Problem Solving in Introductory Physics: Towards a New Understanding of Familiarity', *African Journal of Research in Mathematics, Science and Technology Education*, 8 (1): 29–40.

Ausubel, D. P. (1968), *Educational Psychology: A Cognitive View*, New York: HolCt, Rinehart & Winston.

Black, S. A. (2015), 'Qualities of Effective Leadership in Higher Education', *Open Journal of Leadership*, 4 (2): article ID 57195.

Boaler, J., Williams, C. and Confere, A. (2015), 'Fluency without Fear: Research Evidence on the Best Ways to Learn Math Facts', *Youcubed*, 28 January. https://www.youcubed.org/evidence/fluency-without-fear/.

Bruner, J. S. (1971), *The Relevance of Education*, New York: Norton.

Burke, W. W. and Litwin, G. H. (1992), 'A Causal Model of Organizational Performance and Change', *Journal of Management*, 18 (3): 523–45.

Burnett, P. C. (2001), 'Elementary Students' Preferences for Teacher Praise', *Journal of Classroom Interaction*, 36 (1): 16–23.

Crilly, E. A., Voice, A. M. and Pugh, S. L. (2021), 'Towards a New Equality Narrative', *Physics World*, 34 (6): 19.

Department of Education and Science (1987), Higher Education: Meeting the Challenge, White Paper, Cm 114, London: HMSO.

Eisenkopf, G., Hessami, Z., Fischbacher, U. and Ursprung, H. W. (2015), 'Academic Performance and Single-Sex Schooling: Evidence from a Natural Experiment in Switzerland', *Journal of Economic Behavior & Organization*, 115: 123–43.

Fanghanel, J., Pritchard, J., Potter, J. and Wisker, G. (2016), *Defining and Supporting the Scholarship of Teaching and Learning (SoTL): A Sector-Wide Study*, York: Higher Education Academy. https://www.advance-he.ac.uk/knowledge-hub/defining-and-supporting-scholarship-teaching-and-learning-sotl-sector-wide-study.

French, J. (2015), 'The Shortage of Physics Teachers', *Gatsby*, 29 April. https://www.gatsby.org.uk/education/latest/the-shortage-of-physics-teachers-infographic.

King, A. (1993), 'From Sage on the Stage to Guide on the Side', *College Teaching*, 41 (1): 30–5.

Kolb, D. A. and Fry, R. (1975), 'Towards an Applied Theory of Experiential Learning', in C. Cooper (ed.), *Theories of Group Processes*, 33–57, London: Wiley.

Kotter, J. P. (1996), *Leading Change*, Boston, MA: Harvard Business School Press.

Kouzes, J. M. and Posner, B. Z. (2013), 'The Five Practices of Exemplary Leadership: How Ordinary People Make Extraordinary Things Happen', in E. H. Kessler (ed.), *Encyclopedia of Management Theory*, 435–7, Los Angeles, CA: Sage.

Leithwood, K., Patten, S. and Jantzi, D. (2010), 'Testing a Conception of How School Leadership Influences Student Learning', *Education Administration Quarterly*, 46 (5): 671–706.

Marzano, R. J., Marzano, J. S. and Pickering, D. J. (2003), *Classroom Management That Works. Research-Based Strategies for Every Teacher*, Alexandria, VA: ASCD.

Pace, C. R. (1984), *Measuring the Quality of College Student Experiences*, Los Angeles, CA: Higher Education Research Institute, University of California.

Pennington, C. R., Kaye, L. K., Qureshi, A. W. and Heim, D. (2021), 'Do Gender Differences in Academic Attainment Correspond with Scholastic Attitudes? An Exploratory Study in a UK Secondary School', *Journal of Applied Social Psychology*, 51 (1): 3–16.

Pepper, R., Crawford, K. and Sanderson, R. (2018), *Developing Academic Leadership and Innovative Practice*, London: Leadership Foundation for Higher Education.

Piaget, J. and Inhelder, B. (1969), *The Psychology of the Child*, London: Routledge and Kegan Paul.

QAA (2008), *Subject Benchmark Statement for Physics, Astronomy and Astrophysics*, Gloucester: QAA.

Raine, D. and Symons, S. (2012), 'Problem-Based Learning: Undergraduate Physics by Research', *Contemporary Physics*, 53 (1): 39–51.

Sands, D., Kormos, L., Nowak, J., Vaughan, H., Voice, A. and Zochowski, S. (2020), 'Moving Teaching Online during the COVID-19 Pandemic', *Europhysics News*, 51 (4): 30–2.

Skibba, R. (2019), 'Women in Physics', *Nature Review Physics*, 1: 298–300.

Van Heuvelen, A. (1991), 'Learning to Think Like a Physicist: A Review of Research-Based Instructional Strategies', *American Journal of Physics*, 59: 891–97.

Voice, A. M. and Stirton, A. (2020), 'Spaced Repetition: Towards More Effective Learning in STEM', *New Directions in the Teaching of Physical Sciences*, 15 (1): 1–10.

Voice, A. M. and Vaughan, H. L. (2021), 'Physics Careers Exploration Tool', White Rose Industrial Physics Academy. https://wripa.ac.uk/for-students/career-tools/careers-app/.

Voice, A., Hirst, A., Krauss, T. and Turkenberg-van Diepen, M. (2020), 'Work-Based Learning and Students' Career Readiness', *Prospects Luminate*, July. https://luminate.prospects.ac.uk/work-based-learning-and-students-career-readiness.

Wieman, C. E. (2014), 'The Similarities between Research in Education and Research in the Hard Sciences', *Educational Researcher*, 43 (1): 12–14.

Part 3

The Future of Learning and Teaching Leadership

10

Reflections on Disciplinary and Institutional Leadership: Crossing the Abyss

Ian M. Kinchin

Introduction

This chapter considers the position of the academic leader in relation to their disciplinary home. Most leaders in higher education have not studied leadership (at least not as a first discipline) and have migrated into leadership roles (by accident or by design) through various ill-defined routes and for various reasons. It is important to note that, in many cases, leadership roles are not divorced from academic roles and that formal leadership activities can be variously positioned within an academic team, for example, as a leader of a taught programme, or as a leader of a research project. Many such roles are also associated with (and often conflated with) managerial responsibility, but not always. Some leadership roles maintain the academic's identity within their disciplinary context, while others might be viewed to create tensions with their identity, as the role might require acting as an intermediary between senior management and teachers at the 'chalk-face'. These 'middle leaders' are simultaneously positioned as a 'buffer and bridge' (Bennett et al., 2007, p. 462). Other leadership roles may develop informally as an academic colleague gains the respect of their peers and becomes the go-to person for advice on certain matters, even if this is not within their managerial remit. Therefore, we must acknowledge that when discussing leadership roles in higher education, there is some degree of generalization required to avoid continual reference to contextual variation, and the reader will have to take ideas and contextualize them for their own unique working environment. Whatever the individual context, formal or informal, the acceptance of a leadership role may require an academic to think in various new ways that might not be covered by their disciplinary training. There needs to be an awareness that a PhD in biochemistry or astrophysics, for example, might not be adequate in preparation for leadership.

Here, I also need to emphasize the difference between leadership and management and try not to use the two terms interchangeably. Connelly, James and Fertig (2019) have argued that these are conceptually different things and that clarifying the distinction between the two activities will help those who are developing their leadership practice through further study and targeted research. Essentially, those authors regard educational management as practice that entails carrying the responsibility for the proper functioning of a system. Educational leadership, on the other hand, is more concerned with the act of influencing others in educational settings to achieve goals. It is educational leadership that I am interested in here. Unfortunately, academic leaders working in managerialist university cultures are in danger of having their work subverted by pervasive conceptions of accountability and management that are corrupted by reductive understandings of 'key performance indicators' and short cuts to 'best practice'. According to Edwards-Groves et al. (2019, p. 315), these 'popularized drivers' have 'proved to be little more than destabilizing distractions that divert attention from necessarily *situated* understanding' (original emphasis).

Beyond Disciplinary Boundaries

University academics are typically embedded within the culture of their disciplinary 'home' and will be trained to view knowledge through their disciplinary lens throughout their undergraduate and postgraduate education. Within the typical Western university, the view of knowledge has been dominated by the rational, evidence-based perspective that draws specifically on the dominant scientific paradigm. However, when dealing with the 'wicked' problems that face society, such as climate change, sustainability or (as is discussed in this book) leadership in university teaching, it is apparent that rational 'scientific' thinking is insufficient to account for the personalized and subjective knowledge that colours human understanding or the indigenous knowledges that contribute to a rich patchwork of cultures and traditions. The actions of human beings do not always follow the evidence. This may be why we still see students sitting submissively in lecture theatres even though the weight of evidence strongly suggests that active learning is a more profitable teaching strategy than passive learning (Freeman et al., 2014). The adoption of evidence-based teaching practice is not as simple as it may first appear, particularly when undue prestige is placed upon a single form of evidence that is considered robust because it mimics clinical research as if a teaching intervention was analogous to a vaccination. This is used in a way that recasts teachers in the image of data that ultimately produces conformity and acquiescence, promoted under the guise of best practice (Malone and Hogan, 2020). This apparent misuse of research creates some questions over the nature of evidence and the reason for its collection, leading some observers to question the motives directing the 'industry' of academic research. The singular emphasis on a particular epistemological viewpoint and the resultant monoculture of research approaches has been commented on in the literature as a way of reducing the diversity of thoughts within higher education. For example, MacLure (2006, p. 730) comments that 'state-sponsored intolerance of difference and complexity is now part of the story of education policy and research funding in many countries'. It seems that in some instances, the human connection is still being bracketed out of research in the name of rigour.

I argue here that academics should be encouraged to look beyond the limitations created by their disciplinary blinkers and adopt an epistemologically plural stance when it comes to the 'ecology of knowledges' (as described by Santos, 2014), to overcome the 'epistemological abyss' that separates disciplinary knowledge (considered by many to be 'this side' of the abyss) from knowledge about either teaching or leadership (often considered to be 'the other' or 'dark side' of the abyss – see Chapter 3 by O'Sullivan). This separation of knowledges appears to be particularly marked for colleagues in STEM subjects, whether biology (Chapter 6 by Hosein), chemistry (Chapter 9 by Correia) or physics (Chapter 10 by Voice), where the person is deliberately excluded from scholarly writing. Such a 'them-and-us' binary perspective of knowledge is probably not helpful in terms of institutional health and is likely to contribute to tensions within the neoliberal university. This is recognized by Correia (Chapter 9), who refers to the ideas of C. P. Snow (1959) and the existence of 'two cultures' within academia that separates the sciences and the humanities. It seems such a cultural divide also separates those who work within a disciplinary context and those who focus on leadership, particularly where such roles fall across disciplinary boundaries. Wright and Greenwood (2017, p. 47) comment on the discord between groups operating on the university campus that are isolated by different professional cultures:

> A core pathology of current higher education institutions is that the legitimate participants (students, faculty, staff and administration) are not held together by

shared interests and understandings. They compete with each other rather than being required to harmonise their different interests and operate in solidary ways.

However, a disciplinary heritage is not something to be discarded when the trajectory of an academic's career leads to a shift in focus. In my own career, moving from biology to education, I was conscious of the feeling of loss that stemmed from the idea of a linear progression from one job to another – always having to leave something behind to progress to the next stage of my career. However, by revising my underpinning assumptions about my professional development, I have been able to reframe this in a more positive manner:

> I would now reconceptualise my biological background that I previously referred to as *disciplinary baggage*, as this suggests it creates an impediment to development along a linear pathway of development. Rather, I see it an asset in my own rhizomatic becoming (*sensu* Gravett, 2021) rather than a linear transition. Borrowing from Youdell and Lindley (2019), I need to revise this as part of my *social and biological entanglements of learning*. It seems that old knowledge and ways of thinking are never fully 'over-written' or deleted when learning something new. (Kinchin, 2020, p. 41, original emphasis)

This builds on the idea of a rhizomatic becoming, an idea that has provenance in the work of Deleuze and Guattari (1987) and which has been shown to have application in the field of academic leadership (Benzie, Pryce and Smith, 2017).

From Tree to Rhizome: Becoming Other

Fundamentally, a rhizomatic perspective rejects the twin limitations of binary thinking and linearity. Rather than thinking in binaries (and/or), the grammar of rhizomatic thinking emphasizes multiplicities ('and, and, and'), where every part of the rhizome is connected to every other part (Deleuze and Guattari, 1987). This contrasts with tree thinking (also referred to as arborescent thinking), in which branches of knowledge all arise from a common stem. The rhizomatic acceptance of a complex multiplicity of thought composed of a messy network of interwoven elements, rather than a reductionist binary that projects a false simplicity, offers fresh avenues for consideration and effectively makes thinking in terms of linear processes redundant. So, rather than relinquishing my biologist's hat for an educational leader's hat (transitioning from A to B in a linear manner), I have fashioned an individual identity as an educational leader who is able to draw upon a rich heritage in biology and, in so doing, avoids the classification of 'being' in a group that can be categorized and labelled. Rather, in line with Deleuzo-Guattarian thinking, such an approach accepts 'becoming other' and 'becoming different' rather than 'becoming the same' in order to fit into an established category. Ironically, my academic heritage includes a scientific understanding of the biology of a rhizome (Bell, 1980) and an appreciation of the idea of a consilience, a pulling together of ideas from different academic disciplines to develop a stronger understanding, as developed by the celebrated ecologist E. O. Wilson (1998). And so, I have revisited my understanding of 'this side' of the epistemological abyss (the 'scientific' me) using the lens generated on the 'far side' (the 'post-structuralist' me) so that what was once familiar is seen anew – again emphasizing the lack of linearity in progression.

Leading from the Middle

A rhizomatic perspective requires us to be always in the middle (Deleuze and Guattari, 1987). From that, the only place from which we can lead is the middle. This suggests a need to broaden the idea of leadership from the middle (LftM), which considers a vertical structure to compulsory education systems and their organization (e.g. from school districts upwards towards the state and downwards to school communities, as discussed by Fullan, 2015), and also considers the horizontal dimension within higher education institutions (across disciplinary boundaries, between teaching and research and between academics and administrative staff). Whereas Fullan's vertical dimension exhibits a certain degree of stability, the horizontal dimension exhibits much more fluidity. In rhizomatic terms (*sensu* Deleuze and Guattari, 1987), the middle is not a fixed point. It is a travelling point that moves as conditions move and as the players within it undergo a process of becoming other. But like Fullan's LftM model, the goal is to create a connected strategy 'to develop greater overall system coherence by strengthening the middle in relation to system goals and local needs' (2015, p. 24). Therefore, LftM requires a range of boundary-spanning activities to forge connections between institutional levels, to translate policy into practice and to connect colleagues from disparate corners of the institution.

Expertise in Leadership: Being vs Becoming

Closely associated with the perspective on rhizomatics is the philosophy of becoming (Deleuze and Guattari, 1987), which recognizes change and development to be the natural state. The fluid idea of 'becoming' seems to be in tension with the static idea of 'being' an 'expert leader', where an expert might be seen as someone working on their own in their particular area of expertise (Benzie et al. 2017). However, if leadership is seen as a relational phenomenon that resides in the connections between team members, it seems impossible for an expert leader to function outside the context of the team, that is, the relational assumption of growth-in-connection (Nicholson and Kurucz, 2019). To paraphrase Benzie et al. (2017, p. 233), 'the risk of attempting to build working relationships from the standpoint of an "expert" is that [academics] may be seen as experts in another field trying to colonise an academic's specialist territory in the name of [leadership]'. The becoming-leader is more likely to be effective when they are not set above other team members as experts but are embedded within the team in a parallel state of becoming, and where the activities of leadership are distributed across the team. I should emphasize here that distributed vs centralized leadership is not a simplistic binary as there are many associated concepts that modify and contextualize practices in localized and personalized ways. However, the theoretical extremes of the distributed-centralized continuum are likely to have polarized outcomes for team members. In Figure 10.1, we can see the emergence of 'adaptive expertise' (a precursor to adaptive leadership – Benzie et al., 2017) that is part of the process of becoming through its links with ecological resilience and the learning culture of the institution. This may be inhibited if links are created with routinized practice and non-learning that can lead to academics acting as experienced non-experts.

Becoming 'Leadership Literate'

In order to integrate the conflicting identities of teacher, researcher and leader, academics need time to reflect on these roles and the thinking processes that need to occur to help colleagues reconcile the demands placed upon them from various directions. I draw here upon the case study offered by Kinchin and Thumser (2021), who augmented the model of an integrated academic, offered by Evans et al. (2020), by inserting the concept of epistemological abyss developed by Santos (2014). The concept of epistemological pluralism may be alien to many colleagues as it appears to run counter to the way in which academia has developed and fragmented into specialist areas, each with their own particular ways of working. However, the key to understanding many

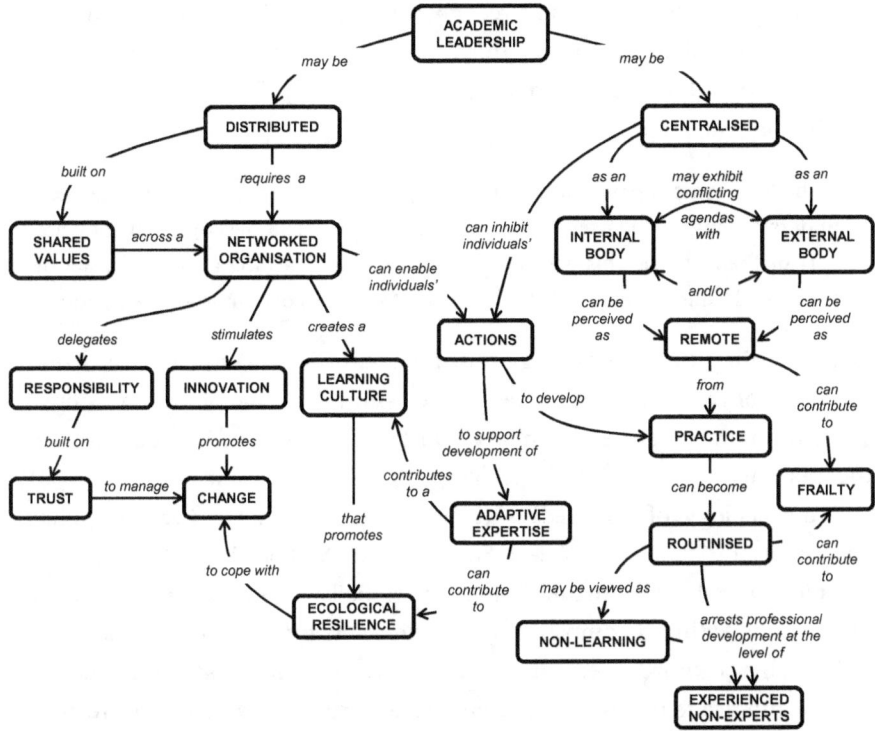

Figure 10.1 A concept map of the potential contributions of centralized and distributed leadership models to the development of adaptive expertise (modified from Kinchin, 2017).

wicked problems may be through the development of a level of epistemological flexibility. As suggested by Andreotti, Ahenakew and Cooper (2011, p. 46):

> Becoming (consciously) bi- or multi-epistemic or operational in two or more ways of knowing, involves understanding different social and historical dynamic processes of knowledge construction, their limitations and the social-historical relations of power that permeate knowledge production. It also involves being able to reference, combine and apply the appropriate frame of reference to an appropriate context.

While the development of epistemological flexibility may present an additional demand on university academics, the explicit recognition of this as a goal and its possible benefits may make the process manageable (Kinchin and Thumser, 2021) and may help colleagues develop their own context-specific 'leadership literacy' by transforming perspectives on leadership and acting as a bridge between different cultures on the campus. Indeed, if it is found that epistemological flexibility has recognizable integrative and transformative functions, we might start to see this as a threshold concept (*sensu* Meyer and Land, 2005) in the development of leadership literacy. To reach this goal, Davis (2010, p. 44) suggests:

> To be leadership literate for the knowledge era, leaders need to develop a deep understanding of themselves and their world and acknowledge that they are part of their world. This goes deeper than simply learning a particular set of functional skills or being able to demonstrate a series of competencies by rote.

Underpinning the binary logic of the traditional command-and-control condition of the 'leaders vs the led' is the assumption that both leadership and academic practice are each unitary constructs. However, if we acknowledge the plurality within both the ecology of practices (Kemmis et al., 2012) and the ecology of knowledges (Santos, 2014), then we need to consider an ecology of leadership (Allen, Stelzner and Wielkiewicz, 1999) in a more complex (non-binary) manner, as a multiplicity of non-linear (rhizomatic) interactions within a complex and evolving network (*sensu* Capra and Luisi, 2016). This acknowledgement of complexity is a more authentic stance to take within academia, where disciplinary experts should be able to recognize parallels with complex conceptual systems in their home disciplines and, by extension, appreciate the problems of failing to perceive the full complexity of educational systems that can result from the filtering out of inconvenient information (Carpenter et al., 2009). This reductionism has been a characteristic of the neoliberal university, where simplicity of measurement (for purposes of accountability) has supplanted the scholarly recognition of complexity.

For many university research staff, 'this side' of the epistemological abyss consists of a comforting solidity built from their undergraduate studies delivered within the Western academic tradition (Santos, 2014). However, the epistemological sovereignty enjoyed in this environment by the natural sciences (*sensu* Healy, 2003) can inhibit the development of post-abyssal thinking (Santos, 2014). As such, the 'other side' of the abyssal line may be considered to consist only of opinions and intangible, subjective understandings. This subjective knowledge has often been discarded, and its value unrecognized, even though it is often the driver for decisions made about teaching activities and human interactions more generally. Colleagues will often know when something 'feels right' even if they have no objective data to back their claim. However, this 'unscientific knowledge' is probably required to address wicked problems, including the complexity of educational leadership. Knowledge from the 'other side' of the epistemological abyss may include subjective views on 'what works for me in the work environment' – a complex and highly contextual cluster of concepts that is not amenable to simplistic description using reductionist metrics. I am aware that the proposal to think differently, and possibly 'unscientifically', to better mirror idiosyncratic human behaviours and strongly held cultural beliefs may introduce a disturbance to established patterns of thought, described as an epistemological shudder by Charteris (2014). But as Garvey-Berger (2004, p. 350) argues, it is at the space at the edge of people's understanding that 'we can find the most fertile ground for transformation'. No one said that leadership was easy.

Conclusion

In this chapter, I have presented some potentially unsettling ideas to reframe the concept of academic leadership. The philosophy of becoming (in contrast to being) underpins this work and challenges the notion of the context-independent expert leader. Becoming has to be viewed as 'a continuous emergent condition' that is 'often a process of struggle, and is always interminably linked to its environs and relationships' (Cristancho and Fenwick, 2015, p. 128). It may be unnerving to know that there is no fixed end point for professional leadership development. Though, for some colleagues, it seems that the concept of 'becoming' might itself be liberating. As one academic recently stated, 'I find it very empowering, in the sense of gaining personal agency. For me, acknowledging that there is no terminal end point to chase releases me from a tick box, to-do list treadmill' (Kinchin et al., 2021, p. 103). Becoming is linked to the reconsideration of knowledge as rhizomatic in structure, where one is always 'in the middle' – always becoming other.

Just as the academic leader is always becoming other, there needs to be an acceptance that everyone else is also becoming other, in different ways and from different starting points. Acceptance of the key role of others in the development of leadership has been described by Davis (2010, p. 45) as 'other-centredness', which 'is concerned with seeing wholeness and interconnections and in leadership theory that promotes relationships, diversity and a post-heroic mindset'. Appreciation of this rich tapestry of becoming is enhanced by an awareness of different ways of knowing. In other words, there are different epistemologies at play across the university, different thought processes and different conceptions about what is valid. As stated by Hoffman (1980, p. 418), 'both poetry and science can be means of validating what we apprehend'. The consideration of different ways of thinking has been described by Santos (2014) as post-abyssal thinking – the ability to use familiar knowledge (from this side of the abyss) without disregarding other less familiar forms of knowledge (from the far side of the abyss). Indeed, adopting the epistemological lenses from the far side of the abyss may offer the opportunity to re-examine our understanding of this side of the abyss to enrich our understanding (explored by Gravett and Kinchin, 2020 in the context of teaching excellence) and to generate greater empathy with colleagues who inhabit the other side of the cultural divide (Snow, 1959). The development of a post-abyssal stance will require openness and dialogue with colleagues from different traditions in order to develop a shared perspective and a shared language. In this context, leadership becomes a parallel process of becoming alongside other team members, giving renewed emphasis to the idea of lifelong learning.

References

Allen, K. E., Stelzner, S. P. and Wielkiewicz, R. M. (1999), 'The Ecology of Leadership: Adapting to the Challenges of a Changing World', *Journal of Leadership Studies*, 5 (2): 62–82.

Andreotti, V., Ahenakew, C. and Cooper, G. (2011), 'Epistemological Pluralism: Ethical and Pedagogical Challenges in Higher Education', *AlterNative*, 7 (1): 40–50.

Bell, A. (1980), 'The Vascular Pattern of a Rhizomatous Ginger (*Alpinia speciosa* L. Zingiberaceae). 2. The Rhizome', *Annals of Botany*, 46 (2): 213–20.

Bennett, N., Woods, P., Wise, C. and Newton, W. (2007), 'Understandings of Middle Leadership in Secondary Schools: A Review of Empirical Research', *School Leadership and Management*, 27 (5): 453–70.

Benzie, H. J., Pryce, A. and Smith, K. (2017), 'The Wicked Problem of Embedding Academic Literacies: Exploring Rhizomatic Ways of Working through an Adaptive Leadership Approach', *Higher Education Research & Development*, 36 (2): 227–40.

Capra, F. and Luisi, P. L. (2016), *The Systems View of Life: A Unifying Vision*, Cambridge: Cambridge University Press.

Carpenter, S. R., Folke, C., Scheffer, M. and Westley, F. (2009), 'Resilience: Accounting for the Non-computable', *Ecology and Society*, 14 (1): 13.

Charteris, J. (2014), 'Epistemological Shudders as Productive Aporia: A Heuristic for Transformative Teacher Learning', *International Journal of Qualitative Methods*, 13 (1): 104–21.

Connelly, M., James, C. and Fertig, M. (2019), 'The Difference between Educational Management and Educational Leadership and the Importance of Educational

Responsibility', *Educational Management Administration & Leadership*, 47 (4): 504–19.
Cristancho, S. and Fenwick, T. (2015), 'Mapping a Surgeon's Becoming with Deleuze', *Medical Humanities*, 41 (2): 128–35.
Davis, H. (2010), 'Other-Centredness as a Leadership Attribute: From *Ego* to *Eco* Centricity', *Journal of Spirituality, Leadership and Management*, 4 (1): 43–52.
Deleuze, G. and Guattari, F. (1987), *A Thousand Plateaus*, trans. B. Massumi, London: Bloomsbury.
Edwards-Groves, C., Grootenboer, P., Hardy, I. and Rönnerman, K. (2019), 'Driving Change from "the Middle": Middle Leading for Site Based Educational Development', *School Leadership & Management*, 39 (3/4): 315–33.
Evans, C., Kandiko Howson, C., Forsythe, A. and Edwards, C. (2020), 'What Constitutes High Quality Higher Education Pedagogical Research?', *Assessment & Evaluation in Higher Education*, 46 (4): 525–46.
Freeman, S., Eddy, S. L., McDonough, M., Smith, M. K., Okoroafor, N., Jordt, H. and Wenderoth, M. P. (2014), 'Active Learning Increases Student Performance in Science, Engineering, and Mathematics', *Proceedings of the National Academy of Sciences USA*, 111 (23): 8410–15.
Fullan, M. (2015), 'Leadership from the Middle', *Education Canada*, 55 (4): 22–6.
Garvey-Berger, J. (2004), 'Dancing on the Threshold of Meaning: Recognizing and Understanding the Growing Edge', *Journal of Transformative Education*, 2 (4): 336–51.
Gravett, K. (2021), 'Troubling Transitions and Celebrating Becomings: From Pathway to Rhizome', *Studies in Higher Education*, 46 (8): 1506–17.
Gravett, K. and Kinchin, I. M. (2020), 'Revisiting "a 'Teaching Excellence' for the Times We Live In": Posthuman Possibilities', *Teaching in Higher Education*, 25 (8): 1028–34.
Healy, S. (2003), 'Epistemological Pluralism and the "Politics of Choice"', *Futures*, 35: 689–701.
Hoffman, R. R. (1980), 'Metaphor in Science', in R. P. Honeck and R. R. Hoffman (eds), *Cognition and Figurative Language*, 393–423, Hillsdale, NJ: Lawrence Erlbaum.
Kemmis, S., Edwards-Groves, C., Wilkinson, J. and Hardy, I. (2012), 'Ecologies of Practices', in P. Hager, A. Lee and A. Reich (eds), *Practice, Learning and Change*, 33–49, Dordrecht: Springer.
Kinchin, I. M. (2017), 'Pedagogic Frailty: A Concept Analysis', *Knowledge Management & E-Learning*, 9 (3): 295–310.
Kinchin, I. M. (2020), 'Concept Mapping and Pedagogic Health in Higher Education (a Rhizomatic Exploration in Eight Plateaus)', DLitt thesis, University of Surrey. https://openresearch.surrey.ac.uk/esploro/outputs/doctoral/Concept-mapping-and-pedagogic-health-in-higher-education-a-rhizomatic-exploration-in-eight-plateaus/99545423202346.
Kinchin, I. M., Derham, C., Foreman, C., McNamara, A. and Querstret, D. (2021), 'Exploring the Salutogenic University: Searching for the Triple Point for the

Becoming-Caring-Teacher through Collaborative Cartography', *Pedagogika*, 141 (1): 94–112.

Kinchin, I. M. and Thumser, A. E. (2021), 'Mapping the "Becoming-Integrated-Academic": An Autoethnographic Case Study of Professional Becoming in the Biosciences', *Journal of Biological Education*. https://doi.org/10.1080/00219266.2021.1941191.

MacLure, M. (2006), 'The Bone in the Throat: Some Uncertain Thoughts on Baroque Method', *International Journal of Qualitative Studies in Education*, 19 (6): 729–45.

Malone, A. and Hogan, P. (2020), 'Evidence and Its Consequences in Educational Research', *British Educational Research Journal*, 46 (2): 265–80.

Meyer, J. H. and Land, R. (2005), 'Threshold Concepts and Troublesome Knowledge (2): Epistemological Considerations and a Conceptual Framework for Teaching and Learning', *Higher Education*, 49 (3): 373–88.

Nicholson, J. and Kurucz, E. (2019), 'Relational Leadership for Sustainability: Building an Ethical Framework from the Moral Theory of "Ethics of Care"', *Journal of Business Ethics*, 156: 25–43.

Santos, B. de S. (2014), *Epistemologies of the South: Justice against Epistemicide*, London: Routledge.

Snow, C. P. (1959), *The Two Cultures*, Cambridge: Cambridge University Press.

Wilson, E. O. (1998), *Consilience: The Unity of Knowledge*, London: Abacus.

Wright, S. and Greenwood, D. J. (2017), 'Universities Run for, by, and with the Faculty, Students and Staff: Alternatives to the Neoliberal Destruction of Higher Education', *Learning and Teaching*, 10 (1): 42–65.

Youdell, D. and Lindley, M. R. (2019), *Biosocial Education: The Social and Biological Entanglements of Learning*, London: Routledge.

Index

academic culture 33, 40
academic identity xi, 171
academic tribes and territories 8, 56, 124
adaptive leadership 132, 176
Australia/ian xi, xiii, 4, 5, 119, 120, 121, 122, 123, 132
autoethnography 4, 86, 147

biochemistry ix, 5, 6, 9, 119, 125, 129, 172
biological sciences ix, xiv, 5, 6, 9, 85, 86, 89
biomedical engineering ix, 89, 91, 93, 94, 96
Brazil xi, xiii, 5, 144, 146

campus-wide 16, 24, 28
Canada xiii, 5, 49, 51, 56, 58, 61, 62
chemistry xiv, 5, 6, 9, 119, 120, 139, 140, 141, 142, 143, 144, 145, 146, 149, 173
collaboration(s) 26, 27, 51, 91, 110,
conservatoire(s) x, 101, 104, 106, 107, 108, 109, 110, 113
critical enquiry x, 66, 76, 77, 78
culture(s) ix, xi, xiv, 4, 5, 7, 9, 16, 21, 22, 23, 24, 25, 27, 28, 31, 32, 33, 35, 37, 41, 53, 54, 57, 77, 78, 106, 113, 121, 124, 125, 126, 127, 128, 131, 132, 133, 134, 139, 140, 142, 143, 144, 145, 146, 147, 148, 149, 150, 172, 173, 176, 177

disciplinary xiii, xiv, xv, xvi, 1, 3, 4, 5, 6, 7, 8, 9, 31, 39, 40, 41, 45, 73, 89, 123, 124, 127, 171, 172, 173, 174, 175, 178

ethics 86, 88, 135
expertise xiv, 39, 44, 57, 60, 61, 65, 71, 85, 103, 104, 105, 106, 130, 134, 135, 175, 176, 177

faculty development ix, 5, 16, 26, 31, 41, 142

hybrid identity 6, 9, 143, 146

identity xi, xiii, 5, 6, 9, 31, 40, 51, 52, 56, 60, 61, 62, 102, 106, 123, 142, 143, 145, 146, 148, 171, 174
interdisciplinary xiii, xiv, 15, 24, 25, 140, 142, 143, 144, 145, 147, 148, 149
integrated scholarship 65, 67, 69, 70, 72, 73, 75, 76, 78
international xi, 7, 51, 71, 90, 91, 94, 96, 101, 120, 125, 139, 144, 146, 161

leadership
    academic leadership xii, xiv, 31, 103, 149, 160, 174, 179
    adaptive 132, 176
    administrative 3
    collaborative 31, 102, 113
    educational development 44
    effective 28, 110, 112
    ethical 110
    journey (s) xiii, xiv, xv, 1, 2, 3, 4, 5, 6, 7, 8, 10, 65, 66, 69, 70, 71, 72, 73, 74, 75, 78, 79, 80, 85, 86, 88, 89, 97, 107
    literacy 177–8
    middle 2
    as position xiii, 1–2, 41, 109, 115, 132, 164, 171
    potential 10
    as process xii, 115
    qualifications and/or training 104, 159
    senior 66, 75, 153, 154, 161
    style 51, 57, 131
learning and teaching x, xiv, xvi, 1, 2, 3, 4, 6, 7, 8, 9, 10, 45, 63, 65, 85, 96, 101, 102, 104, 105, 106, 107, 109, 112, 119, 160, 161, 163
learning and teaching leadership xiv, xvi, 1, 2, 3, 7, 8, 101, 104

mediator 142, 149

methodological tension 145, 146
music x, xiv, 5, 101, 103, 104, 106, 107, 109, 110

partnership(s) xi, 27, 73
pathway(s) xiii, xiv, 1, 2, 4, 6, 31, 34, 41, 66, 67, 69, 71, 72, 75, 122, 123, 153, 155, 158, 174
performing arts 101, 102
Perry xiii, 49, 50, 51, 52, 53, 54, 56, 57, 60, 62, 63
physics xi, xiv, 5, 7, 10, 120, 121, 123, 144, 153, 154, 157, 158, 159, 160, 161, 162, 163, 164, 165, 173

rhizomatic 174, 175, 178, 179

scholarship of teaching and learning 16, 39, 45, 60, 123, 143
scholarly teaching xiii, 31, 39
science(s) ix, x, xi, xiv, 5, 6, 9, 28, 37, 44, 57, 85, 86, 89, 93, 94, 119, 120, 121, 122, 123, 124, 125, 132, 133, 134, 136, 139, 140, 143, 144, 145, 146, 147, 148, 149, 156, 157, 160, 162, 163, 165, 173, 178, 180
small island xiv, 6, 86

social capital xiii, 5, 7, 15, 16, 17, 18, 19, 20, 21, 22, 23, 24, 25, 26, 27, 28
social networks xiii, 5, 7, 8, 15, 16, 18, 19, 20, 21, 22, 23, 24, 28
structure and agency 6

teaching and learning ix, xi, xii, xiii, 5, 15, 16, 17, 18, 19, 20, 21, 22, 23, 24, 28, 39, 56, 58, 60, 68, 76, 93, 113, 123, 124, 128, 129, 130, 133, 134, 136, 143, 145
teaching centre(s) ix, xiii, 5, 26, 31, 32, 36, 38, 39, 41, 42, 43, 44, 56
teaching-focused xi, xiv, 3, 6, 7, 119, 120, 122, 125, 135, 136
transition(s) xiii, 5, 7, 15, 17, 20, 21, 22, 28, 57, 61, 96, 124, 148, 174
Trinidad and Tobago ix, xiii, xiv, 5, 6, 86, 88, 89, 90, 93, 94

UK ix, x, xi, xiii, 5, 10, 49, 51, 52, 53, 54, 55, 56, 57, 58, 60, 61, 62, 65, 66, 67, 72, 74, 103, 104, 108, 157, 160, 164, 165
university-wide xiii, 5, 6
United States xiii, 5, 16, 17, 68, 71, 120, 124

www.ingramcontent.com/pod-product-compliance
Lightning Source LLC
Chambersburg PA
CBHW061832300426
44115CB00013B/2347